AT MEDWAY

BLAIR'S BRITAIN

BLAIR'S BRITAIN

Stephen Driver and Luke Martell

polity

First published in 2002 by Polity Press in association with Blackwell Publishing Ltd

Editorial office:
Polity Press
65 Bridge Street
Cambridge CB2 1UR, UK

Marketing and production:
Blackwell Publishing Ltd
108 Cowley Road
Oxford OX4 1JF, UK

Distributed in the USA by
Blackwell Publishing Inc.
350 Main Street
Malden, MA 02148, USA

A catalogue record for this book is available from the British Library.

Library of Congress Cataloging-in-Publication Data

Driver, Stephen.
Blair's Britain / Stephen Driver and Luke Martell.
    p. cm.
Includes bibliographical references and index.
ISBN 0–7456–2458–8 (acid-free paper)—ISBN 0–7456–2459–6 (pbk. : acid-free paper)
1. Labour Party (Great Britain) 2. Great Britain—Politics and
    government—1997– I. Martell, Luke. II. Title.
JN1129.L32 D748 2002
324.24107—dc21

2002004287

Typeset in 10.5 on 12pt Palatino
by Kolam Information Services Pvt. Ltd, Pondicherry, India.
Printed in Great Britain by MPG Books, Bodmin, Cornwall

Contents

Preface

2001 was the year Tony Blair delivered: a second term in government for Labour with the kind of majority in the House of Commons that politicians dream of. No Labour leader had managed this double whammy. The 2001 landslide followed the 1997 landslide. British politics was getting tired of pinching itself. If Blair was ever to leave his mark on British society, just as Margaret Thatcher had done before, then this was the time.

So how is Blair's Britain shaping up? What did Labour achieve in its first four years of government? Has Blairism broken with Thatcherism or has it just imitated it? How does Labour – and its 'third way' – shape up against European social democracy and against the forces of globalization? Do Labour's constitutional and welfare reforms remake the British state and the role of government in public policy? And what are the challenges Labour faces during its second term in government and beyond? These are the central questions this book seeks to answer.

In our last book on the making of New Labour, *New Labour: Politics after Thatcherism* (Driver and Martell 1998), we argued that the new Blair government had been forged in opposition to Thatcherism and that it wasn't simply defined as Thatcherism Mark 2. In this book, we explore how the Blair government in four years has taken politics and policy-making beyond Thatcherism. We challenge the view that Blair's Labour has simply thrown in the towel to Thatcherite neo-liberalism. But we also cast doubt on the idea that the Labour government 1997–2001 was just like any old Labour government. While Labour's stunning election victories in 1997 and 2001 have given the Blair government an unprecedented opportunity to shape the political and policy land-scape in Labour's (and social democracy's) image, Blair's Britain continues to bear the imprint of eighteen years of radical Conser-vative government.

The book is divided into three parts. Part I, After Thatcherism, surveys the 1997 election result and Labour's first term in govern-ment. Chapter 1 offers an introduction to New Labour, the years of opposition in the 1980s and 1990s, the sliding fortunes of the Conservative government of John Major, and Labour's landslide victory in 1997. The chapter finishes by assessing the two stand-ard interpretations of New Labour: the Thatcherism Mark 2 thesis and the modernization thesis. Chapter 2 examines in some detail the major areas of domestic public policy during Labour's first term: economic policy, welfare reform, public services such as health and education, constitutional reform and law and order. The chapter assesses how far these policy areas show the Blair government to be breaking with the Thatcher legacy or not. It concludes by suggesting that New Labour is not a seamless polit-ical, let alone ideological, project. Like Thatcherism before, Blair's Labour is a political composite, and, rather than search for a sin-gular New Labour, it is better to acknowledge the plurality of New Labours.

The themes of Part II of the book, Rethinking Social Democ-racy, are more conceptual and comparative. Chapter 3 examines Labour's 'third-way' ideas and assesses how successful they are in developing a distinctive politics for the Centre-Left. We argue that New Labour is better seen as an exercise in middle-way polit-ics, where compromises between competing political traditions are worked out in practice, than as some grand transcendence of such traditions. Chapters 4 and 5 look more broadly at the current state of European social democracy. We explore how social demo-crats across Europe in Germany, France, the Netherlands, Scandi-navia and the Mediterranean have responded to the challenges of globalization and social change in terms of domestic policy, the European Union and international affairs.

Part III of the book, New Labour, New Britain, examines four key challenges for the Blair government: the balance between national identities and multi-cultural and multi-national states; strong government and pluralist politics; social justice and eco-nomic efficiency; and life at work and beyond. Chapter 6 looks at how the Blair government has attempted to project a new sense of Britishness in the context of a multi-cultural and multi-national state. Chapter 7 explores in more detail how Labour's constitutional reforms challenge the structure and identity of the United Kingdom and how Labour's pluralist politics struggles with the desire for 'strong government'. Chapter 8 assesses how Labour's commitments to social justice and social inclusion are operating within a work-orientated policy framework. Chapter 9 looks more closely at the Blair government's family policies and at the debate on the work / life balance.

We thank the many people, too numerous to mention, who have offered us advice, help and support with our work.

Versions of chapters 3, 5, 6, 7 and 9 have appeared in the following journals and we are grateful to the following for permission to present them here: the Policy Press for 'Left, right and the third way', in vol. 28, no. 2, of *Policy and Politics* (April 2001), reproduced here as chapter 3; Palgrave, for 'Capitalism, globalization and democracy: does social democracy have a role?' in *Social Democracy: Global and National Perspectives* (2001), reproduced here as chapter 5; Oxford University Press for 'Blair and Britshness' in *British Cultural Studies*, reproduced here as chapter 6; C. D. Howe Institute for 'The new UK: devolution and the union state', in *Inroads* 9, 2000, reproduced here as chapter 7; Blackwell Publishing for 'New Labour, work and family' in *Social Policy and Administration*, vol. 36, no. 1 (February 2002), reproduced here as chapter 9.

Part I

After Thatcherism

1

1997

Eighteen Years is a Very, Very Long Time in Politics

A week, Harold Wilson famously said, is a long time in politics. Eighteen years, then, must feel like an eternity. Certainly that was how it felt for Labour politicians, activists and voters during the party's 'wilderness years' from 1979 to 1997. And just when Labour supporters must have thought that victory would never come – and Wilson was the last Labour leader to win back in 1974 – two landslide wins come in quick succession. Labour, the sick party of British politics in the 1980s, has become its conqueror. The Conservatives, once seen as the 'natural party of government', appear all but dead in the water.

It was not meant to be like this. When Labour lost the 1992 general election, a poll mid-recession they should have won (as Bill Clinton said on winning elections: 'it's the economy, stupid!'), the political pundits delivered their verdict (Heath, Jowell and Curtice 1994). The best the party of the organized working class could hope for was a share in government. The Tories, past masters in winning political power, could not be beaten by Labour alone. For those with an itch to gamble, the Grand National looked a better bet than a Labour administration.

The reasons for such long odds are clear. The Labour Party's 'heartland' supporters were shrinking in number. The world of male, manual work in unionized manufacturing industries was in long decline. In its place was a new economic landscape where women work as much as men, the majority in service-sector, often non-unionized, jobs. Lifestyles and political identities have changed as well. This is due partly to changing patterns of employment and the fragmentation of traditional working-class communities. An ageing population has been a factor too (older people tend to be more conservative), as has the pervasive consumer culture of post-war Britain. Class does remain an important, if not the principal, factor in how people vote (Evans 1999). But voters have become less partisan, more likely to shop around, encouraging political parties to poach opponents' core supporters. Drawn to Thatcherism in the 1980s, the skilled working class – the C1s and C2s – joined the middle classes to keep the Conservatives in government. As we shall see, Blair's success has been to win back these skilled workers plus large sections of the more Tory-inclined middle-class electorate.

None of this in fact is very new. In the post-war decades, Labour modernizers such as Hugh Gaitskell and Tony Crosland were facing similar economic, social and cultural changes. Just as now, the Labour Party had to cast its appeal beyond its core working-class vote. Sociologists charted the rise of a new working class and its increasingly bourgeois lifestyle – though the extent of 'embourgeoisement' was disputed in studies of this new 'affluent worker'. In the 1970s, the American sociologist Daniel Bell argued that long-term shifts away from manufacturing to service-sector employment marked *the coming of post-industrial society*. In France, Alain Touraine claimed that the new information technologies were doing much the same. By the start of the 1980s, the *post-industrial society* had become the *information society*. The French neo-Marxist André Gorz was bidding 'farewell to the working class' and to the partisan politics that went with it. In Britain, Eric Hobsbawm and Martin Jacques suggested that the 'forward march' of Labour had been halted (Hobsbawm and Jacques 1981). The scene was well and truly set for the ascendancy of the New Right.

Taken together, these economic, social and cultural changes have stacked the electoral deck against parties of the Left. By the start of the 1990s, Labour modernizers faced the grim prospect of an electorate with more natural Tories than Labour voters. These electoral numbers meant that, if Labour were to have any chance of winning outright, the party would have to perform at the very top of its post-war range – and the Tories would have to screw up! To form a government, in other words, the Labour Party had to mobilize its own natural supporters – shrinking in number and changing in character – *and* appeal beyond its class roots to non-

Labour voters, both conservative and liberal. Back in the early 1990s, political scientists doubted whether Labour could win. More than likely, they thought, the party would have to make do with a coalition with the Liberal Democrats.

What a difference five years make. By 1997, with a charismatic leader and seemingly election-proof policies – and a Tory government close to collapse – Labour looked set to romp home. On average, opinion polls showed Labour to have a 16-point lead on the eve of voting – a lead they had held for much of the previous parliament. But after 1992, lingering doubts over the accuracy of these polls meant that few took the election for granted – and even fewer predicted a 179-seat majority in the House of Commons. Two landslide victories later, the fears of the early 1990s that the Labour Party was a spent force seem absurd. The question today is not whether Labour can win, but can they lose? In a remarkable turnaround in punditry, the political sage Bob Worcester has predicted twenty years of unbroken Labour government – a prediction which, if made a decade ago, might have seen him committed (Worcester and Mortimore 1999).

Back from the Brink

So how has the Labour Party got itself into such a winning position? The short answer is that Labour listened – not so much to the public but to those who predicted the party's emasculation as a political force. Labour modernizers learnt the electoral lessons of late twentieth-century politics. Society was changing; the voters were changing; political parties had to change; governments had to change. As Philip Gould, one of the architects of New Labour, conceded:

> Labour had failed to understand that the old working class was becoming a new middle class: aspiring, consuming, choosing what was best for themselves and their families. They had outgrown crude collectivism and left it behind in the supermarket car park. (Gould 1999, 4)

Tony Blair's skill as party leader has been to appeal directly to this 'new middle class'. But he alone did not make Labour electable. If truth be told, Neil Kinnock and John Smith as Labour leaders in the 1980s and early 1990s had already pulled the party

back from the brink. Political scientists are still debating exactly
when all of this 'modernization', if that is what it is, started: was
it in 1983 or in 1987, or is it better seen as a gradual and staged
process (see Lent 1997; Heffernan 1998)? Officially, little of significance changed until after the party's defeat in 1987. But unoffi-
cially, Labour's leaders by the mid-1980s had acknowledged that
something had to change (see Jones 1996) – and that the party, as
Blair would later say, had to 'modernize or die'. Two key things
were reformed by Kinnock and Smith in the 1980s and early
1990s: the organization of the party and its policies.

Reforms to the organization of the party fundamentally
changed its structure and character. By the 1992 general election,
Labour had become a centralized and effective campaigning organization with techniques drawn from the media, marketing and
advertising. Some see this as a shift to an 'electoral-professional
party' that has little need for members, but others argue that there
are limits, not least to how far political parties such as Labour can
go without their card-carrying foot-soldiers (see Seyd and Whiteley 2001). Reforms to the organization of the Labour Party have
undermined the influence of trade unions and activists in the
party's affairs, making the party less prone to public displays of
disunity. Labour's left wing was marginalized and, in the case of
the Trotskyist Militant Tendency, expelled. By the time Tony Blair
became leader in 1994, *Old* Labour, Left or Right, had lost its grip
on the party machine.

Moreover, the left-wing policies of the 1983 manifesto – the high-
water mark of the Left's influence – were gradually watered down
and then, sometimes quietly, dropped. After Labour's defeat in
1987, the pace of reform accelerated (see Jones 1996; Shaw 1996). A
policy review was established by Kinnock, and there followed significant shifts in party policy leading up to the 1992 general election manifesto. On the economy, Labour embraced the market; the
commitment to public ownership, such as the renationalization of
those utilities like gas and water privatized by the Conservatives,
was dropped. The role of government in Labour thinking on the
economy became limited to competition policy and to market failures such as training and research and development. The policy
review also sounded the death-knell for Keynesian macro-econom-
ics and withdrawal from the European Community. From now on,
the party became committed to the more orthodox goal of stable
prices and membership of the European Exchange Rate Mechanism. Labour's opposition to the Conservative government's contro-

versial trade-union law, legislation that considerably weakened the power of organized labour, largely evaporated. And what was seen as the party's albatross during the 1987 election, unilateral nuclear disarmament, was buried.

The policy review witnessed significant shifts in Labour thinking on many of the big policy issues: the role of government in the economy, industrial relations, Europe and defence. The genesis of New Labour lies in the process of reform to the Labour Party's organization, politics and policies from 1983 onwards. A lot of the policy positions that are attributed to New Labour thinking are in fact the product of an earlier period. There is little doubt that, on the death of John Smith in 1994, the Labour Party was in an electable state. Its leadership was admired, its policy commitments modest and largely uncontroversial. Some even believe that the party would have won in 1997, Blair or no Blair (Worcester and Mortimore 1999).

The election of Tony Blair as leader of the Labour Party consolidated a process of reform that had been under way for a decade. In many respects, Blair's leadership has been a cautious one: Labour's campaign theme in 1997 was to promise only what it could deliver, and to stick for two years to Conservative spending limits if it won. This caution irritates the Left, who want Blair to be bolder and more radical. Critics accuse New Labour of putting 'safety first' (Anderson and Mann 1997). But the influence of Blair's leadership can be understated. His leadership of the party – in opposition and government – has seen significant shifts in policy: on taxation, public spending, welfare reform, schooling, the role of the private sector in the provision of public services, and law and order. Many of these reforms, as we hope to show in this book, have taken the 'modernization' of the party beyond the policy review – further certainly than those reformers such as Roy Hattersley, the former deputy leader of the party in the 1980s, are happy with. Whether Blair's reforms mark a tightening of the Thatcherite grip on Labour politics, as some believe, or whether they offer a new direction for social democratic politics is, in part, what this book seeks to answer.

The Dark Days of Conservative Government

It is one of the received wisdoms of politics that oppositions don't win elections, governments lose them. 1997 confirms this old electoral adage. The Conservative government blew it. Despite a remarkable recovery in British economic fortunes in the mid-1990s, John Major's government will be remembered as one increasingly remote, abusing its power, which imploded under the weight of party divisions over Europe.

But it is worth remembering how well Major did in April 1992, a tight election that the Conservatives won on a large turnout. The new Tory administration had a working majority of twenty-two – slim, yes, but not unworkable. Prime Minister Major basked in the glory of military victory in the Gulf War. At home his government looked set fair to continue the Conservative revolution in the public services. And Major offered a style of consensual leadership that promised to put cabinet government back at the heart of British constitutional politics after the 'presidential' years of Margaret Thatcher (see Kavanagh and Seldon 1999; Hennessy 2000). But just when John Major must have thought that his day had come, he got hit by a sucker punch: Europe. His government was quickly on the ropes – and there it stayed.

The irony is that Labour supported the very policy that first floored John Major's government: membership of the Exchange Rate Mechanism (or ERM). The ERM was a fledgling Europe-wide monetary policy. Membership of the ERM required participating countries to maintain their currencies within specified exchange-rate bands. Britain joined in October 1990 in the last days of Margaret Thatcher's administration. The Labour Party, under the fiscally prudent hand of John Smith as shadow chancellor, fully endorsed Britain's membership. By this time, Labour had switched from being a Eurosceptic party committed to withdrawal from the European Community to a supporter of far greater European integration. The ERM was one such step towards closer cooperation among Britain's European partners.

But there was a flaw to the pound's participation in the ERM: it was overvalued relative to other currencies. This was hurting Britain's economic prospects. International currency traders knew it, and they hit the pound where it hurt by selling it. By the end of the summer of 1992, the strain of membership was starting to show. The Conservative government parried by raising interest rates, but its defence lacked weight. The dealers scented blood. On 'Black Wednesday', 16 September, the Conservative government was forced to throw in the towel as the pound was sent flying to the canvas – and out of the ERM. And with it went the

Conservative Party's reputation for sound economic management – a reputation that it has still to recover.

The European monetary troubles of the Conservative government were Labour's great chance. They didn't blow it. First John Smith, then Gordon Brown, Labour's shadow chancellors in the 1990s, set out to make the party bank manager-friendly. Certainly the foundations for Gordon Brown's reputation as an 'iron chancellor' were set by Smith as shadow chancellor under Kinnock and then as party leader in his own right. Indeed, over a longer perspective, Smith and Brown completed the shift in Labour's macro-economic policy away from Keynesian demand management to a more orthodox anti-inflationary position first sketched by the Labour prime minister James Callaghan in 1976. This Eric Shaw describes as initially the 'unravelling' and then the 'abandonment' of Keynesian social democracy that is key, Shaw believes, to New Labour (Shaw 1996).

For much of the 1980s, the Labour Party remained committed to an essentially Keynesian view of the world. It believed that the role of government was to manage demand in the economy by taxing and spending in order to create full employment. Some modernizers such as Bryan Gould and Roy Hattersley remained committed Keynesians. Gould in particular was deeply critical of the orthodox economic assumptions of the Bank of England, the Treasury and the City of London generally. He believed that underinvestment in the British economy could be pinned on the monetarist mania with inflation embedded in these institutions. John Smith, however, was far more sceptical of the power of government to manage the economy to stimulate growth and employment. His defeat of Gould in the race to become party leader after Labour's 1992 defeat marks an important development in Labour reforms in the 1990s. Under Smith and then Blair, Labour's economic policies have put the control of inflation above employment as the principal goal of macro-economic policy. Balancing the budget over the economic cycle, not demand management to stimulate growth, has become Labour's economic target. As we shall see shortly, this acceptance of the Conservative macro-economic legacy – especially that articulated by Geoffrey Howe and Nigel Lawson – causes many to believe that New Labour is nothing more than Thatcherism Mark 2.

Labour's good fortune on Black Wednesday was set to continue. The pound's ignominious exit from the ERM was actually pretty good news for the British economy: the late 1990s were set

to be, more or less, boom years. But the question of Britain's place
in Europe was to dog John Major's government for the next five
years. Post-Black Wednesday, those parts of the Tory party that
had always been, or who had become, sceptical of Britain's membership of the European Union turned their ire on the government. For a party that had always prided itself on loyalty, this
was to spell disaster. In 1992, John Major had returned from the
Dutch city of Maastricht believing that he had won a great victory
for Britain. In the negotiations with its continental partners on the
future Treaty on European Union, an enormously significant
treaty that set out the terms and dimensions of European integration for the following decade, the prime minister had secured
British opt-outs on the single currency and the social chapter.
After the 1992 ERM crisis, Major's next battle was with his own
backbenchers on ratifying the treaty in the House of Commons.
Both Labour and the Liberal Democrats supported the treaty, but
Labour was willing to vote against it to defeat Major's government. This it did. Major needed every vote he could get. On 22
July, twenty-three Tory MPs voted against the government, which
lost by eight votes. The next day, the prime minister made the
votes on the Maastricht treaty a confidence motion in his government. He won by forty votes.

Conservative divisions over Europe intensified following the
Maastricht vote. The 'bastards', as Major dubbed the party's hard-
line Eurosceptics not so privately, made his government increasingly unstable. As by-election defeats eroded the Conservatives'
Commons majority, the government found it increasingly difficult
to get its legislative business through parliament: privatizing the
Post Office, for example, was shelved. John Major's leadership
became a matter for continual speculation and intrigue. By May
1993, Norman Lamont, chancellor during the ERM crisis, was replaced by Kenneth Clarke at the Treasury. In a speech to the
Commons, Lamont stuck the boot into Major's premiership by
saying that Major gave the impression of being 'in office, but not
in power'. As the popularity of the government fell, so Major in
June 1995 called his Tory detractors' bluff. He resigned as party
leader (though not as PM) and memorably challenged any opponents to 'put up or shut up'. Arch Eurosceptic John Redwood put
up, resigning from Major's cabinet, and lost – 219 Tory MPs to 89,
with 22 abstentions.

Major was safe, just, until the next general election. But divisions over Europe persisted, divisions that overshadowed much

of the rest of the government's policy agenda on the public services (for example, the private finance initiative), the reorganization of local government (the switch to more unitary authorities),
welfare reform (such as pensions and welfare to work) and law
and order (longer sentences, to name but one of Home Secretary
Michael Howard's attempts to get tough on crime). The Major
government also made a substantial contribution to the negotiations on Northern Ireland that led in August 1994 to an IRA
ceasefire and which paved the way for the devolution of government to Belfast under the Blair administration.

But these many reforms – some of which, such as the PFI and
welfare reform, have been embraced by the Labour government –
have largely been forgotten. Apart from chronic divisions over
Europe, the Conservative government of 1992 to 1997 will be remembered for being caught with its pants down and its hand in
the till. Sleaze, as much as Europe, defines the Major years. From
David Mellor's resignation in September 1992 (for free foreign
holidays; but his beloved Chelsea shorts had already metaphoric-
ally been found around his ankles!), a string of government ministers resigned over personal conduct (the full list of twelve is on p.
15 of Butler and Kavanagh 1997). Part of the problem lay with
Major's 'back-to-basics' speech at the Tory Party conference in
October 1993, which was interpreted, partly unfairly, as marking
a government crusade against lax moral standards. But the allegations of cash for parliamentary questions made against Neil Ham-
ilton and Tim Smith, junior ministers in Major's government,
brought to the fore serious questions about the propriety of the
government. As a result of these allegations, Major established a
Commission on Standards in Public Life under Lord Nolan,
whose first report, published in May 1995, led to a new Commons
Standards and Privileges Committee. This marked the beginning
of the end of parliamentary self-regulation – and is one of the
Major government's enduring legacies.

The 1997 General Election

As all polling evidence shows, the electorate in 1997 were ready
for a change. Voters were as much anti-Tory as pro-Labour. Turnout in the election was low. On almost all policy issues, the Conservatives found themselves trailing Labour. Crucially, the Tories
post-ERM had lost their reputation for sound finances – and this

despite the booming British economy presided over by Chancellor
Kenneth Clarke. 1997 was not to be the year of the economy,
stupid!

But if the Conservatives lost the 1997 election for simply being
Tories – and for being the party that had been in power for eighteen years – so it is also true that Labour played its political hand
skilfully in the years running up to the election. Crucially Tony
Blair and the modernizers made Labour attractive to English conservative and swing voters, especially those in marginal constituencies where general election battles are won and lost. These are
the voters party modernizers thirsted for in the early 1990s:
Labour needed a drop or two of 'southern comfort', they said, by
blending the aspirational values of Thatcherism with Labour's
traditional commitment to the public services (Radice and Pollard
1994). New Labour's message to these voters was that a strong
economy needed a strong society (Gould 1999, 253–6).

It is these voters the Labour Party won in 1997 – or, at least, it is
these voters who deserted the Conservative Party for Labour or
the Liberal Democrats or who didn't vote at all. Labour did do
remarkably well: its vote was up 9 points on 1992; it increased
its share of middle-class voters by the same margin; for the first
time, more women voted Labour than Conservative; the votes of
first-timers and young people were both up by big margins; the
vanguard of Thatcherism, the skilled working class, like their
newspaper *The Sun*, backed Blair, as did the couch-potatoes of
Tory radicalism, the home-owners. Only the over 65s failed to fall
for the charms of New Labour (see Butler and Kavanagh 1997,
table 13.1).

The swings to Labour across the board indicate how successfully the party played the classic politics of 'catch-all'. Seen
through the Downsian model of voter maximization – voters
'shop' with the political party that has the policies they like best,
just like they shop at the supermarket with the best buys – the
Labour Party in the 1990s headed for the middle ground in British
politics: it changed not only its shop window, but what was on
the shelves too. The middle ground is where the majority of
voters are, especially those parts of the electorate that matter:
voters in marginal seats. Labour set about by reassuring these
voters that a Blair government would respect their values, attitudes and ambitions. In doing so, it turned itself from a 'mass' to

a 'catch-all' party, drawing support from a wide slice of British society (Pattie 2001). Crucially, this required Labour to draw a line under some of the central reforms of the Thatcher years. In a largely two-party system, voters on the Left, who are alienated by this accommodation to certain elements of Thatcherism, have nowhere else to go. They will vote Labour anyway – and if they don't it doesn't really matter, because more than likely they live in a safe Labour seat.

But the 1997 general election was not all good news for Labour – or for British politics generally. More people voted for John Major's Tories in 1992 than voted for Tony Blair's Labour Party in 1997: 14 million against 13.5 million. Labour's 1997 landslide was not counted at the ballot box but was a product of the United Kingdom's first-past-the-post system of elections. For good or ill, the newly elected Labour government's commanding position in government was not supported by a majority of the electorate: only 43.2 per cent voted Labour, 30.7 per cent for the Conservatives. So, for every four Labour voters in 1997, three still voted Tory. And, most worrying for British politics, the turnout was only 71.2 per cent, down from 77.7 in 1992 (though the 1992 figure is at the high end of the recent turnout range). This trend in apathy or disillusionment, depending on your view, was set to continue in 2001, when only 59 per cent of the electorate bothered to vote.

The end of macho politics?

1997, many hoped, would mark the end of 'macho politics'. Back in 1993, the Labour Party introduced women-only shortlists for selection for Westminster constituencies, but these were outlawed by the courts in 1996. Still, the 1997 general election saw the number of women MPs jump from 60 in 1992 to 120, 18.2 per cent of the total chamber – 101 sitting on the new government benches. This was hardly revolutionary, or even Scandinavian, in proportion, but it did appear to mark a breakthrough in the political representation of women in Britain.

Hopes were raised that the presence of more women would make a difference to the macho world of British politics: 'The air of excitement around the election of Labour's 101 women MPs came partly from the widespread hope that politics would change. This applies both to the types of policies which are implemented and to the culture, reputation and practices of politics itself' (Eagle and Lovenduski 1998, 3). But would a majority of the female MPs share a distinctive women's perspective on policy issues (if such a perspective exists in the first place); and would they act on the basis of such differences? This debate is ongoing: some studies suggest that the majority of Labour's 101 female MPs are 'attitudinal feminists' (Childs 2001), others that female MPs possess a range of views (Bochel and Briggs 2000).

As we shall see in the next chapter, many of Labour's flagship policies directly concern, and materially affect, women. The national childcare strategy, the working families' tax credit, the increases to child benefit and reforms to maternity leave are all policies that address issues that impact disproportionately on the lives of women. The Women's Unit set up by Labour in the Cabinet Office has done much to press for a progressive political agenda. But there is less evidence to suggest that more women in parliament has affected the culture of British politics – for example, by making it less adversarial.

Many women (and men, for that matter) have become frustrated at the conservatism of parliamentary politics at Westminster. Some even indicated that they would not seek re-election. The Speaker, Betty Boothroyd, proved no ally in Labour's first term for those MPs who wanted to reform Commons practice and procedure – and even those MPs who wished to breast-feed in the chamber. Moreover, the government's commitment to a cabinet post for a minister for women was downgraded. Only in Labour's second term have we seen a significant advancement in the position and status of women in government: seven women were appointed to the cabinet – a record for British politics. Patricia Hewitt was made minister for women alongside her post as Secretary of State for Trade and Industry. Estelle Morris was given the new education and skills department. Tessa Jowell became culture minister; Margaret Beckett, Secretary of State for Environment, Food and Rural Affairs; Hilary Armstrong, Chief Whip; Clare Short, international development minister; and Helen Liddell, minister for Scotland. Harriet Harman made a comeback in the non-cabinet job of Solicitor-General. But at the 2001 election, the number of female Labour MPs dropped to 88 – and the government set out plans in its first queen's speech of the new parliament to change the law to allow positive discrimination in the election of parliamentary candidates.

Style over Substance?

Was Labour's victory in 1997 a triumph of style over substance, as is often claimed? It is certainly true that the modern Labour Party has taken political communications in Britain to new heights: much of what New Labour did on the campaign trail had been learnt from Bill Clinton and the New Democrats in the USA (see Rentoul, 1995, chapter 13; Jones 1995 and 1997). Under the direction of Peter Mandelson (who first became Labour's communication director in 1985) and Philip Gould (who had been on the campaign trail with the Democrats in the 1992 US presidential elections), the Labour Party's political communications were thoroughly modernized. Under Mandelson, a 24–hour campaign and media centre was established at Millbank Tower on the Thames in London, close to Westminster. This centre worked to the party leadership and was single-minded in keeping the party 'on message' as the election approached – much to the envy of Tory strategists. Labour's 'spin-doctors', led by Blair's press secretary, Alistair Campbell (former political editor of the *Daily Mirror*), and Gordon Brown's Charlie Whelan, successfully put across Labour's interpretation of events to the media, albeit bringing accusations of both bullying and flattery. Under Gould's constant prompting, campaigning techniques were brought over from the USA, most famously the rapid rebuttal unit, a computerized database of information for countering the Tory message (it was used, for example, to respond quickly in November 1996 to Conservative costings of Labour's draft manifesto). Under Campbell, Labour courted the tabloid press, in particular *The Sun* and the *Daily Mail*. Hopeful that the Tory tabloids would give Labour an easier ride than they did in 1992, Campbell's strategy proved an even greater success: on the opening day of the election, *The Sun* came out for Blair. Across the country, Labour gathered and collated information on individual voters in key marginal constituencies; and target voters – 'soft Conservatives' and those showing a willingness to switch to Labour – were polled by telephone before and during the election campaign; other computerized marketing techniques such as target mailing were used extensively. Labour also commissioned considerable amounts of market research, including small focus groups, to test the party's message. During the heat of the election battle, Labour candidates were faxed a 'daily brief' at 1 a.m. to coordinate 'the message'; senior Labour figures, among them Mandelson, Gould, Campbell and Brown, met at Millbank at 7 a.m. in preparation for an 8.30 a.m. press conference. Meeting throughout the rest of the day, the Millbank 'war room' reviewed the campaign in the light of market research and other feedback. The 'message' Labour sold at the 1997 election was also much influenced by Clinton's New Democrats: the youthfulness and dynamism of Blair and *New* Labour; the idea of 'time for a change' and of *partnership* between government and the people. The soundbites, as Butler and Kavanagh point out in their review of the campaign, 'were relentlessly repeated': Labour's were 'Two tier health service', 'Britain deserves better' and 'Enough is enough'. And, in this battle of the soundbite, Labour won (Butler and Kavanagh, 1997, 235).

But whatever happened on the 1997 stump, New Labour are not all spin and no substance. Beneath the soundbites and the ever more careful packaging *is* something substantial. Many on the Left may feel uneasy about New Labour's policies, but policies there are in plenty. It is a mistake to miss the substance for the style. Whether voters responded more to New Labour's style is more difficult to judge. Opinion polls suggest that, under Blair's leadership, Labour came to be a party trusted on issues where previously they had been thought of as soft, especially by middle-class voters – in particular, the management of the economy and law and order. Blair himself proved a thoroughly charismatic leader, able to communicate with the electorate directly in much the same way as he appealed to individual Labour Party members over the heads of sectional groups. His appeal to 'one nation' (and, after the election, to a 'patriotic alliance') allowed Blair to distance *New* from *Old* Labour and to project the party as a potential government that would bring unity to the country. Blair's ability to strike a chord with popular sentiments has served Labour well. But this 'popular touch' is not the central point. It may have helped Labour get elected, but in the end what voters found attractive were Blair's policy reforms: on the economy, welfare reform and law and order, which were, in any case, the substantive base of the party's soundbites during the election campaign. Indeed, it was the leading Labour modernizer Giles Radice who argued before John Smith's death in 1994 that the message, not just the messenger, had to change: style alone would not bring the party the votes it needed to win middle-class middle England (Radice and Pollard, 1994). And, according to Butler and Kavanagh: 'Surveys do not suggest that many voters decide how to vote on the basis of the skill with which a party's campaign is presented. In 1987 and 1992 Labour was widely judged to have fought at least as good a campaign as the Conservatives but lost both elections decisively' (Butler and Kavanagh, 1997, 237).

In any case, what New Labour has brought to contemporary British politics is the culmination of longer-term trends. Political scientists have various names for this process: the 'Americanization', 'personalization', 'presidentialization' or 'modernization' of politics (see Norris, 1997). These names reflect the perceived influence of American campaigning techniques and media coverage on British electoral politics. Rather than being of a recent vintage, politics in Britain has taken an 'American turn' since the 1950s, dating to the spread of television and polling (see Rosenbaum 1996). It was in this period that politics was turned into a horse-race: the media treating elections as races between parties, with opinion polls giving a constant up-date on the position of the runners and riders; and the party managers responding by putting more and more attention into grooming the politicians in the media and the public eye.

The central message of Labour's 1997 election campaign was, as one party strategist put it, 'reassurance, reassurance, reassurance'. This hasn't stopped Labour's landslide victory being heralded as a decisive turning point in British politics. It marked a turn away from the Conservatives and their ideological obsessions: it was a time, as Blair has repeated, to move 'beyond Thatcherism'. But was it? Will 1997 go down in political history as a 1945 or a 1979: an election that points to a watershed in political ideas and public policy? To be sure, the whole notion of political watersheds is problematic. Much of the groundwork for Attlee's Labour government was laid by the war-time administration, as well as the Liberal government before the Great War. While 1979 is seen as the birth of Thatcherism, reasonably good cases can be made for saying that Labour under James Callaghan kicked the whole thing off in 1976 during the IMF crisis; or even that Thatcherism proper – the Thatcherism of privatization – didn't really get going until after the 1983 election. Notwithstanding these problems, there is some evidence to suggest that, in terms of party ideologies, party loyalties and other dimensions of political behaviour, 1997 has some of the characteristics of a 'critical election' (see Evans and Norris 1999). But in the end, how important 1997 is depends on what your view of New Labour is. It is to this we want to turn.

Making Sense of New Labour

One of the central themes of this book is to try to make some sense of what New Labour is, what it stands for and how this has been put into practice in government. This attempt to conceptualize the changes to the Labour Party since the 1980s started almost as soon as the process itself did. As we have seen, in the aftermath of electoral defeats in 1983 and 1987, Labour underwent a process of reform – and these reforms sparked a debate about their significance, especially among political scientists. Broadly speaking the interpretations of these reforms fall into two camps: the Thatcherite consensus thesis and the modernization thesis.

The Thatcherite consensus thesis

The first camp believes that Labour, especially after 1987, became more and more like the Conservatives. In playing the politics of 'catch-all', Labour sold its soul to the Tory devil in return for votes. In ditching socialist means, such as redistributive welfare policies, Labour had abandoned socialist ends (Cohen 1994). As a result, Labour became part of a Thatcherite consensus, sharing an 'authoritarian populism', with Blair as 'son of Margaret' (Hall 1994). By the time of the 1997 general election, Labour was offering little more than Conservative policies minus the discredited Tory politicians. In government, its policies continue to reflect a common neo-liberalism and often neo-conservatism with Thatcherism.

Colin Hay argues that after 1987 Labour played the politics of 'catch-up' (Hay 1994). During the policy review, by withdrawing its opposition to privatization and orthodox macro-economic policies, among other things, Labour sought to *accommodate* itself to Thatcherism. Reflecting on the 1997 election, Hay talked of a new 'bipartisan convergence', a 'one-nation polity' that existed in British politics (Hay 1997; see also Heffernan 2001). The post-war 'Keynesian-welfarist paradigm', Hay argued, had been displaced by a new 'neo-liberal paradigm'. And Labour, Hay suggests, had *chosen* to 'modernize' in this way, when they could have chosen to do something much more radical (see Hay 1999).

Critics of the Thatcherism Mark 2 thesis argue that New Labour is much more like Old Labour than most people would care to admit. Responding to Hay's article on the policy review, Martin Smith argued that the accommodation to Thatcherism thesis was too simplistic. Yes, Labour had moved to the right, 'but it shifted policy within its own tradition and returned to the sorts of policies followed by the Labour Government in the past (whether social democratic or not)' (Smith 1994).

The modernization thesis

This continuity with Labour parties and Labour governments past is a critical part of the arguments of the second camp trying to make sense of New Labour. This camp argues that New Labour stands in the long tradition of Labour revisionism, especially that of Crosland and Gaitskell in the 1950s. Just as it was then, the ambition of the current crop of party reformers is to make Labour a progressive party attractive to voters across the political spectrum (Larkin 2001). This view sees the process of *modernization* (the key word) as part of a continual up-dating of the Labour Party and social democratic politics to fit contemporary circumstances. As Andrew Gamble and Gavin Kelly argue, neither social democracy, nor neo-liberalism for that matter, are 'fixed and unchanging' (Gamble and Kelly 2001, 181). So rather than capitulating to the Thatcherite conservative consensus, New Labour is challenging it by modernizing social democracy to fit better the problems and challenges of the contemporary world such as globalization.

While leading New Labour figures such as Gordon Brown have bent over backwards to claim the mantle of revisionist Croslandite social democracy, others are more sceptical (see contributions in Leonard 1998). But Mark Bevir argues that the question of continuity is not just about the similarities between *New* Labour and certain *Old* Labours. Rather: 'to explain New Labour's ideology, we have to trace a historical process in which its adherents inherited a set of beliefs and then modified them in response to salient difficulties' (Bevir 2000, 297). So, simply to equate New Labour with, say, Crosland's brand of social democracy is to miss the contemporary political and policy dilemmas faced by Labour politicians. Equally, to cast it as Thatcherism Mark 2 is to miss the impact of the social democratic tradition – commitments to social justice, citizenship and the welfare state – on New Labour. In some sense, the modernization camp believes that New Labour isn't really very new at all. Labour today is just confronting the same old issues that all progressives from the New Liberals at the turn of the twentieth century to Wilson's modernizers in the 1960s and 1970s have done: that is, the balance of social justice and economic efficiency and the role of the state in bringing such a balance about (Vincent 1998). The difference is that times have changed and New Labour offers a reinterpretation of social democratic ideas for the contemporary world.

Labour modernizers such as Philip Gould, as we have seen, share a version of this argument: times have changed, so must the Labour Party: *New* times equals *New* Labour. As we shall show in chapter 3, Labour's attempt to mark out some kind of 'third way' is voiced as a modernization of social democracy, not its abandonment (Blair 1998c). But New Labour's attempt to establish a new political identity is problematic in two ways. First, New Labour associates itself with social democratic modernizers past, yet disassociates itself by articulating a radical break between *Old* and *New* Labour. Second, while there are clearly novel elements to New Labour, whether these are thought of as neo-liberal or neo-social democrat, the 'one size fits all' approach to Old Labour of Labour modernizers in the end just doesn't work. Even if Old Labour is taken to mean post-war Labour, which exactly of the post-war Labour parties are Labour modernizers thinking of?

Beyond Thatcherism

In assessing the relative merits of these two standard interpretations of Labour reforms under Kinnock, Smith and Blair, we suggest that there are obvious merits in both arguments. As we shall see in the next chapter, the record of Labour in government shows that there are policies that might be seen as Thatcherite, whether neo-liberal or neo-conservative, and others that are more obviously social democratic or liberal-progressive in inspiration and objective. This raises serious questions about the character of the Blair government and its relation to both Thatcherism and Labour's own past.

Central to our argument in this book is that New Labour is not just like any old Labour Party, but neither is it Thatcherism Mark 2. The view, for example, put forward by David Rubinstein, that 'In essentials the party's policies have not changed' (Rubinstein 2000, 161), underestimates the novelty of New Labour and the

Blair administration. To be sure, Rubinstein is right to point out that the rhetoric of Labour politicians in the past is not always matched by their actions. As Tim Bale argues, the 'forgetters' (we plead 'not guilty') tend 'to use the sacred texts, as opposed to the slightly less saintly actions, of Tony Crosland, as a convenient proxy for not just the public ideology, but also the governmental practice of the entire Labour leadership before 1979' (Bale 1999, 196). So, where *Old* Labour 'talked left' but 'acted right', *New* Labour 'talks right, acts left' – and rather conveniently all Labour governments past and present become much of a muchness.

This, we believe, underestimates the novelty of Blair's Labour government. The pragmatic post-war social democratic arguments for a mixed economy have given way, rightly or wrongly, to the celebration of competitive markets and private enterprise. The privatization of public assets and services has continued under Labour. The Blair government has become the champion of public-sector reform. Labour is business-friendly as never before. The government is committed to maintaining Britain's status as a low inflation and low-tax economy. Despite new legislation on trade-union rights, there has been no return to the pre-Thatcher days of labour law. Those such as Rubinstein who want to emphasize the continuities between the Blair government and other post-war Labour administrations are right to point out that Labour governments, for example, have attacked trade unions in the past. But in the Blair era, after two decades of Tory reforms and industrial decline, trade unions are a shadow of their former selves – and, under John Monks, the TUC has sought out a new role under the banner 'new unionism'. At the 2000 Labour conference, the union barons gave Tony Blair a bloody nose over pensions – just like the good old days of Labour governments past. But the influence – real and symbolic – of unions, as well as the political Left, in the Labour Party has diminished. By and large, Labour now supports the idea of flexible labour markets – with the usual 'not as flexible as the Tories' caveat. The government's reforms of the welfare state reflect this. Building on Conservative pilots, Labour is promoting work, not welfare. Benefits entitlements have become subject to participation in work and training programmes, and time-limits have been introduced. There is, as Gordon Brown likes to say, no 'fifth option' of staying at home for those capable of work. To this government, any job is better than a life of dependency on the dole.

These shifts in policy – shifts that Rubinstein himself acknowledges – are not consistent with his conclusion that Blair's Labour 'is the direct successor of the Labour Party of the past'. Far from rejecting the 'current orthodoxy' that 'New Labour represents a clearly defined break from the Labour Party's past', Rubinstein's own balance sheet of changes seems to support it, with all his qualifications about continuity accepted. _cory_

But this government is not a facsimile of previous Tory ones – and here we want to break with the Thatcherism Mark 2 thesis. The minimum wage has been introduced, child benefit upgraded, free nursery places funded, childcare provision secured and tax revenues redistributed to the public services and the working poor. The government has introduced new workplace regulations such as the working time directive and other limitations to the market economy that are anathema to economic libertarians. These policies are things we might expect from a Labour administration and represent a social democratic and progressive ethos to New Labour.

What made New Labour new is important for understanding the novelty of Blair's government. As Michael Kenny and Martin Smith suggest, no account of New Labour can ignore the constraints facing the Labour Party in the late twentieth century, the dilemmas the party faced and the responses to such constraints and dilemmas by Labour reformers (Kenny and Smith 2001). Labour faced in the 1970s and 1980s an economic environment that was rapidly changing. These changes, rightly or wrongly, were conceptualized in certain ways – as 'globalization', for example – and this led to certain arguments about how best to respond in policy terms to them. Labour faced, too, a political system that was straining at its constitutional seams and a set of political numbers that, as we have seen, did not make pretty reading. The Labour Party, as Kenny and Smith argue, was confronted with a series of dilemmas arising out of these constraints: could the party ever be trusted to manage the economy again? How could it build an electoral coalition capable of taking on the Tories? And how should Labour deal with the legacy of Thatcherism?

The modernizer camp (and Labour modernizers themselves share this view) sees the reforms undertaken by Kinnock, Smith and Blair as a rational response to the profound economic and social changes that have taken place since the 1970s. A world increasingly shaped by globalization and the erosion of traditional economic, social and cultural roles was never likely to leave the political ideologies of the Left or Right untouched. As we shall examine in chapters 4 and 5, social democrats across Europe and beyond spent most of the 1980s and 1990s considering how best to respond to the challenges of globalization. It seems highly unlikely that the Labour Party would not have done the same. But would the Labour Party have 'modernized' in the way it did if it hadn't been for Thatcherism?

The 'new times' argument is missing a certain something – and that certain something is Thatcherism. Martin Smith (Smith 2001) suggests that there is an element of 'path dependency' to what New Labour is and what it has tried to achieve in power – and both Thatcherism and Old Labour are part of the New Labour story. As Mark Wickham-Jones argued about the policy review, the reforms undertaken by Kinnock are better seen as an attempt to recast social democracy in the light of the changes brought about by Thatcherism (Wickham-Jones 1995). Without falling into the 'New Labour equals Thatcherism' trap, we believe that the story of the Labour Party in the last decades of the twentieth century would be very different if Thatcherism had not existed in Britain. There is something more important about the impact of Thatcherism than simply an accommodation to it.

Steve Ludlam is, of course, right to argue that many New Labour themes reflect the failure of the post-war Labour Party to find a workable and coherent political package in a deteriorating economic and political climate, as much as they reflect Thatcherism (Ludlam 2001a). But Thatcherism was itself part of the 'new times' in Britain – and it is inevitable that, after Thatcherism, Blair's (and Kinnock's and Smith's) Labour has responded to the Thatcherite agenda on 'new times'. For us, Thatcherism was always more than just four Tory governments in a row. Yet, Thatcherism, just like the 'post-war consensus', was never as seamless as it is often portrayed. But there was at the heart of Conservatism in the 1980s a fundamental challenge to the values and policy instruments of the Left. As Michael Harris argues, the Centre-Left was forced, in particular, to rethink the role of markets in social democratic politics (Harris 1999). To be sure, this rethink would have happened anyway, just as it did in the rest of Europe and in Australia and New Zealand. But would it have happened quite the way it did if it hadn't been for Thatcherism?

For more than a decade, the ideas of the Right in Britain were hegemonic – perhaps more useful a concept here than 'consensus' – just as the ideas of the liberal Left were the leading ones in the post-war period. The reform of the Left grew out of a changing

economic, social and political context – and the challenge from the
Right was part of that context. But the political war between Left
and Right was an engagement, not a battle fought at a distance.
And the new 'New Left' that emerged in the early 1990s was, in
part, shaped by these engagements with the forces of Thatcherism. In part, this meant drawing a line under many of the fundamental reforms of Conservative governments in the 1980s and
1990s. In this sense, Labour did accommodate itself to Thatcherism. But the engagement was not one-sided: Labour (and the Left
more broadly) brought something to the intellectual and political
table – something more rooted in its own past – that has allowed
the Blair government to move beyond Thatcherism: to take public
policy-making beyond the domain of the New Right. This is what
we mean by 'post-Thatcherism'. This is why Blair's New Labour
is not just like any old Labour government – or any old Tory one
either.

2

Labour in Power, 1997–2001

In the aftermath of the 1997 general election, opinion was divided on the significance of Labour's victory. Was it the start of something new or business as usual? Would the new Labour government turn out to be, as the editors of the centre-left *Political Quarterly* posed, 'a great reforming administration' or 'one that broadly accepts the agenda it inherited' (Gamble and Wright 1997, 315)? Would *New* Labour map out a *new* social democracy? Or was the central message of 1997, as it would be for 2001, as William Rees-Mogg put it, that 'Thatcherism is safe with New Labour: that is the core message' (Rees-Mogg 1997 and 2001)?

How does Labour measure up in power? Are we witnessing government by neo-liberals or neo-social democrats? Or does the study of Labour in power offer a more complicated picture, one that reveals an administration both embracing yet pushing beyond Thatcherism? In this chapter we shall sketch out five areas of domestic public policy and examine Labour's record in government.[1] These are: economic policy; welfare reform; public services such as health and education; the constitution; and law and order. Then we want to return to the question: what kind of administration is the Labour government? What are the criteria for evaluating the Labour Party's first term in power for a quarter of a century? Is there even one New Labour or are there many sides to Tony Blair's administration? The central theme of the

1 Studies of Labour's record in government include: Powell (1999), Savage and Atkinson (2001), Toynbee and Walker (2001), Ludlam and Smith (2001), Coates and Lawler (2000), White (2001) and Rawnsley (2001).

chapter is that Labour's policies reflect both continuity and change of previous Conservative policy-making: the New Labour government is neither wholly Thatcherism Mark 2, nor wholly a modernized social democracy. Instead, we argue, the study of Labour in power reveals a government taking politics and policy-making *beyond* Thatcherism.

Economic Policy

The strange case of the Labour Chancellor the City came to trust

In political folklore, the election of a Labour government is followed by a run on the pound, just as night follows day. The financiers in the City of London don't like socialists at the Treasury. They don't trust a Labour government not to hock the crown jewels to pay for lavish public-spending projects. So, they sell sterling and the government quickly finds itself facing a monetary crisis. Such crises – 1931, 1967, 1976 – are etched into the collective memory of the Labour Party. The party's left wing never forgives the inevitable 'betrayal of socialism' as Labour leaders stop doing the things that socialists are meant to do in power. But New Labour, as Martin Smith points out, 'has learnt the lessons of old Labour in government' (Smith 2001, 256). Gordon Brown was not about to go down in history as yet another Labour chancellor who blew it. Here was a man who believed he could combine 'prudence' with 'purpose'. But how prudent? What purpose?

Labour won the 1997 election partly because the Conservatives had lost their reputation for sound economic management. After eighteen years of Tory governments, the electorate was willing to give Labour a chance at the control of the economic levers of power. Already by 1992 Labour had gone some way to appeasing the City of London. As we saw in chapter 1, the policy review had made the prospect of a Labour government far less daunting for business. But Labour made a fatal political error in the 1992 general election campaign. Not unreasonably for a party of the Left, it promised to raise pensions and child-benefit levels and to pay for them by increasing the top rate of income tax and middle-income national insurance contributions. The Tories seized on these throw-backs to Old Labour, labelling John Smith's shadow budget 'Labour's tax bombshell'. Labour's campaign was holed below the water-line.

By July 1993, these rather modest tax proposals had been abandoned. And in the run-up to the 1997 election, Labour was making a virtue out of *not* spending extra money on the public services, as well as promising not to raise higher income tax rates. Labour leaders bent over backwards to assure business, and the City of London in particular, that a New Labour government would not be like any old Labour government. Following John Smith's lead in the early 1990s, Gordon Brown committed the party to the traditional economic virtues of low inflation, a balanced budget, reducing the national debt – and *not* taxing and spending like Labour governments are supposed to. Labour, if elected, its leaders promised, would help set an economic framework – of low inflation, low taxes, flexible labour markets and modest public spending – to create the kind of incentives and stable expectations that are meant to encourage investment, entrepreneurialism and new business formation.

All of this sounded rather like what the Conservatives had been preaching for twenty years under chancellors Howe, Lawson, Major, Lamont and Clarke. It didn't exactly endear *New* Labour to the Left, who argued that the party had sold out to Thatcherism. In a wonderful role reversal, one of many the party would play in the run-up to the 1997 election, Labour leaders accused the Tories of mismanaging the economy – in 1987 (the Lawson boom) and 1992 (the ERM crisis); of 'boom- and-bust' economic cycles; and raising taxes after 1992, when they promised to cut them. A Labour government, they promised, would do better (see, in particular, Blair 1995b).

Monetary policy

Once in government, Labour delivered its masterstroke. Despite an oblique reference in the manifesto (and an old pamphlet by Brown's chief economic advisor, Ed Balls), the decision to give independence to the Bank of England days after its landslide victory caught everyone by surprise. To those who doubted Labour's new-found monetary prudence, it was rather a pleasant one at that. Independence to the Bank of England meant that the month-to-month setting of interest rates – i.e., monetary policy – would shift from the Treasury, in consultation with the bank, to a Monetary Policy Committee of the Bank of England alone. This committee is

he governor of the bank, and five of its eight members
of the Treasury. The remit of the committee is set by
.⌐ury: to keep inflation within 1 per cent, up or down, of 2.5
˧ cent. If it fails in its mission, the governor has to write a letter to
the chancellor explaining what has gone wrong. So far, the bank
has delivered.

Giving the Bank of England control over monetary policy was a
key marker set down by the incoming government: Labour could
be trusted with inflation because one of the central tools of macro-
economic policy, the setting of interest rates, would not be under
the government's direct control. The bank, which in the 1980s had
gained a reputation for monetarism, would keep a lid on prices
by guarding the growth of money. This was at odds with the
Labour Party's post-war commitment to Keynesian economics.
Keynesian theory said that interest rates should be kept low to
maintain the supply of cheap money and that aggregate demand
should be managed by governments taxing and spending (i.e., an
active fiscal policy) in order to bring the economy into equilib-
rium at full employment.

These assumptions were publicly questioned by the Labour government led by James Callaghan in 1976. But it was the Conservatives who brought about a fundamental shift in the direction of
economic policy. At the heart of economic Thatcherism was the
turn away from Keynesian demand management and the balance
between fiscal and monetary policy. For the Conservatives, governments should cut taxes and public expenditure; the only thing that
needed managing was the supply of money in order to control inflation. This would be done through an active monetary policy, with
the setting of interest rates as the principal economic lever of power.

The government's decision, then, to let the Bank of England set
interest rates established Brown as a Labour chancellor the City
could trust. It would, more or less, be business as usual. Those
opposed to Labour's decision tended to be Keynesians who believed that giving the bank complete control over interest rates
was giving in to monetarism. Governments, they argued, should
have direct control over monetary policy in order to pursue a
more expansionary macro-economic policy based on cheap
money to stimulate growth and employment, especially in Britain's hard-pressed (and shrinking) manufacturing sector, which
suffered as the government's sound money policies kept the value
of sterling high relative to other currencies, thereby making British exports expensive and difficult to sell.

Fiscal policy

Having given up control over the monetary levers of power, Brown was left with his hands on fiscal policy: on levels of taxation and public spending. In theory, an independent central bank, as the Bank of England has effectively become, sets interest rates on the basis of its expectations of what will happen to prices in the future. The trick is for the Treasury and the Bank of England to set complementary fiscal and monetary policies. The Treasury's fiscal policies need to keep taxes and public spending at such levels that the bank is willing to keep interest rates at relatively low levels. Being *prudent*, as Gordon Brown likes to think of himself, is partly about keeping the bank happy. In the first two years of government, Brown was prudent by agreeing to stick to the previous Conservative government's spending plans, even if this meant cutting social-security payments to lone parents, as the government did in 1997 to the uproar of some Labour MPs. So, in May 1997, Conservative Chancellor Kenneth Clarke's spending plans became Labour Chancellor Gordon Brown's spending plans. Those who wanted the new Labour government to behave more like Labour governments of old and increase spending on welfare and the public services were to receive short shrift.

Chancellor Brown enshrined his 'prudence' in Treasury practice by establishing a 'code for fiscal stability' with its two rules: the 'golden rule' states that, over the economic cycle, governments will borrow only to invest and not to fund current spending; and the 'sustainable investment rule' states that public-sector net debt as a proportion of GDP will be held over the economic cycle at a 'stable and prudent level'.

The Conservative economic legacy had a profound influence on the shape and direction of policy-making in Labour's first term. By 1997, Britain was booming – if not uniformly. Under chancellors Lamont and Clarke after 1992, the Conservatives steered the British economy away from the rough waters of recession. They cut public deficits, curbed inflation and introduced greater stability into the economic cycle. Unemployment fell as the economy took off. But, sadly for the Conservatives, no one really noticed – or, if they did, none of the credit went to the government. Labour taunted the Tories for twenty-two tax rises after 1992 – when Major had promised to cut taxes – and few were in the mood to give the Conservatives the credit for unpopular policies (higher taxes) that were necessary to get the economy back on track. After all, the Conservative government had helped get Britain into the mess in the first place.

If the Labour government's economic inheritance was a rich one, it has done little to squander it. Since 1997, the British economy has performed well as real gross domestic product has increased annually: by 2.6 per cent in 1998, 2.3 per cent in 1999 and 3.1 per cent in 2000. By European and world standards, Britain received top marks. At the same time, unemployment fell, from 4.5 per cent in 1998 to 3.6 per cent in 2000, and household incomes rose. But British manufacturing, which accounts for about 20 per cent of the economy, continued to suffer under the pressure of a strong pound or, more specifically, a weak Euro, which made British exports relatively expensive. By the summer of 2001, with the slow-down in the world economy hitting British companies, the UK manufacturing sector went into recession after the second successive quarterly fall in output. The problem monetary policy-makers faced was that something quite different was happening on Britain's high streets, which were still booming.

On tax, following the sound liberal, though not socialist, principle that taxes on consumption are better than taxes on income – they do less to distort work incentives (socialists prefer taxes on incomes because the rich pay more than the poor) – Gordon Brown raised taxes on tobacco, insurance and fuel (though after the 2000 fuel protests the chancellor cut the fuel duty). Income-tax rates under Labour were cut: in 1999, 1p was slashed from the basic rate and a new lower rate of 10p was introduced. The 40p top rate of tax has, as promised, not been increased. Brown abolished two well-known tax allowances: the notoriously middle-class mortgage-interest relief and the married person's tax relief. The chancellor also abolished the dividend credits for pension funds. To raise the finance for the government's welfare-to-work programme, the New Deal, it levied a one-off 'windfall tax' on the privatized utilities – gas, electricity, water and telephones.

These tax changes, including the government's so-called stealth taxes, have helped increase the overall tax burden from 35.2 per cent of national income in 1996/7 to 37.7 per cent in 2000/1 and to swell the Treasury coffers since 1997. The booming economy has seen tax takes increase and social-security payments fall as more people work and pay taxes and stop claiming welfare. Moreover, the government's self-imposed public spending straitjacket was so successful that the proportion of government spending as a percentage of gross domestic product fell from 41.2 per cent in 1996/7 to 37.7 per cent in 1999/2000. As the neo-liberal New Right always wanted, the state under New Labour was being rolled back.

By 2000, then, Gordon Brown had money to play with. But what would the chancellor do? Cut taxes in neo-liberal style or increase spending on collective public services in social democratic fashion? While Brown stuck largely to the Conservatives' spending plans in the first two years of government, he had in fact juggled the books in the spring of 1998 by taking £2.2 billion from the contingency reserve (the government's rainy-day account), giving £1 billion extra to education and £1.2 billion extra to health. As a new millennium turned, Brown was looking at far bigger numbers. In July 2000, the chancellor announced a spending package that would see total managed expenditure by government increase by £68 billion over three years – the equivalent of more than £1000 for every person in the country (Dilnot and Emmerson 2000). Spending on education was set to increase in real terms by 5.4 per cent a year; that on health by 5.6 per cent; and that on the Department of Environment, Transport and the Regions (mostly on transport) by 15.8 per cent. The size of the state was set to grow again. The Treasury forecast that government spending would top 40 per cent of GDP by 2002/3. But this, analysts pointed out, was still less than in all but three years of Conservative government in the 1980s and 1990s.

Brown's budget was not much of a socialist revolution. But neither was it very neo-liberal. Labour was to trust government, not the market, with spending decisions on welfare. Whitehall, under Chancellor Brown, knows best. Indeed, the Treasury has had so much money that Brown has been able to play both the social democratic chancellor – increasing spending on public services – and the prudent neo-liberal chancellor – cutting tax rates and paying off the national debt (helped by £22.5 billion from the sale of third-generation mobile-phone licences in 2000). And if Gordon Brown set the Labour government on course to increase spending on collective public services, so the chancellor has also overseen a redistribution of resources to the poorer sections of British society, especially those in work. The fruits of the booming economy have been targeted by the Labour government on the less well off. As we shall examine in more detail in a moment, welfare and social-security payments to the poor, especially the working poor with children, have risen significantly. While top-rate tax payers haven't been squeezed very much, as Labour chancellors of old liked to boast, the Labour government of 1997–2001 will go down as one that engineered a modest redistribution of resources to the poorest members of society. Whether these redistributions have made Britain a less unequal society remains to be seen.

Chancellor Brown's 'prudence' and his 'purpose', then, are clear: to be prudent is to balance the nation's finances and keep inflation under control. The purpose is to spend the fruits of a strong economy on collective public services and welfare to the working poor, especially those with children. Brown's prudence echoes Thatcherite economic philosophy; his purpose doesn't. But whether Brown can sustain this strategy of investing in the public services over the full economic cycle, without increasing taxes or government borrowing, remains one of the central questions for Labour's second term and beyond.

We're all supply-siders now

Gordon Brown, like Nigel Lawson before him, is a supply-sider. This means that the focus of government attention shifts from the total amount of demand in the economy – spending and investment – to the capacity of the economy to supply that demand without causing inflation. The government's supply-side strategy is aimed at drawing those out of work into the labour market, thereby raising tax revenues and putting downward pressure on wages. Brown's supply-side strategy has had the good fortune to be tested when demand has been buoyant. But, as we shall see in chapter 8, some doubt whether Labour's supply-side assumptions hold where there are regional concentrations of high structural unemployment. Supply, they argue, does not always create its own demand.

The Conservatives in the 1980s believed that the supply-side of the economy had become too inflexible over the post-war years. Businesses had been caught up in a web of laws, regulations and taxes that undermined their competitiveness. Trade unions had become too powerful and were preventing managers from managing. And government had become too big and the state was doing things that were better left to the private sector. The inflexibility of the supply-side, the Conservatives argued, constrained the capacity of the British economy to grow without generating inflation. Supply-side Thatcherism was, then, about deregulating the economy, cutting taxes, reforming labour-relations laws, reducing public spending and privatizing government activities. The Conservatives also believed that those on welfare needed more incentives to take work, so they cut the real value of social security and introduced an in-work benefit, family credit. Conservative ministers such as Keith Joseph also set about reforming the education system to increase the supply of better trained workers (known in the academic literature as the 'new vocationalism'). Taken together, the Conservatives believed, these policies would make British business more competitive and increase in the longer term the non-inflationary economic growth rate.

The Labour Party of old opposed most if not all of these policies. But bit by bit Labour came to terms with them. As we saw in chapter 1, under Neil Kinnock, John Smith and then Tony Blair, Labour started to draw lines under these fundamental features of supply-side Thatcherism, just as it reconciled itself to the anti-inflationary focus of Conservative macro-economic policy.

But New Labour's supply-side agenda was meant to be very different from the neo-liberal agenda of Thatcherism. It was about making British business more productive and competitive by promoting a more skilled workforce ('education, education, education', as Tony Blair famously put it) and the diffusion of new technology in business and society. This was, the government said, to be a new economic revolution based on information. In a global economy, where knowledge is king, business can no longer compete by 'piling high and selling cheap'. It needs to raise its productivity, develop higher quality products and services, often in smaller runs, made by skilled workers whose wages reflect the premium their labour, and the products and services they make, attract in the market. This was New Labour's supply-side dream. It was about empowering both workers and business in the global knowledge economy (see Department of Trade and Industry 1998b; Leadbeater 1999).

It is certainly true that the Labour government of 1997–2001 will go down as one that liked to micro-manage certain aspects of the supply-side of the economy. Its targets to increase the use of information technology in schools and colleges and small and medium-sized businesses, as well as among the 'socially excluded' (partly defined as 'information have-nots'), were attached to a range of government incentives and programmes to deliver the targets. The government, Labour argued, had an important role in bringing about the new 'information age'.

But, in other respects, the fact that the Labour government has retained many of the Conservative supply-side reforms leads some to conclude that it is business as usual. And, on the face of it, the record of Labour in power shows much continuity and little change. The government's message over four years in power is that taxes must be kept low, business freed from 'unnecessary' regulation, competition laws enforced and the trade unions receive 'fairness not favours'. The idea of an industrial policy – aside from a bit of supply-side meddling – appears anathema to Labour modernizers: governments set the general economic framework rather than interfere with the 'business of business'.

Certainly Labour has promoted competition policy with all the zeal of a convert. Indeed, the government has intervened strongly in the market to promote competition. The 1998 Competition Act tightened rules for mergers and gave greater powers to a new Competition Commission and the old Office of Fair Trading. Reflecting Labour's wider 'rip-off Britain' campaign, a 2001 white paper proposed taking on 'hard-core cartels' by making price-fixing a criminal offence, abolishing the 'public interest test' and giving the independent competition authorities, rather than ministers, the final say (Department of Trade and Industry 2001). As we shall see in other sections of this chapter, the Labour government has also continued to increase the role of the private sector in public services; to make work rather than welfare pay; and to make British education at all levels more vocational and business-orientated. *Plus ça change?*

In fact, Labour's record is rather mixed on these ambitions. The tax burden, as we have seen, has risen. The government has intervened (as the Conservatives did too) to prop up the odd 'lame duck' of British industry, although generally Labour has focused state aid to the retraining of workers made redundant. Labour has been as keen on introducing red tape as it has been on cutting it. It signed the social chapter of the Maastricht treaty, implemented the European working time directive, introduced a minimum wage and passed new laws covering maternity and paternity leave. Many of these new regulations reflect long-standing progressive and social democratic concerns on the length of the working day, low pay and the balance between work and family life. On the minimum wage, the government clearly struck a deal between the interests of employers and employees: business would rather not have their hands tied on how much they paid their workers; and workers would like government to set a much higher minimum-wage rate. The result, a starting rate of £3.60 and young people exempt from its main provisions, pleased neither side of industry. But that, the government said, was exactly the kind of balance between economic efficiency and social justice that *New* Labour and its 'third way' was all about. Indeed, the fact that the government intervened to regulate the market economy to the advantage of workers, as well as parents, is significant for defining its political character.

It is true that the Labour government has resisted (and continues to resist) many features of the European 'social partnership' model of market regulation. These include legally binding laws requiring employers to consult with employees on, for example, future redundancies. While in the early 1990s Labour modernizers were often drawn to a model of stakeholder capitalism found on the continent, by 1997 the American model of deregulated markets was more to Labour's liking, and that of Gordon Brown especially.

But the Labour government did establish a review of company law. The final report, published in July 2001, recommended changes to corporate governance in the direction of greater business transparency. The report proposed a new operating and financial review that will require large companies to disclose information on their relationships with customers and suppliers, their financial risks, environmental costs and plans for technical change. The review also suggested that businesses disclose some information on management structure and employment policies. These changes, if acted upon by Labour in its second term, would not exactly deliver a new framework of stakeholder corporate governance, but they would be a small step in that direction.

Equally, the Labour government's reforms to labour-relations law indicate a government pushing beyond the boundaries of Thatcherism. *New* Labour had, to be sure, defined its political identity by distancing itself from its union paymasters (see Ludlam 2001b). In opposition, Blair insisted that there was no going back to the pre-Thatcher state of labour law. While the 1999 Employment Relations Act certainly didn't show the Labour government in the pockets of the unions, it did give workers a statutory right to union recognition where 50 per cent of employees were union members, or where 40 per cent of employees voted for union representation. The Act also reduced the minimum qualifying period from two years to one year for claims against unfair dismissal, and extended paid maternity leave to eighteen weeks. The Act did not take trade-union rights back three decades – most Labour modernizers were horrified at such a prospect. But it did offer public policy *beyond* Thatcherism – and with what some saw as a recognizably social democratic element (Gamble and Kelly 2001).

Welfare Reform

By the mid-1990s, work not welfare became the central theme of New Labour's social policies. But was this another example of Labour modernizers throwing in the towel to Thatcherism? Or did it mark out a bold new approach for Labour post-Thatcherism? In government, supply-side Thatcherism sought to reform the labour market by making paid work more attractive to those on welfare. This it did by reducing the real value of welfare by switching the link between benefit rates and wages to prices, which tend to increase less than wages. Under John Major in 1996, the Conservatives piloted a welfare-to-work programme, Project Work, which included a programme of interviews, 'job search' and compulsory work experience for those unemployed for more than two years.

In opposition, Gordon Brown responded by announcing Labour's own 'new deal' on welfare. A Labour government would require young people after six months on its welfare-to-work programme to participate in one of four options: subsidized paid employment; work with a voluntary-sector employer; a job with an environmental task-force; or a place on a full-time training course. There was to be, Brown said, no fifth option of just staying at home on the dole. Combating 'social exclusion', one of New Labour's central policy themes, was about welfare promoting paid work.

Once in government, Labour launched the New Deal with two programmes, one covering the young (those aged eighteen to twenty-four) unemployed and the other the older, long-term unemployed. Subsequently, New Deal programmes were introduced for the over 50s, lone parents, disabled people and partners of the unemployed. In effect, by 2001 Labour's welfare-to-work programmes covered a majority of those not working or in full-time education.

The New Deal has changed the rules of entitlement to social security, making the right to welfare support more conditional on the search for paid work. But the New Deal programmes offer help as well as hassle: they include support with basic skills, finding work and job interviews – and those unemployed with little education could return to full-time study for up to a year. The rationale of the New Deal is that those not working could be made more 'employable' by carefully targeted help from a personal advisor in the Employment Service. To encourage the unemployed to move from welfare to work, policies such as the working families' tax credit (paid through wage packets and replacing the in-work benefit family credit) and the minimum wage, to 'make work pay', were designed first and foremost to remove the disincentives for those on benefits to take jobs. Making low-paid work more attractive was key to the Labour government's welfare-reform strategy.

The big story, then, of Labour's first-term welfare reforms has been making the receipt of welfare subject to more stringent work tests – and, in return, providing greater state support to individuals to find work. These tests differ in severity from group to group. For young people, the tests are tough and kick in after six months. Sanctions are applied to those young people who refuse a New Deal option or who leave an option without good cause. These sanctions increase in severity with repeated refusals. The New Deals for lone parents and the disabled are effectively voluntary, although an annual interview was made compulsory in April 2001.

These work tests are controversial – for the Left at least – because post-war social democracy in Britain was wedded to the idea that the right to state welfare was unconditional. As we shall see in chapter 8, the combination of work tests and what is seen as a lack of interest in labour-market inequalities causes alarm among social policy analysts on the Left. Such controversies look set to continue during Labour's second term. Proposals in the June 2001 Queen's Speech included a Welfare Reform Bill that will make it obligatory for mothers with young children and women whose partners are unemployed to attend job interviews, although no one will be forced to work under the proposals. The Bill will also require those on incapacity benefit to attend more frequently assessments to see if they could work. Both measures come under the new Department for Work and Pensions, which brings together the old Department for Social Security with much of the employment functions of the old Department for Education and Employment.

But the Labour government's welfare reforms have also brought a small measure of egalitarian policy-making back onto the policy agenda. During the 1980s the income gap between rich and poor widened. Various factors contributed to this growing inequality, including a booming and increasingly deregulated economy, globalization, and new technology, as well as Tory fiscal reforms that disproportionately favoured the better off. After the recession in the early 1990s, the income gap stabilized. By the end of the decade, however, the income gap was bigger than at its peak in the 1980s (Goodman 2001).

National statistics show that, before any state intervention, the income gap between the top 10 per cent and the bottom 10 per cent of the population is 17:1. Cash benefits reduce this gap to 7:1; and once direct and indirect taxes, as well as benefits in kind such as health, housing and education, are taken into consideration, the gap between top and bottom is reduced to 4:1 (Office for National Statistics 2001). The effect of Labour's fiscal reforms has been to make the tax and benefit system more equalizing (Clark, Myck and Smith 2001), certainly by comparison with Conservative fiscal policy under Margaret Thatcher and John Major. These reforms, aimed principally at welfare dependency, have increased the incomes of the poor. According to the Institute for Fiscal Studies, the post-tax income of an average household in the bottom decile of income rose by 8.8 per cent between 1997 and 2001. Higher earning households benefit proportionally less, and the highest 30 per cent of households on average saw their post-tax income fall. The picture of winners and losers is made more complex by patterns of consumption and the impact of direct taxes: smokers, drinkers and drivers in all income groups have been hit by tax hikes.

The real winners of Brown's fiscal reforms have been the 'working poor', especially those with children. Tony Blair's pledge to end child poverty in twenty years starts here. Child benefit, at least for the first child, has been increased well above the rate of inflation, as has income support for children. The working families' tax credit, a scheme more generous than the family credit that it replaced, also increases incomes for low-paid workers already in employment, as does the minimum wage. In 2001, the chancellor introduced a new children's tax credit, replacing the old married couples' allowance. During Labour's second term, Brown plans to integrate these benefits into a single tax credit payable to those in and out of work.

While Brown's budgets have been embraced by the Left as 're-distribution by stealth', there is nothing very underhand about the Labour government's commitment to increasing the income of those at the bottom of the labour market and to families with children. The poor who have benefited least from Labour's reforms are the unemployed without children (or those with grown-up children), whose benefits have risen only with price inflation. The government has remained true to its *New* Labour colours by not raising the income-tax rates of high earners, though many higher earning households have been hit by increases to national insurance and the abolition of mortgage tax relief and married couples' allowance. But the extra money flowing into Treasury coffers after four years of Labour government has been targeted on those households at the bottom of the income scale. After two years of sticking to Tory spending limits, this is a government striking out beyond Thatcherism.

Whether Labour's fiscal reforms reduce the income divide in British society remains to be seen. During its first term, the government's commitment not to raise income taxes for higher earners acted to constrain Labour's egalitarian ambitions, if it had any. Certainly the Blair government has done little to change the highly unequal distribution of wealth in society, with the bottom third of the population holding almost no assets (Goodman 2001). If the government's stated ambition is to make Britain a more meritocratic country, then its policies to enhance educational opportunities, and reduce poverty and social exclusion, may go some way to assist upward social mobility. Whether Labour will follow the recommendations of a 2001 Cabinet Office paper (Performance and Innovation Unit 2001) to increase downward social mobility – including higher taxes on income and wealth and the abolition of inheritance – is unlikely. The challenge for Labour's second term and beyond is whether it can fulfil its commitment to tackling poverty and social inclusion – and mildly progressive fiscal policy – as the economy turns down. Can a policy strategy dependent on Britain at work still deliver when unemployment rises and when many of those on benefits face rate rises linked only to prices rather than wages?

The modest element of redistribution in Labour's social policies is linked to a far greater emphasis on the targeting of welfare reforms. This raises fundamental questions about the future of social democratic social policy, in particular, the balance between universal and targeted benefits. In the post-war period, social democratic social policy was committed to the universality of the welfare state: that it should be available on the same terms (free at the point of use) to everyone. Of course, not all of the welfare state was universal, but the principle became central to the theory and practice of post-war British social democracy. But, as unemployment grew in the 1970s and 1980s, more and more people found themselves subject to means-tested social security (which, in Beveridge's model, was a benefit of last resort: he assumed that most men would be working and would, therefore, be entitled to social security if they lost their job because they had paid their national insurance contributions). The Labour social-security expert Frank Field argued that a Labour government must reverse this trend (Field 1995). Once in government, he was appointed by Tony Blair to 'think the unthinkable' on welfare. Field's time as minister for welfare reform under the social security minister Harriet Harman was neither a happy nor a very long one (see Rawnsley 2001). His proposals for reintroducing the insurance principle into social security, including the creation of new 'stakeholder' institutions, were not well received by the government, especially by Gordon Brown at the Treasury. The 1998 welfare-reform green paper looked like it had been written by Brown at the Treasury, not Field at the Department of Social Security.

Instead, the thrust of the government's welfare reforms has been to target extra help on those in need – such as the low paid, poorer families with children and poor pensioners. In some cases, as with the working families' tax credit (and its associated childcare credit, which meets up to 70 per cent of childcare costs for low-income families), the test of need is being done by the Inland Revenue, not the Benefits Agency. Critics, such as the Conservative MP David Willetts, argue that Brown's reforms have made the tax- and-benefit system too complex and that too little pressure is being put on the jobless to take work (Willetts 1998a). Certainly, what some call 'progressive universalism' is not very universal at all. Labour's reforms target welfare on those groups in need. In this sense they are progressive. Benefits are available to everyone, so they remain in theory universal. But crucially benefits are not the same for everyone: they are means-tested.

Labour's pension plans clearly illustrate Brown's philosophy. The government has increased the basic rate of the state pension in line with inflation. It has not restored the link with earnings, as pensioner groups demand, although in the 2001 budget the chancellor increased the state pension above the rate of inflation. Instead, Labour's approach has been to target help on poorer pensioners by increasing the value of special payments and introducing a minimum income guarantee. In 2000, Brown announced that the guarantee would be increased to £92.15 and linked thereafter to increases in earnings. This, as Polly Toynbee and David Walker note, was just above the minimum of £90 a week Age Concern calculated as the pensioner poverty line (Toynbee and Walker 2001, 25). At the same time, the government has introduced new 'stakeholder' pension schemes as an alternative to private pension plans; and a second state pension is to be phased in for low earners. So, the basic pension remains universal, but extra help is targeted on those in need. The government's policy is thus to redistribute income to poorer pensioners while, at the same time, encouraging greater self-reliance for future generations of old people. Whether Labour's strategy to provide adequate incomes for today's pensioners by means-tested transfers squares with protecting incentives for tomorrow's pensioners to save remains an unanswered question for Labour's second term (see Edwards, Regan and Brooks 2001).

Reforming the Public Sector

The creation and then defence of public services was at the heart of the Labour Party's political identity in post-war Britain. Moreover, the collective provision of education, health, housing and social services by public-sector institutions funded by the government out of general taxation was central to the theory and practice of post-war social democracy. Politically, the public services remain Labour's trump card at the polls. On the eve of the 1997 election, Tony Blair told the voters that they had 'only 24 hours to save the National Health Service'. In 2001, Blair warned the electorate that, if they didn't trust Labour to reform the public services, then the Conservatives would dismantle them.

But Labour's record in power on public-sector reform has been mixed. In 1997, expectations were high, fuelled in part by Labour's pledges to cut hospital waiting lists and primary-school class sizes. A Labour government, its supporters believed, could be relied upon to support the public sector, not attack it like the Tories had. In many cases, Labour voters had failed to read the *New* Labour small print. They still believed that a Labour government would ride into government and throw money at the public sector.

But Labour modernizers had been saying nothing of the kind. In fact, they argued that the problem with the public services was less a lack of resources, more a problem of how those services were delivered – or not delivered – to the required standards. With distinct echoes of James Callaghan's 1976 Ruskin College speech – when the then Labour prime minister had shocked his own supporters by suggesting that the funding of education was not the real issue when it came to school standards – Labour modernizers argued that the public sector needed to be reformed; and that Labour had to abandon its post-war commitment to the centralized collective delivery of public services by public-sector institutions. The Left, they argued, had to give up its ideological commitment to the public sector and take a more pragmatic approach to the delivery of services: 'what works' should guide public policy, not what's Left.

In part, this meant a shift in emphasis away from the interests of public-services producers to the interests (high standards) of the users (or consumers) of those services. Here Labour echoed the shift in emphasis under the Conservatives. It also signalled a shift in Labour policy away from the direct provision of services by the public sector to 'partnerships' between the public, private and voluntary sectors. Again, this mirrored the shift that had taken place under the Conservatives.

So, New Labour was interested in what the role of the state should be in the provision of public services; how far those services should actually be delivered by the public sector (and, crucially, public-sector workers); the duties of the state in providing public services; and the rights and responsibilities of those who use those services. For Labour modernizers, the question of how services are managed and delivered is secondary to the basis on which those services are available to the public. So long as they are funded by the tax payer and free at the point of use, then it doesn't matter who delivers them if they are delivered efficiently and to a high standard.

Labour's pragmatism on public-service provision is, as we shall see in chapter 3, a key element of its 'third way' politics. This apparent turn away from an ideological approach to who delivers the public services has seen Labour embrace the use of private-sector ideas in public-sector provision. Under the Conservatives, British public administration was subject to a managerial revolution that saw the application of market models of governance applied to the civil service, local government and the delivery of public services such as health and education.(These reforms included the market-testing of civil-service work, the creation of 'Next Step' agencies (such as the Benefits Agency), the compulsory tendering of local services to the private sector and the introduction of internal markets into the NHS and schooling.) These reforms, known as the new public management, embraced the market, the manager and the private sector. Markets were preferred to hierarchies; the management of outcomes to the process of governing itself; and the private (and voluntary) sectors to the public sector as the delivery mechanism for services. This revolution was based on the idea that power should be taken away from public-sector monopolies and their self-serving members and given to the consumers of public services. This, it was believed, would make the public services more efficient and accountable to individual people.

During Labour's first term, this pragmatism on means was clearly evident – no less than in the decision by the then Labour majority on Islington Council in north London, fully supported by the Department for Education, to privatize its local education services. This agenda for reform – or 'modernization' – of the public services has not gone away. Indeed, it appears that Labour's second term will see the pragmatism at the heart of Blairism tested to the full as the government confronts head-on public-sector reform. The ruthless pursuit of public-sector reform by the Blair government has witnessed, as we shall see, the visible hand (or the big stick, depending how you view it) of government much in evidence. The frustration expressed by ministers over the slow pace of many reforms has only strengthened Labour's resolve to 'get things done' in its second term.

But significantly, by the mid-point in Labour's first term, the emphasis on public-sector reform shifted: money crept back on to the political agenda. Soon Labour was heralding – often two or three times over, which didn't help the management of expectations – new tranches of spending (the government preferred to call it 'investment') for health, education and other public services. By 2000, as we have seen, the chancellor was pulling large sums of public money out of his Treasury hat. Was this the return to good old-fashioned Labour public administration – throw money at the problem? It certainly didn't look like a government in thrall to neo-liberalism. Was it, then, a government with a post-Thatcherite agenda for the public services?

From the 2000 comprehensive spending review, Brown set government on a traditional Labour course to increase spending and investment on the public services, especially on education and health. The biggest problem facing the government has been not a lack of cash but getting public-service bureaucracies, long accustomed to cuts, to spend the new money. The key aspect to Chancellor Brown's new-found generosity was that in most cases the extra resources came with strings attached. In return for more money, the public services had to 'modernize' – that key *New* labour term. But what does modernization of the public services amount to, both practically and politically? How is this new money going to be spent? What strings are the Treasury attaching?

Public–private partnerships

The welfare state has always been a 'mixed economy' of public-, private- and voluntary-sector providers, as well as informal networks of family and friends. In government, Labour has set about challenging one of the fundamental tenets of post-war social democratic theory – and the practice of Labour governments: that public is good and private bad. So, when Labour, as promised, embraced the Conservatives' private finance initiative (PFI), the government was unlikely to win many friends among public-sector unions and more broadly on the Left. The PFI, or public–private partnerships (PPP), as Labour now calls it, is a fairly simply idea: the private sector invests in public-sector capital projects, such as building and managing new schools, hospitals, prisons and roads, and the government then effectively rents the new facility from the private-sector provider. So, today's private-sector capital investment is tomorrow's public-sector spending.

Under PPP, the private sector brings not only money to the table but management and employment contracts; it also undertakes to bear the risks of overruns in costs. Since 1997, 150 public–private partnership contracts worth £12 billion have been signed for thirty-five hospitals, 520 schools and four prisons (Toynbee and Walker 2001, 105). Controversially, the government proposed that the London Underground be upgraded by a public–private partnership, despite opposition from the London Mayor, Ken Livingstone.

The extension of these public–private partnerships looks set to be one of the key battlegrounds in Labour's second term. Labour modernizers claim that these partnerships are not privatization because the public services themselves remain available on the same universal and free terms. The Commission on Public–Private

Partnerships of the centre-left Institute for Public Policy Research couched its support for such partnerships in third-way terms. PPP, it said, offered an alternative to the (new right) private provision of public services and the (old left) public-sector monopoly provision. The commission suggested that PPPs, which between 1997 and 2000 accounted for only 9 per cent of total public gross capital spending, can improve services by bringing diversity and innovation, and introducing private-sector skills and expertise, to public-sector provision. As long as the conditions were right, the commission argued, PPPs would allow governments to get more from public assets over their life-cycle (Commission on Public Private Partnerships 2001).

Critics of public–private partnerships are not impressed. Gordon Brown's 'golden rule', as we have seen, does not rule out borrowing to invest – and the public sector often gets better deals on loans than the private sector. Britain's public finances are certainly in the kind of state that would allow such an investment. Critics of public–private partnerships also argue that the private sector doesn't always provide value for money and that private-sector management has often proved incompetent. This was certainly the government's case when transport minister Stephen Byers brought Railtrack, the private company controlling Britain's railway infrastructure, back under public control in October 2001 (though this was not a case that Railtrack shared). Many professional bodies and public-sector trade unions have also been critical of the introduction of the profit motive into such public services as health and education, arguing that resources have been diverted from frontline services and that service priorities have become distorted.

Health

The relationship between the public and private sectors has been one of the most controversial areas of Labour's health reforms. Indeed, the relationship between public and private health has caused controversy and acrimony since the NHS was founded by the post-war Labour government. By encouraging the private sector to build and run NHS hospitals, the Blair government has drawn the wrath of professional health bodies and public-sector unions. Need not greed, Labour's critics say, should determine health priorities. The profit motive, they say, should play no part in shaping the state of Britain's health service.

Labour came into government promising to save the NHS. It said it would cut waiting lists and that it would abolish the 'internal market'. This market had been the central feature of the Conservatives' health reforms in the 1990s. It split the purchasers of health care (mainly GPs) from the providers of that care (mainly hospitals) and allowed the purchasers to shop around for the best deals in health care among hospitals in a new internal market. Theoretically at least, GPs, some of whom controlled their own budgets as 'fund-holders', were able to exert influence over hospitals (who themselves became self-governing 'trusts') by forcing those hospitals to compete for their business. Whether it actually worked is a matter of some debate. When the political chips were down, it proved almost impossible to let hospitals close under market forces. Labour's position was clear: it would abolish the internal market and concentrate resources on clinical procedures, not management red tape. But was it so simple? Was Labour setting out a different model of NHS governance to the market-led reforms of the Conservatives?

In power, Labour has reformed Conservative reforms, not abolished them. While the Blair administration has not returned the NHS to a state before the Conservative reforms, it has adjusted the balance of those reforms. The changes that Labour has made to the NHS have altered the structure and character of the internal market in such a way that make it much less like a market. As set out in a 1997 white paper, *The New NHS: Modern, Dependable*, Labour has retained the split between 'purchasers' and 'providers'; and all GPs have effectively become fund-holders as the control of budgets by individual GP practices has shifted to larger primary care groups. These groups, 481 of them, are larger than the old fund-holding practices, and are made up of groups of GP practices, plus other health professions. As primary care trusts, they will take with local health authorities overall responsibility for health services and for developing 'local improvement programmes' with the health providers. The intention is that the new primary care trusts will act cooperatively rather than competitively by bringing together all the primary health professions in an area; and that they enter into longer-term (three years not one year) and more collaborative contracts with hospitals and other care providers for health services. Whether this reduces the leverage trusts have over hospitals remains to be seen.

So, Labour's approach to NHS reform has been to shift away from competition as the main tool to increase standards of health.

It has retained the central feature of Conservative reforms, the split between purchasers and providers, but it has made the relationship between them less like a market by creating large primary care trusts and by altering the relationship between the purchasers and the health providers. In this way, it has taken NHS reform beyond Thatcherism.

This approach came to the fore as the NHS hit its annual winter crisis in January 2000. As the country's health services were tested to breaking point by the flu virus, Professor Robert Winston (Labour life peer) suggested that the NHS wasn't up to the standards of Poland's health service. Indeed, Labour's approach to reform the NHS, despite all the headlines about private money, has been rather Eastern European, if not downright Soviet. Labour created two new health regulators. The job of the first, the National Institute for Clinical Effectiveness (NICE), is to bring order ('evidence-based medicine') to the rationing of health treatments; the nasty one, the Commission for Health Improvement, is meant to act as an inspector, monitoring the relative effectiveness of hospitals and attempting to improve health care across the country from the centre. The commission has been assisted by the government's attempts to establish national standards of treatments under national service frameworks. Labour also set up NHS Direct, a telephone health service that allowed the public to call health workers directly for clinical advice.

But central to Labour's health reforms in its first term was the promise of more resources. As the 1999–2000 winter health crisis prompted damning headlines, Tony Blair promised that by 2006 health spending in the UK would reach the European Union average. The chancellor's 2000 comprehensive spending review, as we have seen, set government investment on health to increase by 5.6 per cent per year over three years. But just as the government promised the NHS extra resources, so it set out how it should spend the new money. After wide consultation, in July 2000 the government published its NHS plan.

For all Labour's critics on the Left, the NHS plan was as close to old-style central planning as a government embracing market forces was likely to get. This really was the gentlemen in Whitehall knowing best. The plan listed government-set targets that filled in the detail of how the chancellor's extra money should be spent. Targets included waiting times for casualty, for operations and to see a GP. It set targets for the number of beds, doctors, nurses and other health workers. After reading the NHS plan, no one in the health service could doubt what the government wanted. The plan was particularly controversial because of the strings attached: the government would give the NHS more money but only if some of the old professional demarcations, between doctors and nurses for example, were broken down. Like the Thatcherites before them, Labour modernizers were squaring up to the medics, who seemed to be part of what the prime minister called 'the forces of conservatism'.

The Blair administration is having to confront a problem all governments face in Western societies: however much money you spend on health, the demands on the health service continue to rise as the population's expectations go up and the range of new treatments expand. But the cost of these treatments outpaces inflation in other sectors of the economy, particularly because health is labour intensive and earnings outpace prices. Technological change does little to bring down the cost of medicine, if anything quite the reverse.

As far as Britain is concerned, the Treasury fears that the NHS is a never-ending hole that can take as much money as you throw in. There is, simply put, never enough NHS around to supply what people want, when they want it. The private health sector exists, in part, to deal with this. The Left doesn't like private medicine because it rations health care not by need but by ability to pay. Significantly, Labour in government has steered a pragmatic course. It has not gone down the health insurance route taken by many Western European countries and the United States. Instead, to bring the capacity of the private sector into supply, health minister Alan Milburn in October 2000 signed a 'concordat' that sanctioned and regulated the use of the private sector by the NHS for more routine procedures. The Labour government also looked to health services on the continent to provide extra capacity for Britain's hard-pressed hospitals. Labour modernizers claimed the pragmatic use of the private sector was putting the interests of patients first. Critics on the Left argued that it amounted to privatization; critics on the Right, that it was a return to nationalization. Maybe it was a 'third way' after all.

Furthermore, as Jennifer Dixon points out (Dixon 2001), the Blair government's approach to NHS reform is caught between encouraging local partnerships and consensus-building and good old-fashioned 'command and control' management from the centre. Local partnerships take time to develop, and Labour has relied more and more on dirigism to get things done – or not.

'Command and control' policy-making can inhibit local partnerships, let alone local health professions; it can lead to government overload at the centre; and it relies on the Whitehall bureaucracies knowing what's going on locally, when very often they don't.

Education

After Tony Blair's three famous words 'education, education, education', the state of Britain's schools and colleges was always going to help define Labour's first term – and the shape of Blairism to come. As with health, the focus of Labour's attacks in opposition to Conservative education policy had been on the structure of those reforms. A Labour government, Blair and his education spokesman David Blunkett said, would concern itself with what parents cared about most: 'standards, not structures'.

But, as with the NHS, the story is a little more complex. Central to Conservative reforms to schooling in the 1980s was the creation of an internal market. The landmark 1988 Education Reform Act allowed parents to choose the school for their children and for schools to admit any pupil up to its physical capacity ('open enrolment'); for school governing bodies to manage their own affairs ('local management of schools', or LMS); and for schools, if they wanted, to opt out of local education authority (LEA) control and become 'grant-maintained' by central government. The Conservatives also encouraged greater diversity in education by allowing schools to specialize in certain areas, such as technology (the 'city technology colleges') and languages, and by allowing an element of selection on the basis of aptitude for a particular specialism. Further, the 1988 Act introduced a national curriculum and a testing regime that would provide information (school league tables) on comparative educational performance. In theory, these reforms forced schools to compete for the well-informed choices of parents because the funding of schools became attached to school enrolment. Bums on seats became the name of the education game.

The Conservatives, then, had pinned their hopes on the market delivering higher standards. Good schools would prosper, attracting pupils and funding. Poorer schools would either have to improve standards or close. And, under LMS, all schools would flower free from the day-to-day control of local government. This at least was the theory – and, just as with the NHS internal market, there is much debate about the effectiveness and justice of the Conservatives' competitive regime.

Under Blair, Labour accommodated itself to these major planks of Tory education policy: parental choice, open enrolment, LMS and the National Curriculum would all be retained, as would the revamped schools inspection service, Ofsted. Indeed, the retention in government of Ofsted's controversial head, Chris Woodhead, signalled that Labour's education policies would be marked as much by continuity as by change. Only the grant-maintained schools, as Labour promised, have been abolished under the 1998 School Standards and Framework Act, to be replaced by a new category of schools, foundation schools, that partly bring the schools back under the LEA umbrella. In any case, the advent of LMS made the question of LEA control less controversial, given the much reduced powers of LEAs under LMS. The Labour government, like the Conservatives before them, has also promoted a new vocationalism in education. Following the 1996 review of qualifications for 16-to 19-year-olds by Lord Dearing, the Labour government has gone ahead with the reform of vocational qualifications, albeit alongside the traditional 'gold standard' of English schooling, the A Level (see Department for Education and Employment 1999).

But if Labour in power retained these central features of Thatcherite public policy – and the 1988 Education Act was about as High Thatcherite as they came – it is also true that Labour does not share the Conservatives' faith in market forces as the main tool for raising standards. Instead, Labour is thoroughly dirigiste in its approach to school reform. To be fair, the Conservatives could never make up their minds about how best to raise standards. The neo-liberal 'voucher-men' believed the market knew best; the neo-conservative 'preservationists' believed that a state-sponsored national curriculum was the best way to preserve academic values. In the end, the 1988 Act was pure New Right: part neo-liberal, part neo-conservative – a real belts and braces piece of public policy-making.

Labour in government has shown none of the neo-liberals' faith in market forces. Indeed, Labour's first education act was to abolish the assisted places scheme, which provided government support for bright children from poorer families to attend private school. Instead, Labour's approach to education reform was to get its hands on the levers of power – and damn well use them to make education institutions do what they told them. As in health,

Labour established a school standards unit, under Michael Barber, to provide central steerage to education policy. The Department for Education and Employment under David Blunkett used its full powers to intervene locally, both with LEAs and with schools, to 'name and shame' poor performers. Ofsted under the Labour government has remained a key tool in policy enforcement. On the National Curriculum, Labour has developed in primary schools (Key Stages 1 and 2) specialist literacy and numeracy hours that develop the main thrust of Conservative education policy towards more formal, traditional teaching methods – and to greater central control over the curriculum.

This shift away from market to state governance can clearly be seen in terms of the provision of education and childcare for pre-school children. The Conservatives under John Major opted for nursery vouchers for four-year-olds. Labour developed a government-led national childcare strategy for providing free education and childcare places for four- and three-year-olds, delivered by early years development and childcare partnerships bringing together local government and voluntary- and private-sector providers. In addition, its 'Sure Start' programme, combining family support and health and education provision for pre-school children, sought to tackle social exclusion by catching problems early in a child's development.

As with the NHS, by 1998 the government was shifting the emphasis of reform in education from 'modernization' to 'money and modernization'. And more money meant more strings. Under Chancellor Brown's spending reviews, as we have seen, education has seen substantial increases in resources. But – and it's a big but – schools and other education institutions would have to reform. In particular, they would have to accept a greater role for the private sector in the building and running of schools and education authorities, as well as the introduction of performance-related pay, something to which teacher unions were bitterly opposed. Schools would also have to show a willingness to promote school standards, especially in basic subjects such as maths and English, by embracing government reforms to the curriculum and school governance.

By and large, the focus of Labour's education reforms have been the primary school and early years education. The literacy and numeracy hours, and the integration of early years education and childcare provision, have been at the forefront of the government's drive to raise standards in schools. But the focus of

Labour's second term shifted to secondary schools. The key issue then became the future of comprehensive education.

No party is so wedded to the comprehensive model as is the Labour Party. Despite the fact that more comprehensives opened in England and Wales when Margaret Thatcher was education minister in Edward Heath's Conservative government, the development of comprehensive schooling was driven forward by Labour at national and local level. Comprehensives are, essentially, mixed-ability schools. Early on, New Labour got itself into a mess over the issue of selection, anathema to the comprehensive ideal. Blunkett promised in opposition 'no selection' – which many took to mean the closure of the remaining 100–odd grammar schools in England and Wales. Supporters of comprehensives were to get a rude awakening. In government, Labour set the rules for parental ballots in such a way that the supporters of the local grammar school were likely to win.

By the end of its first term, Labour was signalling the end to what it called the 'bog-standard comprehensive'. And, to add insult to injury, Labour in power has supported the extension of 'diversity' in schooling started under the Conservatives. The Tories had pioneered specialist city technology colleges – and encouraged other schools to specialize in other areas such as languages and music. Labour has continued this policy – and has promised that it will be radically extended during the government's second term: it hopes that 46 per cent of all secondary schools by 2005 will have a specialism. Specialist schools can select on *aptitude* 10 per cent of their intake – though, in practice, a majority of specialist schools don't. Labour has also signalled that the policy of allowing businesses and voluntary groups to takeover the running of 'failing' schools will continue; and that the Church of England and churches will be encouraged to develop more 'faith-based' education (see Department for Education and Employment 2001; Department of Education and Skills 2001). Does New Labour's model of 'post-comprehensive' education mark the end of the comprehensive ideal – or its modernization?

Housing and the social services

Health and education have been the focus of Labour's policies on the public services since 1997. In two other areas, housing and the social services, Labour's first term has been marked by the same mix of continuity and change. The government's housing policy has seen a continuation of the trend towards social housing by housing associations initiated by the Conservatives. As promised in opposition, Labour released funds from the sales of council housing under the Conservatives, much of it to be spent on renovation to the social housing stock. But Labour has drawn a line under the Conservative 'right-to-buy' policies and accepted, pragmatically, that the private market, rented and owner-occupied, has a major role in the provision of housing. Where Labour has departed from this market model of housing provision is in its analysis and policy prescriptions for 'problem estates' and neighbourhood renewal in its New Deal for Communities. This return to a form of localism aims to be an interventionist and multi-agency (so-called joined-up government) approach to what are seen as multi-dimensional social problems requiring 'joined-up' thinking (Cabinet Office 1998 and 2001).

As with housing, health and education, the key to Conservative reforms to social services in the 1980s and 1990s was the introduction of internal markets. Local government authorities were no longer to be the main providers of social services but were to purchase such services from the private and voluntary sectors. In government, Labour published a 1998 white paper, *Modernising Social Services*, that promised £3 billion of extra funds over three years. The white paper also laid out specific grants for channelling resources to social services. The Conservative internal markets have been reformed, not abandoned. The Conservatives' compulsory competitive tendering (CCT) has given way to 'best value', which imposes on local authorities a requirement to set objectives and performance indicators and ensure that the purchasing of social services by local authorities reaches the standards set by these indicators. Under Labour, the sourcing of social services from the private and voluntary sector remains, but the competitive market is seen as insufficient on its own to ensure efficiency, high standards and social justice and is to be tempered by models of community partnership (see Johnson 2001), as well as central government regulation: in October 2001, the health minister Alan Milburn 'named and shamed' fourteen local authorities as poor providers of social services, threatening that the best performers would be encouraged to takeover the worst if no improvements followed (*The Times*, 20 October 2001).

Constitutional Reform

The three areas of domestic policy we have looked at so far –
economics, welfare reform and the public services – are controversial, not least because they touch on the novelty of New Labour
and on the future of social democratic politics. Labour seems to be
both accommodating to Thatcherism *and* striking out beyond
Thatcherism. The Blair government may be drawing lines under
certain key aspects of Conservative reforms, but it is also
reforming these reforms in a significantly different way.

The issue of constitutional reform has been controversial in
other ways. It clearly breaks with the non-constitutional politics of
the Thatcher/Major years (beyond, that is, the issue of Europe,
which we will examine in more detail in chapter 5). It also reflects
a quite different side to the Labour government, one more rooted
in the liberal pluralist tradition.

Labour's constitutional reforms have devolved political power
from parliament and the Whitehall machine to new representative
institutions. But it has been a painful process for a party that has
turned control from the centre into an art form. Labour's reforms
to the public services, as we have seen, have a strong whiff of
centralization. But just as the Labour government has been
driving public-sector reform in health and education from the
centre, so it is a government that has devolved significant responsibilities for domestic policy to the periphery. As we shall examine in chapter 7, its devolution programme was one of the most
significant features of Labour's first term. Devolution has seen the
creation of new governing institutions in Scotland, Wales and
Northern Ireland. Devolution under Labour has been asymmetrical: that is, some devolved institutions (the Scottish parliament)
have more power than others (Wales and Northern Ireland). Certainly the process of devolution challenges the centralization of
the British state by introducing what has been called 'quasi-federal' features.

This devolution of responsibilities for many areas of domestic
public policy, such as health and education, has introduced a new
political dynamic into British territorial politics – a dynamic
Labour 'control-freaks' are having a hard time coming to terms
with. But devolution has introduced a much more pluralist structure to UK politics. The devolved institutions in Edinburgh, Cardiff and Belfast are all elected by systems of proportional

representation – though the government has resisted such a reform to elections to Westminster. Coalition government is the norm (and, in the case of Northern Ireland, the constitutional requirement) in the new devolved administrations (one of the reasons why Labour has problems with the idea of voting reform for general elections). While the powers of these new devolved governments remain limited by the Treasury in London, a new form of pluralist politics is emerging under Labour in which multi-party politics and the sharing of political power have become the norm.

In power, then, the Blair government made good on the devolution promises made by John Smith in opposition. But in opposition, too, Labour promised to be a great champion of local politics. Its policy statements were replete with ambitions to empower local politics and local government and reverse the centralizing trends of the Conservative years. But its actions in power do not always live up to these ambitions. The Labour administration has been less willing to give up the centralist controls over local government put in place by the Conservatives. As we shall see in chapter 7, the Labour government has faced a genuine dilemma. Its decentralist ambitions are constrained by its lack of trust in the responsibility of local politicians and local institutions – a lack of trust it shares with previous Tory governments. And the basis for that lack of trust has some foundation. Local government in Britain lacks legitimacy. The stripping away of local power by central government has not helped matters. Governments, Labour and Conservative, have been unwilling to give greater fiscal powers to local government when so few voters turnout for local elections. Labour is pushing ahead with reforms to local government that might go some way to restore that legitimacy. These reforms include measures to increase turnouts in local elections and to make local politicians more directly accountable. The mayoral model adopted in London may be one direction for local government and politics nationwide. But the election of former Labour MP (and leader of the former Greater London Council in the 1980s) Ken Livingstone showed how far Labour modernizers have to go in coming to terms with the political dynamics of devolved administration.

On the question of 'strong government', Labour has drawn the criticism that it is just another 'elective dictatorship': that, unconstrained by a written constitution, it can use its huge majority in the House of Commons to do, more or less, what it likes. Cer-

tainly, Labour's first term was marked by the executive largely
ignoring parliament. Pre-election pledges to strengthen parliament have been limited largely to reform of the House of Lords.
But even this was limited in the first term to abolishing the right
of hereditary peers to sit in parliament. The government's lack of
a 'second stage' model for Lords reform did little to mark Labour
down as a radical reforming administration. And when that
second stage was announced in November 2001, with only 120
members in a reformed chamber to be elected and the powers of
government patronage largely intact, Peter Riddell's comment in
The Times (8 November 2001) that the plans were 'shallow, minim-
alist and deeply conservative' reflected the view across the political spectrum (even, it was suggested, of Robin Cook, who
announced the measures in parliament).

'Modernization' of the Commons was even more limited, and, if
anything, the Blair government behaved like many governments
over the past two decades and simply ignored MPs. Moreover,
Blair, like Lady Thatcher before him, has taken the job of prime
minister to be more presidential than 'first among equals'. But, as
historians of contemporary British politics point out, there is a
longer-term trend away from cabinet government. Headlines about
'control freaks' make good copy, but Labour modernizers have a
point when they argue that British public administration is fragmented and this can inhibit effective policy-making and delivery.

But the Labour government did make good on its promise to
sign into British law the European Convention on Human Rights –
a measure that will have a significant long-term impact on public
administration. The 1998 Human Rights Act is not a bill of rights in
a written constitution but is a step in that direction. Its impact is to
create for the first time in British history a positive statement of
rights in English law; and to alter the balance of power between
parliament and the judiciary – giving more power to the judges. In
the longer term, the Human Rights Act may pave the way for some
kind of supreme court, a measure supported by many in the judiciary. Another opposition promise, to create a legal 'right to know',
was enacted although in a much weakened form.

Taken together, these constitutional reforms stand as the enduring legacy of Labour's first term. But these reforms, as we shall see
later in the book, have their critics. Constitutional conservatives
say that Labour has done too much: that it is a constitutional
vandal. Constitutional radicals believe it has done too little: that
Labour, like its predecessors, remains a party of traditional loyalty

to the Westminster model of government. Certainly, Labour's constitutional reforms have put in train a process of reform that is set
to continue. They reflect the constitutional turn taken by the party
under Neil Kinnock and John Smith and mark a clear break with
the non-constitutional politics of Thatcherism. But, despite the
Blair government's constitutional radicalism, Labour remains open
to the charge that it has failed to break with the 'levers of power'
Westminster politics so beloved by Labour politicians of old.

Law and Order

Tony Blair first came to attention at Westminster as a member of
the Commons committee scrutinizing the Conservative government's trade-union reforms. He had been picked by John Smith,
then shadow employment secretary. Blair was, wrote the Conservative diarist and then junior minister at the Employment Department, the late Alan Clark, one of Labour's 'two bright boys' – the
other, not surprisingly, was Gordon Brown (Clark 1994, 54).
Indeed, throughout much of the 1980s and early 1990s it was
Brown, not Blair, who looked destined for Number 10. But Blair
found a wider audience as Labour home affairs spokesman in
John Smith's shadow cabinet. After a trip to the USA where Blair
and Brown inhaled the sweet smell of Bill Clinton's presidential
success, Blair caught the headlines echoing one of Clinton's
themes, that Labour should be 'tough on crime, tough on the
causes of crime'. Brown, in fact, had already used the line, but
that, as they say, is show business (see Rentoul 1995, 285–6).

The interesting bit, as far as Labour was concerned, was the part
that Labour should be 'tough on crime'. The party was well known
for being tough on the causes of crime – high unemployment, poverty, inequality and so on – but were less well known for getting
tough with criminals themselves. Indeed, the Tory gibe that
Labour was 'soft on crime' sunk home with the voters. The Conservatives were well entrenched as the party of law and order – and it
won them votes. Labour modernizers in the early 1990s knew this.
Leading Labour reformers such as Blair and Jack Straw were keen
that the party do something about its perceived 'softness' on crime.
When Blair became leader, there was a perceptible hardening of
Labour's stance on law and order issues. The party's 'hostages to
fortune' – support for striking miners, rioting youths, radical political movements and liberal laws – were dumped (Downes and

Morgan 1997). In the run up to the 1997 general election, it was difficult to work out who would make the most right-wing home secretary, the then holder, Tory Michael Howard (not noted for his kindness towards law breakers), or Labour's Jack Straw. It was enough to drive a liberal to, well, vote Liberal!

So how has Labour measured up in power? Did it push a New Right socially conservative, even authoritarian, agenda on law and order issues, as its critics argue? Was Jack Straw the most right-wing home secretary since – since Michael Howard?

Tough . . .

Rhetorically at least, Straw played with aplomb the part of the home secretary liberals love to hate – but then most liberals hate all home secretaries, even that most liberal of them, Roy Jenkins in the 1960s. The Labour government, like previous Conservative ones, remained committed to tough sentencing. Straw implemented Howard's 1997 Crime (Sentencing) Act, which introduced minimum and mandatory sentencing. Labour followed the Conservatives by taking a more corrective approach to the criminal justice system (though the probation service got extra staff). The 2000 Football (Disorder) Act empowered the authorities to prevent anyone travelling abroad even if they have not been convicted of a crime. The government sought, not with any great success, to make Britain less attractive to asylum-seekers by making the regime of claiming welfare (vouchers, not cash) and asylum tougher. Labour attempted, again unsuccessfully, to abolish the automatic right to jury trial (though a 2001 report by the senior judge Sir Robin Auld supported limits to jury trial) and proposed the abolition of the 'double jeopardy' rule in a new Criminal Justice Bill at the start of its second term. Here is a government, civil libertarians argued, that is bending over backwards to appear tough on those not accused of crime, those accused of crime, those guilty of a criminal offence – and those who just wanted to live in the United Kingdom.

. . . and tender

It is certainly true that the central piece of law and order legislation during Labour's first term, the Crime and Disorder Act 1998, contains 'tough' measures. Examples include 'anti-social behaviour orders', 'child curfews', the monitoring of convicted sex offenders, and reforms to the youth justice system to make it quicker and more effective. But the Act also departed from the deterrence/punishment regime of the Conservatives. Instead, the Crime and Disorder Act rests on an approach based on crime prevention and community safety. One study suggested that it 'has the potential to become an essentially liberal and progressive piece of legislation, one accepting of the criminological research on the most effective strategies for crime control' (Savage and Nash 2001, 114). The approach taken by the legislation is to make local authorities, the police, health authorities and the probation service work in partnership to make communities safer in the first place. New local authority 'youth offending teams', for example, aim to bring together programmes of education and training with parenting classes, drug treatment and bail supervision for young offenders. On sentencing, the government pushed 'restorative justice', such as making good damage to the community such as graffiti. The 1998 legislation also introduced new offences relating to racial violence, a measure which, along with the 2000 Sex Offences Amendment Act, which lowered the gay age of consent to sixteen, gladdened the hearts of all die-hard liberals. There was, after all, a tender side to Jack Straw. But the problem, as Carolyn Hoyle and David Rose point out (Hoyle and Rose 2001), may be that there is a very real tension between the 'zero tolerance' of Labour's tough approach and the welfarist logic of its tender approach. The former approach must exclude; the latter demands inclusion. It is not surprising, then, that prison numbers continued to rise under Labour.

Whether Straw's successor at the Home Office, David Blunkett, another of New Labour's social conservatives, will respond to this challenge remains to be seen. After Blunkett's decision in 2001 to overhaul asylum policy (including the scrapping of the voucher scheme), as well as the downgrading of cannabis in drug laws, pigs were universally acclaimed as capable of flight. But Blunkett's response to the war in Afghanistan, involving internment without trial of suspected terrorists, indicated that New Labour's illiberal reflex was still in operation.

New Labour or New Labours?

A sketch, then, of what Labour has done in power over four years confirms a mixed bag of public policies. In some cases, this government has behaved rather like previous Tory ones. In other cases, it feels rather more like Labour governments of old – though, very often, being rather more successful. One of the essential arguments of this book is that there are important continuities with the Conservative governments of the 1980s and 1990s. Given that the Tories were in power for eighteen years, this is hardly surprising. But there are also significant discontinuities with the Thatcher and Major years. These breaks, we argue, reflect long-standing progressive, liberal and social democratic concerns – concerns that, to a greater or lesser extent, will have been felt by Labour governments past and present.

The case for New Labour as an accommodation with Thatcherism or neo-liberalism has obvious strengths. As we have seen in this chapter, Labour in government has pursued an anti-inflationary macro-economic policy, drawn lines under the Thatcherite supply-side reforms, promoted work not welfare, continued the managerial revolution in the public services (including private-sector involvement), and retained some of the central features of the internal market reforms to health and education. This, it could be argued, has been a government committed to the free-market economy and to promoting the interests of private enterprise and one which is unwilling to tackle the entrenched powers of the business class and the inequalities across society. Away from political economy, Labour has proved to be a government with a taste for getting tough on law and order, short of liberal justice and committed to traditional constitutional institutions. Its agenda of radical modernization has been thoroughly conservative in all senses of the word.

If these really were the limits of Tony Blair's government, then the Thatcherism Mark 2 thesis would win hands down. But there is another side to Labour in power. Once it got past its self-imposed two-year fiscal strait-jacket, it began to act more like a reformist social democratic government. To be sure, the government's economic policies are clearly designed to promote business in Britain. But, then, social democracy has always been committed to the mixed capitalist economy. While Gordon Brown has been hawkish on inflation, the chancellor has proved more pragmatic on fiscal matters, increasing public expenditure in 2000/1 as the economy slowed in what could be read as good old-fashioned counter-cyclical demand management. This may be a government that cares about the money supply, but it is not one that is a slave to it. Indeed, the Bank of England's (and the US Federal Reserve's) willingness to cut interest rates in the face of the global economic recession shows that some central bankers have rediscovered a degree of sanity on monetary policy. Labour has also raised taxes, increased spending on the public services, introduced a range of policies directed at the poverty trap between welfare and work, and engaged in a modest, but not insignificant, bout of redistribution to some of the poorer sections in society. At the same time, Labour reforms to the public services have in places marked a clear shift away from the market-based reforms of the Conservatives. Labour, unlike the Conservatives, has a clear interest in, and strategy for, social exclusion – and retains a commitment, unlike the Tories, to social justice. This, Andrew Gamble and Tony Wright argue, is a government committed to 'inclusive modernization' within a market economy, not 'market modernization' in a market society (Gamble and Wright 2001).

There is something challenging about New Labour. This is a government committed to monetary and fiscal prudence, but (and the *but* is important) it is also an administration that is spending the national surplus on collective public services and redistributing resources to the poor. It is not a government that has radically cut taxes, as the Bush administration advocated in the USA. The Labour government is a champion of free markets and free trade, but it is also one that has introduced new regulations in the workplace. In addition it is a government that tried to restrict the right to jury trial, but signed the European Convention on Human Rights into English Law. The government's law and order policies have led to a higher prison population, but the focus of its reforms has been to prevent crime in the community, not bang people up for committing criminal offences. And, while extending the role of the state to promote opportunities 'to the many not the few', it has done so in ways that deepen the 'new managerial state'.

The Labour government of 1997 to 2001 has, in short, done much that confirms the neo-liberal consensus established by the Conservatives in the 1980s and 1990s. A number of key policies fall under the neo-liberal principle of putting free markets first.

But it is also a government that has broken with that consensus in significant ways. This has not been a simple return to Old Labour ways of doing things. But it has meant a return to concerns and approaches that bear the hallmarks of social democracy and progressive liberal thinking towards the regulation of markets – and particular policies, such as the minimum wage and the new labour-relations law, show a clear social democratic imprint. Certain government policies, as Colin Crouch identifies, *mix* neo-liberal and social democratic priorities. The New Deal, for example, puts work before welfare and has introduced measures to make the labour market work more efficiently. But it also includes elements such as training and childcare support that are much more like the active labour-market strategies of Scandinavian social democracy (Crouch 2001). To dismiss these social democratic and progressive elements as irrelevant is to miss one aspect of what is quite distinctive, challenging and successful about the Blair government. Labour has, for good or ill, taken public policy *beyond Thatcherism*. Herein lies the novelty to *New* Labour and the challenge it offers to British politics.

New Labour, then, is not a seamless political, let alone ideological, project. As a result it resists simple characterization. Like Thatcherism before it, Blair's Labour Party is a political composite and, rather than search for a singular New Labour, it is better to acknowledge the plurality of New Labours. Michael Freeden (Freeden 1999) locates New Labour within the three major Western ideological traditions: liberalism, conservatism and socialism. These traditions provide an 'ideological map' for New Labour – though it is not 'equidistant from them'. For Freeden, each of these traditions raises central philosophical and practical questions: liberalism and the freedom of the individual and the role of governments; conservatism and the social and moral order; socialism and the structure of society and the (unequal) relationship between groups in communities.

As we shall argue in the next chapter, Labour's attempt to provide an overarching theory of New Labour thinking – the 'third way' – ultimately fails because of the tensions between the traditions Freeden identifies. While it is true that, in the world of politics and policy-making, fashioning compromises between different positions is the name of the game, this does not mean the original positions disappear. However many times Gordon Brown may like to say 'prudence with a purpose', sometimes prudence demands one thing and purpose something quite different. This, as we suggest, is not to deny the efficacy of Labour modernizers' quest for a middle way – such middle ways are endemic to political theory and practice – but it is to question whether some reconciliation between different political traditions and their interests and values is possible. It is to these issues that we shall turn next.

Part II

Rethinking Social Democracy

3

New Labour's Third Way

Labour modernizers see New Labour as a 'project' that is taking politics 'beyond Thatcherism'. New Labour believes in the values of social democracy but has devised radically new means for pursuing them different from those used by Old Labour or Thatcherism. New Labour is taking a path that is neither the first way of the old Left nor the second way of the New Right. Being post-Thatcherite involves taking a 'third way'.

In this chapter we shall argue that Labour's third way does not transcend 'Old Left' and 'New Right'. Left and Right remain important markers for contemporary policy and politics. But the third way does combine them in significant ways. In fact the third way is often best defined by the manner in which it has taken up positions on both Left and Right – perhaps sometimes more on the side of the latter than might once have been expected from social democracy, but by no means only on the Right. Furthermore, between Old Left and New Right, we suggest, there is space not just for one third way but for many, with different values and policy positions. In future chapters we shall show how varying third ways, and positions from Left to Right, lead to different third ways across national boundaries, albeit with common concerns, and to different responses to changes such as globalization and to institutions such as the European Union.

The third way is one of a number of attempts by modernizers to find a label to capture New Labour politics. The name 'New Labour' itself was one of the first, signalling to the electorate a turn away from the unpopular policies of Labour in the past by the constant distinction of 'new' from 'old' – and indicating a government that wished to create a modernized 'new Britain'. New Labour has also been projected as a party of 'one nation', 'community' and 'social inclusion'. On the election night of 1 May 1997 candidate after candidate making their acceptance speeches invoked the phrase that Labour would 'govern for the many and not the few'. Related ideas of 'stakeholding' also featured temporarily (see Driver and Martell 1998, 51–60). The idea of a 'third way' is attractive to Labour modernizers because it challenges conventional notions of Left and Right – and thus reinforces the 'newness' of New Labour. It allows them to distance themselves from the alternatives of Thatcherism and Old Labour. Speaking just a month after Labour's landslide victory in 1997 to a meeting of the European Socialists' Congress in Malmö, Sweden, Blair said: 'Our task today is not to fight old battles but to show that there is a third way, a way of marrying together an open, competitive and successful economy with a just, decent and humane society' (Blair 1997a). As we shall see in the next chapter, this is not quite how all those in the same room saw things.

Some of the concepts that New Labour has used in the past to define itself have faded away. Stakeholding, for example, was abandoned largely because of left-wing associations. Community and social inclusion, however, became encompassed within the notion of a third way that became Blair's favourite means of evoking what New Labour stands for. Yet Labour's search for a 'third way' between the 'Old Left' and 'New Right' came at the end of a century littered with other attempts to break the mould with some political new way. Some of these – for example, Lloyd George's coalition government and later the Social Democratic Party – have searched for a political middle ground between Left and Right. Approaches such as theirs have often been compared to that of New Labour under Blair (on parallels with the Liberal Party, see Beer 2001). Some have come from the Right, whether from mainstream conservatism (e.g., Macmillan's 'middle way') or from far-right political movements – Mussolini being a self-proclaimed third-wayer whom even Tony Blair would not include in his 'big tent' politics. Other third ways have emerged from the Left: democratic socialists, social democrats and market socialists searching for third ways between social democracy and Stalinism, reform and revolution, or capitalism and communism. These do not match with Labour's centrist search for a third way between old-style social democracy and neo-liberalism.

Contemporary third-way thinking in Britain emerged out of the reform to the Centre-Left worldwide since the early 1980s (see Sassoon 1996). In Britain and the United States, New Labour and the New Democrats, faced with the hegemony of radical conservative governments espousing economic liberalization, were concerned with finding a politics that would mark a break with their own parties' past and with conservative governments in office. Ideas of a third way have been particularly relevant in such contexts – and the New Democrats are often credited with first popularizing the phrase in its current usage (on Clinton's third way, see Jaenicke 2000). It is also seen as having had wider reverberations – from like-minded reforms in Dutch and Swedish social democracy and among the Italian ex-communists and German social democrats to interest from the Spanish conservatives on the Right. Beyond Europe, one of the third way's most prominent exponents has been the sociologist and Brazilian president, Fernando Enrique Cardoso, and it has attracted sympathizers in the Labour parties of Australia and New Zealand. We shall return to such international comparisons in the next chapter.

Whether the idea of the 'third way' has preceded and guided policy development or resulted from *ex post facto* rationalizing of ideas and policies or, most likely, a bit of both is open to debate. In this chapter our concern is with what Labour modernizers such as Blair mean by the third way. Is being post-Thatcherite and 'beyond old Left' simply a receptacle for all things New Labour is not, too vague to have any definite positive implications? Or does it have some substantive meaning which provides a useful guide for public policy-making? Does it make the old politics of Left and Right redundant or does it just end up combining them in a contradictory and incoherent way? And, if it aspires to transcend traditional political divides and labels, to what extent can the third way still remain a political project for the Centre-Left? Does it, in fact, disguise a shift to the Right, marking a new consensus between Labour and the Conservatives?

The Third Way – and the First and Second Ways

The third way starts off from what it is not. A third or middle way must necessarily stand in relation to two others. What the nature of the relationship is between the different ways is one important issue in defining the third way: is it a compromise, a

synthesis or just the third of three, for example? Within New
Labour politics, the third way is defined as 'beyond Old Left and
New Right' (see, for example, Blair 1998c; Blair and Schröder
1999). The definitions of 'Old Left' and 'New Right' used in third-
way thinking are thus significant – as is the meaning of 'beyond'.
By 'Old Left', Labour modernizers have in mind the social democratic Labour politics of the post-war period – in particular, of a
post-sixties liberal hue. Generally, by 'Old Left' (or 'old Labour'),
Labour modernizers mean the Keynesian, egalitarian social democrats who tended to favour state and corporatist forms of economic and welfare governance within the context of a mixed
economy. Labour modernizers accuse this 'Old Left' of being too
statist; too concerned with the redistribution (and tax-and-spend
policies) and not the creation of wealth; too willing to grant rights
but not to demand responsibilities; and too liberal and individualist in terms of social behaviour and social relationships such as
the family. So, if the 'Old Left' is all of these, then New Labour's
third way is concerned to find alternatives to state provision and
government control; to promote wealth creation by accepting inequalities and being fiscally 'prudent'; to match rights with responsibilities; and to foster a culture of duty within 'strong
communities'.

By 'New Right', Labour modernizers mean Thatcherite conservatism. New Labour accuses successive Conservative governments – and here they echo significant voices on the Right
(Gilmour 1992; Gray 1993; Scruton 1996) – of being the slave to
neo-liberal dogma by favouring market solutions in all cases; by
having a laissez-faire view of the state; by promoting an asocial
view of society; and by championing an economic individualism
that places the value of individual gain above wider social values.
When New Labour opposes the 'New Right' way, as well as the
'Old Left' way, it argues for a third way that will promote wealth
creation *and* social justice, the market *and* the community; that
will embrace private enterprise but not automatically favour
market solutions; that can endorse a positive role for the state –
for example, welfare to work – while not assuming that governments provide public services directly (these might be done by
the voluntary or private sectors); and that can offer a communitarian rather than an individualist view of society in which individuals are embedded in social relations which give structure and
meaning to people's lives; and that it is the role of governments to
promote 'the community' as a way of enriching individual lives.

There are obvious problems with defining the third way simply in terms of what it is not. It can appear negative, lacking substance. As Stewart Wood suggests, it is 'product differentiation without really knowing what the product is' (Halpern and Mikosz 1998, 7; see also Dahrendorf 1999). There is also the tendency to create caricatures of the alternatives. New Labour's view of the 'Old Left', for example, is a catholic one (Shaw 1996; Hirst 1999). It combines disparate political positions under one label – from the social democracy of Tony Crosland in the 1950s and 1960s (itself a 'middle way') to the state socialism of the Alternative Economic Strategy in the late 1970s and early 1980s. New Labour's view of the 'New Right' has similar faults. In particular, it suffers from an exaggeration of the neo-liberal influence on Conservative governments in the 1980s and 1990s – any government that continues to spend over 40 per cent of GDP can hardly be described as laissez-faire – at the expense of acknowledging their conservative social interventions, the growth in economic regulations and the centralization of government.

The advantage to Labour modernizers of this negative or relational approach is to highlight – and exaggerate – the novelty of New Labour. Continuities with the 'Old Left' can be downplayed (except where, before a Labour audience, it is opportune to claim inheritance of traditional left values). Discontinuities with Conservative policy-making in the 1980s and 1990s can also be drawn (except where it suits New Labour to appear 'tough', on inflation or trade unions, for example). This is not to suggest that New Labour is simply a more up-to-date version of a post-war Labour government – there are too many important discontinuities – and nor is New Labour simply a continuation of Thatcherism. But if a third way is neither 'Old Left' nor 'New Right', then it – or the political territory where it might be found – can cross the centre ground of politics from Left to Right, and a third-way politics might embrace not just the Centre-Left but include more traditional 'one nation' strands of Toryism, as well, perhaps, as notions of 'compassionate conservatism' (see Dionne 1999). It is a perspective that might combine different traditions (Powell 2000; Deacon 2002). We shall return later to the issue of the broad ground within which the third way – or third ways – may co-exist.

This brings us to the question of what 'beyond' means and to the nature of the relationship between the various ways. For instance, does 'beyond' mean a break with the past or a continuation of it? Blair's position is that the third way represents a 'modernized social democracy' – in other words, a path on the *Centre-Left* of modern politics (see also Giddens 2001). This qualifies the meaning of 'beyond'. While it retains progression – the third way is at a better point further on – there are strong connections with the past. So, Blair argues, the third way offers an opportunity to advance traditional centre-left values using new policies that reflect the changing circumstances of the modern world.

Globalization, Information, Individualism: Bases of the Third Way

Blair's attempt to substantiate a third way falls into three parts: first, the general conditions or bases for the third way; second, its values; and third, the new means required to achieve these ends, taking into account the new conditions.

The general conditions for third-way politics rest on the argument that late twentieth-century society underwent profound and irreversible changes; and that these 'new times' called into question established political and policy-making frameworks. A central theme here is 'globalization'. In a speech in South Africa in January 1999, Tony Blair suggested:

> The driving force behind the ideas associated with the third way is globalization because no country is immune from the massive change that globalization brings...what globalization is doing is bringing in its wake profound economic and social change, economic change rendering all jobs in industry, sometimes even new jobs in new industries, redundant overnight and social change that is a change to culture, to life-style, to the family, to established patterns of community life. (Blair 1999b)

A third way, then, is required to cope with these 'new times'. For Blair, the Old Left – post-war social democracy – 'proved steadily less viable' (1999b, 5) as economic conditions changed as a result of globalization. In particular, Keynesian economic management to achieve full employment, partially repudiated by James Callaghan in the mid-1970s and again under question during Labour's policy review in the late 1980s, is seen as redundant in the context of a global economy. The economic liberalism of the New Right

Thatcher governments, which 'in retrospect' brought about 'necessary acts of modernization' (in particular, 'exposure of much of the state industrial sector to reform and competition'), ultimately failed because of a political dogmatism which prevented it from dealing with consequences of globalization, such as social dislocation and social exclusion, which required more active government (Blair 1999b, 5–6).

Third-way thinking supports the view that globalization brings with it greater risk and insecurity, and that it is the role of policy-making not to shield individuals from these but to provide the 'social capital' and 'proactive' welfare states that enable them to respond to such changes and prosper in the global age. For some of its proponents, the third way is in part a response to the development of post-traditional individualism and choice in a risk society (Giddens 1998). Traditional modes of behaviour, such as marriage, the family and women's roles, are breaking down, as is the security perceived to have been provided by institutions such as science and the welfare state. People are having to make more choices themselves as individuals in an increasingly fast changing world, whether about lifestyle, health risks, changes in employment status or other issues. The third way is in part about adapting to these new circumstances – formulating policies that recognize, for instance, the need for protection from risk (through education and training, for example, or new forms of pensions and savings), and developing policies on the family, including its relationship with work, especially flexible patterns for female workers and parents. And where globalization is bound up with the new digital information and communication technologies and the 'knowledge economy', individuals need the education and training appropriate to these conditions. Public policy should support business in the creation of 'knowledge-rich products and services', which will be the source of future economic growth (Leadbeater 1998 and 1999). As a result, it is suggested, the competing goals of economic success and social justice/cohesion can be squared. Government promotes economic growth by creating stable macro-economic conditions; and its supply-side social interventions enhance individual opportunity (social justice) and increase non-inflationary growth, which together bring greater social cohesion by reducing social exclusion, enhancing choice and protecting from risk.

But within and beyond third-way thinking there are, as we shall see in chapter 5, important divergences over the significance of globalization and how a third-way politics might or should respond to it. There are different views on the extent to which governments can or should control, regulate and respond to the global free markets at the heart of economic globalization. There are also markedly different responses to the other social changes seen as behind the third way. The main issues here are twofold: first, whether there is agreement in a sociological sense on the changes Blair and third-wayers identify; second, where there is agreement on the nature of social change, whether the normative implications flow clearly. As Finlayson (1999) has pointed out, the third way is as much about sociology and its political implications as about politics in isolation (see also Leggett 2000; Hay 1999).

As we shall see in chapter 5, Giddens and Blair, for instance, while often speaking a similar language, do not always share the same picture of social change. Their concepts of individualism differ, as do their analyses of policies required to tackle inequality and globalization. We shall return to this shortly. Other contributors also differ in their interpretations of globalization, the extent and nature of change involved in it, and consequently the sorts of politics implied. For some, nation-states retain significant powers as shown by national differences in, for instance, welfare policies and regimes. For others, the era of the nation-state is coming to an end (for the variety of interpretations, see Held et al. 1999; Hirst and Thompson 1996; Dearlove 2000; see also chapter 5). Even if the extent or nature of globalization is agreed upon, commentators such as Hay (1999) argue that the response to it is contingent. For him the third way is sociologically deterministic, portraying as economically fixed what is actually a matter for political choice. Anthony Giddens may be particularly vulnerable to this criticism, frequently seeing third-way values as an issue of social necessity in a global age.

One symbol of this is the evolving position of some of the earliest advocates of 'New Times'. In the 1980s those associated with *Marxism Today* argued that the Left was advocating a politics associated with the male working-class world of production and the nation-state. The Left, it was argued, needed to adapt to consumer capitalism, post-Fordism, globalization, women's changing position and new cultural identities (Hall and Jacques 1989; Hall 1988). The magazine closed down soon after, arguing that its case had been widely accepted, but published a one-off special issue in 1998. The cover featured a photograph of Blair with, emblazoned across it, the word 'Wrong'. *Marxism Today*'s contributors returned to condemn New Labour for a neo-liberal and conservative choice of response to 'New Times' that acquiesced far too much to the values of the Right. They argued for more social democratic and progressive responses. The message was that there is a very different reading of the possibilities inherent in the 'New Times' to that taken by Blair and the third way (see also Callinicos 2001).

'Traditional Values in a Modern Setting'

If these, then, are general conditions for a third way, what about the values that third-way politics promotes? There have been a number of attempts to pin these values down, and we shall focus on the four identified by Tony Blair in his third-way pamphlet for the Fabian Society: 'equal worth', 'opportunity for all', 'responsibility' and 'community' (see also Le Grand 1998; Giddens 1998; Hargreaves and Christie 1998; White 1998; Latham 2001).

Blair's first value, 'equal worth', is the old liberal nostrum that all human beings are equal and should be treated as such and not discriminated against. It should be noted here that equal worth is not the same as equality of *outcome* – having equal worth with others does not itself mean you are entitled to the same income or wealth if, for instance, you work harder than others do. Equal worth itself also does not necessarily imply equal *opportunities* – it is consistent for someone not to get the same opportunities as another if there is a right to private education, for instance, or if one person works harder to earn greater opportunities or has greater luck. Nevertheless it does seem to imply in New Labour hands that everyone should have some *minimum* opportunities or some basic fair chance in life and that no one should be excluded from this, even if beyond these basic opportunities there isn't necessarily equality of opportunities or of social and economic outcomes.

The second value, 'opportunity for all', reflects the New Liberalism in New Labour's third way: that substantive (or positive) freedom requires that individuals have the resources to develop their talents and exercise their liberty – rather than being concerned solely with the legal conditions which support individuals to lead free lives (negative freedom). In this case those resources include such things as educational opportunities and access to the labour market (see the ideas of Amartya Sen 1992 on social capability, referred to supportively by Giddens 2001). Equal opportunities do not only go beyond the New Right, though. Blair attempts to make a distinction crucial to the third way: that 'opportunity for all' is concerned principally with opportunities and not outcomes: 'The Left...has in the past too readily downplayed its duty to promote a wide range of opportunities for individuals to advance themselves and their families. At worst, it has stifled opportunity in the name of abstract equality' (Blair 1998c, 3; see also Brown 1997). By 'abstract equality' Blair means equality of outcome.

While he goes on to suggest that 'the progressive Left must robustly tackle the obstacles to true equality of opportunity', and that these might include 'gross inequalities...handed down from generation to generation', Blair offers what has widely been interpreted as a meritocratic understanding of equality. Inequality is a necessary part of a market economy, an important incentive and often deserved. White and Giaimo argue that one reading of this is as a 'Left Thatcherism' – 'an ideology which says that we should try to ensure citizens roughly equal initial endowments of marketable assets and then let the free market rip' (White and Giaimo 2001, 216). As Merkel puts it, the trend in social democracy under the British third way has been 'to the recognition of societal inequality as a legitimate and functional stratification pattern in highly developed market economies under the conditions of globalised economic transactions' (Merkel 2001, 50). Supporters of the third way 'seem fully prepared to accept greater income inequality as a market and policy outcome. Their acceptance ends only at the point where this leads to voluntary and involuntary exclusion in the higher and lower strata of society' (ibid., 53). In Blair's case the focus may be more on involuntary exclusion at the bottom than voluntary exclusion at the top. Furthermore, Giddens argues that equal opportunities cannot be divorced from more equal outcomes because some commitment to redistributional equality, in which income and/or wealth is more equally spread, is a precursor to equal opportunities. Inequalities in economic outcomes are themselves a basis for unequal opportunities. For Callinicos (2001) New Labour's neo-liberalism has led the party to abandon the sort of redistributional egalitarianism that is necessary for equality of opportunity: here is a place where a tension between Labour's neo-liberalism and its egalitarianism has had to be resolved, and it has been done so in favour of the former over the latter.

So New Labour's focus is more on opportunities than on greater equal outcomes. And, as far as opportunity goes, its focus is as much on greater chances for those excluded from basic, minimum opportunities as on equalizing opportunities. This leads, to some extent, to greater equality of opportunities as those excluded from fair chances get better access to them and, consequently, more equal opportunities relative to others than before. But a key characteristic of this approach is an orientation to *inclusion* into the world of opportunities as much as *equality* of opportunity within it. On the basis of minimum opportunities for the socially excluded there can still be inequalities in opportunities. So when speaking to a 1999 conference of third-way politicians, the political philosopher Ronald Dworkin warned that the third way had replaced 'equality' as an objective with 'sufficiency' in which, 'once those minimal standards are met, government has no further obligation to make people equal in anything' (Dworkin, 2001, 172). 'Does a political community owe only "sufficiency" and not equality to its members?' (ibid., 172), he asked. The consequence of choosing the former undermines achieving even something as modest as equal worth – 'If some political community really did succeed in guaranteeing the material means for a decent life to even its poorest citizens, but allowed some citizens to become rich, and to have the opportunity not just for a minimally decent life but for a fascinating one, the question would remain whether that result was consistent with equal concern for all' (ibid., 174). A commitment to minimum opportunities is a laudable policy objective and something which marks out the third way from the conservative Right, but authors such as Merkel, Giddens and Dworkin cast doubt on whether it amounts to equal opportunities or even equal worth, and whether such objectives could be achieved anyway without more equal outcomes.

The third of Blair's four values is 'responsibility' and links closely with the fourth, 'community'. 'Responsibility' reflects Blair's ethical turn, spelt out in his 1995 *Spectator* lecture that 'we do not live by economics alone': 'a society which is fragmented and divided, where people feel no sense of shared purpose, is unlikely to produce well-adjusted and responsible citizens' (Blair 1995a). In a decent society, individuals should not simply claim

rights from the state but should also accept their individual responsibilities and duties as citizens, parents and members of communities. A third way should promote the value of 'community'
by supporting the structures and institutions of civil society –
such as the family and voluntary organizations – which promote
individual opportunity and which ground 'responsibility' in
meaningful social relationships.

It is notable that New Labour's discourse of community differs
in emphasis from more traditional social democratic ideas of
social and economic community based on greater equality and
universal experience of services such as welfare, health and education and with a stress on the obligations of business to the
community (even if this was not always followed in practice as
effectively as it could have been). The third way is based more on
opportunities than on greater equality of outcomes. It retains an
emphasis on universal, collective services such as health and education, but some of its social policies make welfare more selective
and targeted. The third way has a more business-friendly tone
that stresses, rhetorically at least, moral as well as socio-economic
community and work. Responsibility of the citizen to the community is emphasized relatively more than corporate obligations.
Community is linked less to class than to moral cohesion and
social inclusion. (We discuss New Labour's communitarianism in
greater depth in Driver and Martell 1997.)

As we shall develop in this chapter, there is broad agreement
over these values among third-way writers, though problems
emerge over the interpretation of them and the extent to which
they define a centre-left political project (White 1998). For Blair,
his values are old values of the Left even if circumstances mean
new means are needed for achieving them (see also Giddens
2001). But one question is whether they do represent the values of
the Left or are something broader and representative of other
traditions. If the latter, do they create a new ideology that breaks
with its predecessors or one that merely recombines old ideas?
This raises a concern about the extent of the values' coherence or
internal contradictions, and whether together they make up a
philosophy or ideology or whether it is more the case that they
are a framework for policy (White 2001). In other words, is there a
systematic approach that gives guidance to policy in different
areas (a philosophy or ideology), or is it more of a case of a
political space without a coherent set of ideas but within which
different policy options are possible (a framework)?

'What Matters is What Works'?
New Labour's New Means

Blair's claim to a pragmatic view of means is indicative of much third-way thinking: 'These are the values of the Third Way. Without them, we are adrift. But in giving them practical effect, a large measure of pragmatism is essential. As I say continually, what matters is what works to give effect to our values' (Blair 1998c, 4). For Blair, as times change, so must the means to achieve centre-left values; and it is these values, not the policies in themselves, which matter. To be pragmatic rather than ideological about the choice of means is central to New Labour's case for a third way between Old Left and New Right – and to aspire to continuity in values is central to Blair's assertion that the third way is a centre-left political project.

The third-way debate about public policy reflects the Left's long preoccupation with the appropriate role for government in a market society. Bill Clinton and the New Democrats argued that the third way offered a new role for government between the Left's 'big government' and the Right's attempts to dismantle it; and this, in part, can be seen as a debate about the balance between the state and the market and the character of public policy instruments. What is common to the third way is the notion that there is an active role for government in contemporary market societies; and that this breaks with the state versus market approach which, it is suggested, typified the Old Left and New Right. New Labour's third way pragmatism, Le Grand (1998) argues, lies in the fact that it has no automatic commitment to either the public sector (as Old Left social democrats did) or the private sector (as New Right neo-liberals do). New Labour's third-way approach to public policy is said to break with the state/market approach by being more pragmatic and less ideological about them.

Put more concretely, a third-way approach to public policy encompasses a number of features: the state working in 'partnership' with the private and voluntary sectors (e.g., the New Deal and public–private cooperation in health and education, such as hospital building or private-sector school management); government regulating and acting as guarantor but not direct provider of public goods or of basic standards (e.g., of the minimum wage and local government services such as refuse collection); the reform or 'reinventing' of government and public administration (e.g., government departments and agencies working together to tackle complex social problems – so-called joined-up government); the welfare state working 'proactively' to help individuals off social security and into work ('employment-centred social policy' or the 'social investment state'), not leaving this to market forces or direct state provision of welfare or jobs; government working to provide public goods (such as childcare, education and training) to underpin greater equality of opportunity ('asset-based egalitarianism'); government targeting social policy on the socially excluded, and at the same time encouraging greater individual responsibility for welfare provision (e.g., 'stakeholder pensions'); and government redrawing the 'social contract': rights to welfare matched by responsibilities, especially regarding work. A third-way government can, then, be distinguished from an 'old left' one by its willingness to find new forms of public intervention in the economy and society – in particular, by giving up its role as the direct provider of public goods – and from a 'new right' one by its willingness to embrace a wide definition of public goods, especially in social policy, and a more active and interventionist role for the state.

Not all New Labour policies, on the definition we have outlined, can be seen as third way. Attempts to give a third-way meaning to foreign or defence policy, for example, artificially expand the third way to anything that can be defined as different to two alternatives, whatever they may be. Furthermore, the fact that a government espousing a third way pursues such policies does not make them original or exclusive to the third way. Many of the public policy instruments and reforms, such as public–private partnerships or 'reinventing government', now seen as being at the heart of New Labour's third way, were features of previous Conservative administrations from which the third way is meant to be clearly distinguished. In this manner, current third-way thinking can be seen as marking some degree of consensus between Left and Right, and the Labour government's reforms as revising previous Conservative reforms, not as overturning them entirely. The fact that governments of the Right, whether at state level in the USA or such national governments as that of José María Aznar in Spain, are attracted to so-called third-way public policy instruments also presents problems for any attempt to identify the third way as a uniquely centre-left political project.

There are further reasons to doubt whether Labour's new approach to means remains a centre-left or even pragmatic approach. One is that, in situations where it has been faced with decisions over the role of the public or private sectors in the provision of services, the government has consistently favoured increasing the role of private-sector money and management, but has not done so with regard to extending the role of the public sector in private-sector services. The government has controversially increased the role of the private sector in health and education while partly privatizing air traffic control and pursuing plans for part privatization of the London Underground. Conversely, when there was public sympathy for renationalizing the railways after a series of crashes, inefficiencies and price rises in rail travel, the government resisted, as it has done in other areas. It could be argued, in short, that Labour's approach to public–private partnerships appears not to be entirely 'what works matters' but just as much an ideological commitment to an increased role for the private sector in provision of previously public services. Hence some see it as one traditionally more associated with the Right and ideological sympathy for increasing the role of the private sector than with the Left or pragmatism (Shaw 2000).

For Plant (2001) New Labour fetishize means too much, stressing them as the arena in which change has happened and underplaying the extent to which the third way also involves shifts in ends. The third way argument is that centre-left ends have stayed constant while the means for achieving them have been changed from an item of political dogma to something that can be decided on pragmatically. Yet this separates means from ends too much, because changing means may affect the ends they are supposed to achieve. So a shift from policies of public ownership, Keynesian economics and tax redistribution affects whether centre-left ends such as equality can be pursued. Without such means the ends they were intended to achieve may become less realizable. A bias to private ownership and supply-side economics and inclusion strategies is amenable less to egalitarian redistribution and more to minimum opportunities within an inegalitarian market economy. Similarly, a shift away from ideas of, for instance, a universal welfare state and the comprehensive ideal in education affects the goals of certain kinds of equality and community. Targeted welfare and a pluralistic education system, whatever their vices or virtues, undermine egalitarianism as a goal and take away some means for achieving community. In short, the New Labour contention is that new times require new means, while ends can stay constant. The problem with this is that it underestimates the extent to which changing means affects ends also.

In the rest of this chapter and the next we shall raise two inter-related issues that have already been brought up by the discussion so far. First, we shall examine whether the third way marks a significant break in political thinking and policy-making; whether it moves 'beyond' notions of Left and Right – and what 'beyond' really means in this context. Second, we shall ask if there is one third way or a number of possible third ways and whether, if there is more than one, they are all equally social democratic. Do the kind of values which Blair and others suggest clearly define a third way? Or is the debate over the interpretation of third-way values (the question of what kind of equality, for example) indicative of significant lines of division within the third way?

Is the Third Way Really *Beyond* Left and Right?

As we have seen, third-way arguments claim that, with changing economic and social circumstances, a new politics is required that departs from the major political paradigms of the post-war years: namely social democracy (Old Left) and Thatcherism (New Right). But to what extent does the third way dispense with the traditional divide between Left and Right, and with the established political categories of liberal, conservative and social democrat? Does it, as Bobbio (1996) has asked, transcend and make such categories redundant? Or is it simply a cobbling together of different intellectual positions combining principles and practices which could cohere or be contradictory and mutually undermining?

There is a degree of ambiguity on these questions. Blair, for example, argues that 'the Third Way is not an attempt to split the difference between Right and Left', suggesting not a middle way but something more novel. He also states that the third way offers a new synthesis between liberal and socialist thinking: the third way 'marks a third way *within* the left' (Blair 1998c, 1, original emphasis). But some commentators have their doubts. Stuart White argues that the third way 'can all too easily be taken to imply that we need, not to modernise, but to exit the social democratic tradition in pursuit of something wholly new and distinctive' (White 1998; see also Marquand 1998).

John Gray is a leading advocate of the argument for a new politics that transcends established political frameworks: 'The place we occupy is not a halfway house between rival extremes. Our position is not a compromise between two discredited ideologies. It is a stand on a new common ground' (Gray 1997). Elsewhere he argues for his 'conviction that the established traditions of British political thought: liberal, conservative and socialist, cannot meet the challenges posed by the technological and cultural environment of Britain in the late modern period. New thought is needed, in which debts to the past are light' (Gray 1996, 7). The 'debts' to which Gray alludes include, crucially, political values, not just policy instruments – the dominant theme in New Labour thinking. He argues for a politics 'beyond the new right' (Gray 1993) and *'after* social democracy' (Gray 1996). Significantly for any debates about the third way, he suggests that 'Social democrats have failed to perceive that Thatcherism was a modernising project with profound and irreversible consequences for political life in Britain. The question cannot now be: how are the remains of social democracy to be salvaged from the ruins of Thatcherism? but instead: what is Thatcherism's successor?' (ibid., 10). For Gray, the 'communitarian liberalism' that he advocates rejects the social democratic value of equality and seeks instead to develop notions of 'fairness' and 'local justice'.

Others have suggested that contemporary politics is undergoing a 'cultural turn' in which questions of identity have become paramount, and that this culturalization of politics is blurring left/right political distinctions. Anthony Giddens (1994 and 1998; see also Driver and Martell 1999 for a discussion of this) argues that 'emancipatory politics' – concerned with questions of political economy and with the distribution of rights and resources – is giving way to 'life politics' – concerned with questions of identity and the quality of life. Giddens suggests that these shifts in contemporary political culture blur distinctions between Left and Right outside the domain of party politics: 'a whole range of other problems and possibilities have come to the fore that are not within the reach of the left/right scheme. These include ecological questions, but also issues to do with the changing nature of the family, work and personal and cultural identity' (Giddens 1998, 44). Left and Right concerns cut across these areas and, it is argued, fail to encapsulate differences between points of view on life politics.

Giddens also argues that traditional attachments of Left and Right to radicalism and conservatism respectively were becoming less and less meaningful after a decade of Thatcherite neo-liberal radicalism and in a cultural environment he calls 'post-traditional'. New Labour has since conformed to Giddens's thesis with a social conservative strand to their politics. For Giddens this makes it seem that old left–right associations do not work any more: particular views are no longer exclusively the property of one or the other. This is reinforced by the fact that popular attitudes do not so easily divide into consistently Left or Right positions as they used to. On many issues people divide into liberal or communitarian camps, for example, rather than left and right ones.

Such views suggest the moving of politics to areas beyond categories of Left and Right. But does this mean that Left and Right are transcended or synthesized or that they merely co-exist? We believe that the third way involves the combination rather than the transcendence of these traditional foes. Principles such as equality, efficiency, autonomy and pluralism, over which the Left and Right have long been divided, get mixed together rather than left behind. The novelty of the third way lies in this combination: it is a mixture which is exclusively neither of the Left nor of the Right. In this manner, the third way offers a politics which is beyond the closed ideological systems of the past, but which still combines them and remains within the tradition of middle-way politics that was a feature of much of twentieth-century British politics – most notably New Liberalism, post-war social democracy and one-nation conservatism.

Blair has argued that public policy 'should and will cross the boundaries between left and right, liberal and conservative' (Blair 1995a). In his Fabian pamphlet, he suggested that the third way offers 'a popular politics reconciling themes which in the past have wrongly been regarded as antagonistic' (Blair 1998c, 1). So, a third way stands for social justice *and* economy efficiency, rights *and* responsibilities, a successful market economy *and* social cohesion. It overcomes these bipolar divisions by suggesting that they are mutually supporting. Social justice, for instance, can be supported by ensuring everyone has the education and training needed to give them a fair chance in life; this also underpins economic efficiency by providing a skilled workforce which can attract investment and enhance productivity in the new global economy. You can have social justice and economic efficiency at the same time.

Blair offers practical examples of third-way policy positions which he sees as crossing traditional political divides: cutting corporation tax *and* introducing a minimum wage; giving the Bank of England independence *and* developing a programme of welfare to work to promote social inclusion; reforming schools to give marginalized kids better chances *and* tough policies on juvenile crime; giving central government 'greater strategic capacity' *and* introducing devolution; more money for health and education *and* tight limits to the overall level of government spending or limits on income tax. For Blair, the distinctiveness of these policies in terms of a third way is the italicized *'and'* in each case: it is in the combinations that the originality of third-way thinking lies. And it is the combination that produces a politics which is both new – 'beyond Old Left and New Right' – yet also rooted in centre-left values.

The notions that freedom might need equality; that a strong community is the basis for individual autonomy; that economic efficiency should be tempered by social justice; and that rights must be balanced with responsibilities are hardly original – these are concerns which run right through, for example, New Liberalism. There are, of course, essential and irresolvable tensions between liberalism, conservatism and social democracy and their principal values – equality, liberty and authority. But what the third way tries to do is not to reconcile but to manage the relationship between these political traditions: to find compromises not resolutions (see Martell 1993). For Salvati (2001), New Labour's third way is the latest in a long line of liberal-socialist compromises that have defined social democracy, in this case one that tries to strengthen the liberal side.

This is one way of encapsulating what the third way is: a pragmatic politics which tries to break with what it sees as the strait-jacket of left/right politics (see also Powell 1999). From this perspective, the third way offers a wide and potentially fertile landscape for public policy-making. Such a political project could be seen as in a better position to tackle complex social problems, such as social exclusion, because it is light on ideological baggage. Or at least it is willing to make compromises on its contents – and so can approach policy analysis and prescriptions in terms of what works rather than always on the basis of ideological origins (Glennerster 1999). The New Deal illustrates how the principles of autonomy, opportunity and rights balanced with responsibilities might actually complement one another. The third way also allows the Labour government to have a more pluralistic approach to policy-making, in the sense that certain principles operate in some spheres of policy-making and not in others: for example, rights-based liberal individualism in constitutional reform but social conservatism in education and the criminal justice system.

This notion of a mix of values and approaches better encapsulates the third way than the more radical definition of it as a synthesis or as transcending Left and Right. Finding some balance or *modus operandi* between the demands of competing political values and recognizing that different values (or combinations of values) may be more suited to different policy areas better defines the third way and what the Labour government is doing in practice. But such compromises come with price tags as principles and values have to be traded off against one another. What Blair's third way often appears to do is to try to combine what are in the end contrary principles. New Labour's third way can at times appear as if, as Albert Hirschman (1996) puts it, all good things go together – when very often they don't. While reciprocity and mutual dependency between different values and policies is possible in particular circumstances, there are also different interests at work, and tensions remain permanent features of the political and policy-making landscape.

It follows that, as a perspective that combines different principles, the third way cannot be said to be a coherent ideology or philosophy. There is no systematic, consistent guide to action or to which principles should be favoured in circumstances where they clash. So the third way is more of a framework than a philosophy, more of a space between other alternatives within which policy can be developed (White 2001; Giddens 2001). What decisions and 'hard choices' should be made in adjudicating between contrary principles is left open. So, in criminal justice liberal and conservative views can co-exist, but sometimes they come into conflict and choices have to be made between them. In economic policy the commitment to minimum opportunities may come into conflict with the success of a market economy, and so choices have to be made between these two: in fact choosing the market economy is one key reason why the principle of egalitarian redistribution has been considerably downgraded in Labour's approach. Giddens (2001) expresses sympathy for egalitarian redistribution, the European social model and global economic regulation, including policies such as taxes on currency speculation. Yet he also rejects demand management and a role for government in supporting ailing industries and enthuses about flexible labour markets. Where some commitments undermine others, and how choices might be made between them where they clash, is not considered. Callinicos (2001) acknowledges the mixed nature of the New Labour agenda but argues that the hard choices, where they have to be made, nearly always favour the further embedding of market relations throughout society and of the neo-liberal element in New Labour. For him, therefore, there is a consistent pattern in Labour choices between competing values, and that is a tendency to choose a continuation of the New Right.

It would, then, be mistaken to see the third way as only pragmatic, as leaving behind ideology and values and being just about 'what works best'. Raymond Plant (2001) argues that pragmatism involves deciding what works best in the pursuit of something in particular. What that something is involves values, ends and ideology. So greater pragmatism is not post-ideological or a substitute or a replacement for ideology or values. The third way has value and ideological dimensions.

Thatcherism Mark 2?

But is this third way simply the mark of a new consensus between Left and Right – in particular, a consensus based on the Thatcherite reforms of the 1980s and 1990s which New Labour has adopted and which has replaced the post-war social democratic consensus on Keynesianism and the welfare state? Does the third way debate symptomize the more significant development of a post-Thatcherite consensus where there is agreement between the major parties on the big issues and it is only on detail that political actors part company? And does the notion of a third way, and the consensus which may lie behind it, raise concerns that debate about genuine contested political alternatives, the heart of an open, liberal democracy, is being foreclosed? For many critics the consolidation of Thatcherism is what New Labour amounts to, and Blair is little more than the 'son of Margaret' (Hall 1994; Hall and Jacques 1997; Hall 1998; Hay 1999). In being more pragmatic about what works best, the third way has opened the Left up more to non-left inputs. Pragmatism has allowed an ideological shift in which the Left has become more open to right values. For one commentator the third way, mixed as it is, has continued and even radicalized neo-liberal policies: 'It does not follow that no more beneficent measures have been passed, but the balance is greatly outweighed by those that further entrench market relations in every corner of social life' (Callinicos 2001, 121–2).

Certainly the political agenda shifted to the Right under Mrs Thatcher and the main political parties now are fighting on a similar post-Thatcherite terrain. This is not evidence for the 'beyond Left and Right' view. The new consensus consists of a shift from Left to Right, not one which goes beyond both to something new. The occupancy of positions has moved, but the old divides on which they are based remain. But the 'beyond Left' view is also, on a factual level, too simple. The case for consensus is based on Labour's adoption of an orthodox macro-economic policy that has low inflation as its central policy objective and interest rates as the key policy instrument. While giving the Bank of England the power to set monetary policy marks a point of departure from previous Conservative governments, it is in other public policy areas – the labour market (the minimum wage, the social chapter), constitutional reform, public spending on health and education, the scale and scope of the New Deal – in which it is possible to identify imprints of the Left. Those who advocate the 'Labour as Thatcherism' view downplay or even ignore social democratic elements to the third way (as is the case, for instance, in Hay 1999). Many of these differences involve a combination of small practical measures based in centre-left values and embrace important symbolic differences from the Right. Put simply, the third way is worth taking seriously because, while the Labour government is doing things previous Tory administrations did, it is also doing significant things that they didn't do and wouldn't have done, and this combination has challenged the Right to think again. 'Beyond Left' is also too simplistic, because the third way beyond Blair, and politics beyond the third way itself, still includes distinctively left-wing positions.

We have suggested that the space between Old Left and New Right may not be as narrow as it first appears. There is a mixture of Left and Right in there, a mixture of ideology and pragmatism and of different responses to differently interpreted social changes. If there is one third way in that space, there may be room for others (see Dahrendorf 1999; Freeden 1999; White 1998). Different third ways might be more or less centre-left in orientation: some social democratic, others not – and some to the Right of the political divide. We wish to go on to argue in this chapter and the next that there are different third ways, both domestically in Britain and across Europe. These vary on the left–right axis but also on other grounds. In the following chapters we will show how third way responses vary at a wider level, in response to European policy, international affairs, foreign policy and globalization.

Giddens and Blair:
New Times and Social Democracy

Anthony Giddens is often styled as Tony Blair's guru. But in terms of what Giddens sees the third way as being a reaction to, on what he says underlies and shapes it, and, consequently, on some of the positive meanings of the third way, there are differences of emphasis between him and Blair. What kind of individualism? What kind of civil society? What kind of politics? What kind of equality? In Blair's and Giddens's answers to these questions there are divergencies in third ways between Old Left and New Right. Giddens gives different emphases to the social trends he sees as important – globalization, 'detraditionalization', value change in society, changes in social structure and ecological problems. Where they do identify similar significant social changes (e.g., globalization and individualism), Giddens and Blair define them differently. As we shall see, Blair sees globalization and the rise of individualism differently to Giddens and places less emphasis on factors such as the growth of ecological problems. Variations in the positive content of their third ways arise from such underlying divergencies in emphasis. To put it another way, there are differences in Giddens's and Blair's sociologies of the modern world, and in the normative responses to whatever social changes each perceives.

While they both stress the role of globalization, Blair does not put the emphasis that Giddens does on institutions of global governance that might counteract economic globalization (see also Held 2000). Blair stresses the need to accept, and actively participate in, the global market economy. For critics such as Hutton (1995), for example, Blair is too acquiescent to the perceived globalization of the world economy and to the limits this places on national economic policy-making (see also essays by Marquand, Vandenbroucke, Hirst and Hutton in Gamble and Wright 1999; Callinicos 2001, chapter 4; Held 1998). Where Blair does discuss transnational political coordination, it is focused mostly on leadership in the European Union and prioritizes the need for transparency and democracy in EU institutions rather than the more expansive ideas for global governance that Giddens discusses. Blair's emphasis is more adaptive to globalization than that of Giddens. This may be less the case when it comes to military intervention: during the Kosovo crisis Blair did talk of permanent structures for international intervention in humanitarian crises and played a proactive role in the creation of a European defence identity and coalition-building during the war in Afghanistan. We shall return to this issue in chapter 5 (see also Martell et al. 2001).

The growth of individualism is another phenomenon Giddens and Blair both see as an important influence on politics – but they have different analyses of it. Giddens argues that the sort of individualism that has grown in society is not economic egoism and cannot be attributed to Thatcherism (Giddens 1998, 34–7, and 2001). It is a product of detraditionalization and increases in choice, and more about moral uncertainty than moral decay. For Giddens, the growth of this sort of individualism requires, as a response, more active responsibility, reflectiveness and democratization. There are crossovers here with Blairite ideas of individual responsibility and self-reliance concerning welfare reform, but also key differences. Blair explicitly locates the growth of individualism in, among other things, the Right's economic egoism, the Left's social individualism and a more general process of moral decay. The active, reflective citizen in a radical democracy is Giddens's model. Blair puts more emphasis, in his response to individualism, on the notion of duty, on moral cohesion and institutions such as education, family and the welfare state that he believes can and should enforce good behaviour. The post-traditionalist Giddens's solution is to emphasize active individualism, where the communitarian Blair's is to stress moral responsibilities and standards as an antidote to the individualism he identifies. In this respect, third-way ideas can be divided between more progressive 'post-traditionalists' such as Giddens and more conservative 'social moralists' such as Blair.

Giddens also gives greater emphasis to post-materialist attitudes and quality of life issues expressed in 'life politics'. He is conscious of risk, scientific uncertainty and ecological problems. He does not propose replacing governmental politics with 'life politics', but does suggest the latter should have a more important role. Blair's politics are less about quality of life issues beyond conventional economic and social policy concerns: while the Labour government has developed a quality of life index, it remains peripheral to the main body of policy-making. The core of New Labour has little interest with active democratizing processes for citizens in everyday life outside mainstream politics and elections. To the disappointment of many environmentalists, feminists and others, there is little in Blair's politics that is a direct response to contemporary radical social movements or incorporates their concerns. The democratization programmes of New Labour are *of* government, not *beyond* government. When Blair discusses the need for 'a strong civil society' and 'civic activism', it is not social movement politics he has in mind. His concern is with individuals fulfilling their responsibilities as parents and the role of the established institutions of the voluntary sector and the family rather than radical, informal social movements. The life politics which preoccupy Giddens plays less of a part in the politics of New Labour.

Third-Way Values in Question: Equality and Community

On closer examination there are further ways in which there are differences within third-way politics. Stuart White offers his definition of third-way values (White 1998). These, he suggests, are: 'real opportunity', 'civic responsibility' and 'community', and offer a 'general normative framework'. They tally more or less with the values offered by the Labour leader we examined earlier. However, unlike Blair, White suggests that they are open to different interpretations, not all of which will fall on the Centre-Left. This leads him to suggest two lines of division within the third way. The first between 'Leftists' and 'Centrists' concerns the nature of equality. Like Bobbio (1996), White identifies equality as a crucial issue that divides those on the Left from those further on the Right. The second line is between liberals and communitarians and concerns the degree of individual freedom in relation to community-enforced norms.

There are two points of note which we shall pick up and develop from White. First, the interpretation of third-way values is significant and marks out different political positions within the third way. What kind of equality is involved and what kind of community, and how much of each? There are divergences among third ways on such questions. Second, the third way is concerned with means as well as ends. The varying means intended to achieve third-way ends – governmental or more voluntaristic, for example – may also lead to a differentiation of third ways.

White's first line of division is between leftist-egalitarian and more centrist-meritocratic third ways (see also Holtham's distinction between the 'Centre-Left' and 'radical centre' in Halpern and Mikosz 1998, 39–41). Leftists would like to see greater redistribution of income and wealth rather than just of asset-based opportunities; and critics such as Roy Hattersley (1997a and 1997b; see also Levitas 1998) have condemned New Labour's shift from equality of outcome to meritocracy and inclusion as the principal aims of the third way. Giddens (1998, 2001, 2002) launches a stern attack on the inadequacy of meritocracy and equality of opportunity alone.

A second line of division identified by White is between communitarians and liberals: between those who have a broad understanding of the range of behaviour for which the individual may be held responsible to the community, and for which the state may legitimately intervene, and those who have a much more limited notion. White argues that any third way view must have some commitment to civic responsibility. And it is New Labour's communitarian understanding of civic responsibility – its apparent willingness to set public policy that challenges liberal notions of the private sphere – which is distinctive and which has drawn fire from, among others, the liberal Left for being too conservative, too prescriptive, even socially authoritarian (*Marxism Today* 1998; see also Dahrendorf 1999; *The Economist* 1999).

This liberal–communitarian distinction conceals further differences in third ways – among liberals and among communitarians. Some who are liberal on social matters, for example, may be left-egalitarian – less interventionist socially but in favour of greater economic interventionism and equality. It is conceivable that some who are liberal on social intervention could be more centrist-meritocrats, although this combination begins to move us to the Right rather than Left of Centre. Similarly those who are sympathetic to Labour's communitarian interventionism on social matters may be leftist-egalitarians or more centrist-meritocrats when it comes to questions of economic equality. So between liberal and communitarian third ways there may be differences, and within each yet further third-way approaches can be distinguished. How such positions may be viewed in the space between Old Left and New Right can be seen in figure 1.

These distinctions leave out a third axis, to do with the nature of communitarianism, along which there is space between Old Left and New Right for third ways to differ. Different sorts of communitarianism can be progressive or conservative, voluntaristic or statist. As we have suggested, criticisms of Labour's communitarianism are often liberal and suspicious of prescriptive moralism. But another line of criticism could come within communitarianism from anyone at odds with its conservative content (again, see *Marxism Today* 1998). This raises issues not of whether community should be promoted but of what sort of community – a 'progressive' community (which promotes modern teaching methods and support for non-nuclear family forms, for instance) or a more 'conservative' sort of community (which emphasizes more traditional norms for education and the family). Alternatives here may concur over the idea that it is the role of government to have a moral agenda about what kind

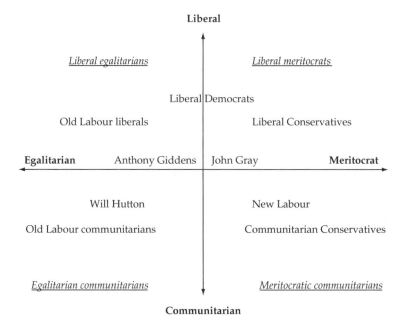

Figure 1   Liberty, equality and community in
contemporary British political debates

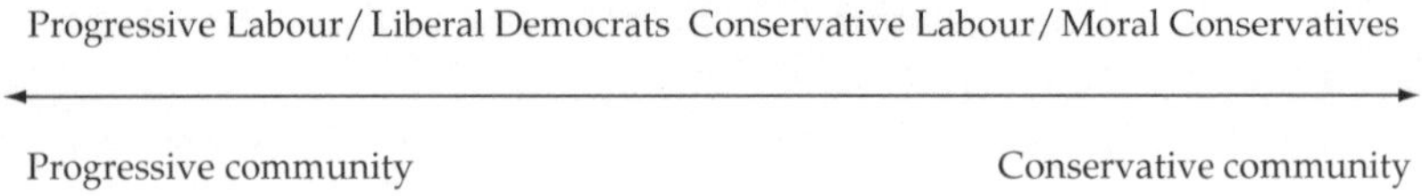

Progressive Labour/Liberal Democrats Conservative Labour/Moral Conservatives

◄──►

Progressive community   Conservative community

Figure 2   Progressive and conservative community

of community is desirable, but disagree over the sort of community prescribed.

Also glossed over by the liberal–communitarian distinction is a difference between voluntaristic and top-down communitarians. Again, the difference is not over whether greater community or shared moral norms are needed but, in this case, where these come from – state action or more organically. Those who stress the latter can include one-nation or 'compassionate' conservatives or leftist-communitarians of more voluntaristic, civil society and social movement traditions, in search of more community but not through state action. Those, like New Labour, who stress the former see governments – through exhortation, symbolic action and legislation – taking the lead in fostering community in society, even if they are also open to some forms of community action from below in New Deal in the Community programmes, for instance.

This is one example of where third ways diverge on means. The third way can involve the initiative of civil society or state or delivery of, for instance, welfare by the state or by greater delegation to the private and voluntary sectors. The question here is whether a government committed to strong social objectives can deliver on them without the old levers of power – at least without resorting to new 'cattle prods' (see Coote 1999). There might be divisions over whether welfare is universal or more targeted, with any implications this may have for impinging upon social democratic values. There can be third ways pursued via global governance or national or local action or through cooperation between state and other actors, whether governmental or non-governmental. In this manner, the third way can diverge on means – and the choice of means in each of these cases will affect the character of the ends reached.

Conclusion

The third way is initially a negative programme, to go beyond Old Left and New Right, especially applicable, as we shall see shortly, to Anglo-American contexts, where these alternatives have been prevalent. This is combined with an attempt to modernize in tune with new times in the economy, society and culture. But beyond this basis in negative opposition and modernization there are positive meanings in terms of values (versions of equality and community) and means (the role for government). On such issues, Blair's third way combines rather than transcends Left and Right but, in doing so, produces new configurations which in themselves may not be easily identifiable as being strongly either Left or Right. Combining Left and Right can lead to contradictions or be mutually undermining. It may lead to situations where choices have to be made between Left or Right over the other, but not necessarily so. In some circumstances Left and Right can co-exist in the third way. In fact they can on occasion form mutually dependent and reciprocal relationships.

The positive implications of taking a third way are not pre-determined or singular. There are different possible meanings of what can be between Old Left and New Right. Variations in social changes identified will lead to different positive contents for the third way. And third ways can vary on the content of values such as equality, community and individualism, what these should mean and how much of each there should be. In identifying third ways old political labels continue to be useful. Versions of the third way are more Left or Right, more or less social democratic, more liberal or conservative; and criticisms and defences of Blair's third way often break down along such lines. This casts doubts on Blair's oft-repeated claim that the third way is necessarily a centre-left project. A social democratic third way, whether it is actually called that or not, is discernible (see Gamble and Wright 1999 and the 'new social democracy'). Equally apparent are third ways to the Right, including strong elements in Blair's own approach, which share less with the Centre-Left, however defined. In this way, Left and Right divisions, as Bobbio (1996) argues, as well as those between liberals and communitarians, progressives and conservatives, have not been left behind. Such divisions also mark out social democratic paths taken beyond Britain and underpin the reception of the third way elsewhere. It is to the significance of national institutions, traditions and cultures that we turn now.

4

The Third Way beyond Britain

Tony Blair has had his moments of evangelism in trying to promote the third way abroad – and this has led to a certain degree
of irritation among some listeners. When Blair spoke (in French)
to the French National Assembly, Lionel Jospin, the centre-left
prime minister, was said to scowl and read his mail while all
around him listened attentively. But there is no doubt that across
Europe and in many countries abroad the sort of third-way ideas
being pursued by Blair have caught on. Commentators such as
Sassoon (1999) and Vandenbroucke (2001) are keen to stress com-
monality rather than difference, and there are notable similarities
in agendas across Europe and in other parts of the world. Blair
has been keen to promote the third way abroad – not just through
fitting in with Europe or playing a part in it, but through actively
exercising leadership in creating a third-way model that other
European social democrats will go along with (Blair 1997a, 1998c).
But it is not only Blair who has helped these ideas to catch on.
Many other centre-left parties before Blair were pursuing what
have become known as third-way policies. For some, commonalities around third way ideas are due to the fact that shared processes of globalization are leading to the same sort of logical
adaptations (Giddens 1998; Sassoon 1999). But there may be many
other common problems that different national governments have
been facing – pressures following from European integration, or
demographic change and other difficulties for European welfare
states, for instance. In this chapter we shall look at common patterns in third ways across Britain, the USA and Europe, before
moving on to examine the manner in which national institutions

and cultures lead third ways to take different forms in different places.

The Third Way across the Pond

Some credit US President Bill Clinton as the first real popularizer of the idea and policies of the third way and with whose New Democrats Blair's New Labour came to have much in common. Both Clinton and Blair came to power against the backdrop of years of radical neo-liberal governments, as moderates within their own parties convinced that modernization and a move to more central ground was necessary for electoral success, placing importance on globalization and the information economy and the priority for welfare reform, economic stability and fiscal prudence. Both tended away from isolationism on the international stage. Robert Reich, former secretary of labor under Clinton, declared in 1999 that 'we are all third wayers now' (Reich 1999). Reich argues that Western Europe and the USA shared a commitment to reducing budget deficits and to deregulation (in the USA) or privatization (in Europe), an acceptance of globalization in trade and the mobility of capital, and commitments to flexible labour markets and reductions in welfare. The US Democrats and New Labour, he argued, were also committed to reducing burdens and regulations on business and accepted the growth of inequality. On these issues there may be some difference between the Anglo-American partners and their European counterparts, differences being an issue we shall return to shortly. Yet alongside this neo-liberalism there is also a commitment to government activism, making the British and USA ways *third* ways, departing from the old left but also more than just neo-liberalism (Jaenicke 2000). Both US and UK policies on social inclusion have involved education and training, special support for families with children, and making sure that work is worth-while for the poor, through tax credits for instance. In both the US and the UK one factor that limited such attempts was an emphasis on fiscal prudence and restrictions on tax rises for those who benefited under two decades of Reagan and Thatcher (Reich 1997 and 1999), not to mention other institutional and political obstacles faced especially in the USA (Weir 2001; Jaenicke 2000). As we show in chapter 8, both Clinton's and Blair's welfare reforms have also been marked by conservative emphases, imposing obligations in return for welfare rights, or, in some cases, limiting rights to, or amounts of, benefits.

The Third Way across the Channel – and Before Blair

But the spread of third-way ideas and policies can be seen beyond Britain and the USA. Other leaders, such as D'Alema in Italy, Gerhard Schröder in Germany and Cardoso in Brazil, not to mention leaders not of the Left or Centre, such as José María Aznar in Spain, have explicitly praised Blair's third way or allied themselves with it, attended third-way conferences or developed written joint platforms with Blair reflecting third way policies (e.g., Blair and Schröder 1999). This is not to mention policies which, named as third way or not, seem to match neatly with those of the third way. In the 1980s, 1990s and afterwards other parties have reinvented themselves in ways that could be seen as going in a comparable direction to Blair's (albeit with specifically national or some ideological differences) – the PSOE in Spain under Felipe Gonzalez, the Dutch PvdA under Wim Kok, and the Swedish SAP, for instance. Overall the political centre of gravity among social democratic parties has shifted rightwards to a more centrist position.

Beyond Britain, other social democratic parties have long been struggling to win middle-class and popular support outside their shrinking working-class constituencies. In Sweden, for instance, middle-class support has always been central to the success of the SAP. By the mid-1990s Europe's social democrats were also in principle accepting the market economy they had long learned to live with in practice. For some, this path traces back to the 1950s, through Crosland and Gaitskell in Britain, through Bad Gödesborg in 1959 for the SPD in Germany and through related reforms in this period in countries such as Italy, Norway and Sweden.

In some places, social democratic modernization preceded that recently carried out by the British Labour Party – seen by most as, for good or ill, presently the furthest down the road of liberalization. At the 1959 Bad Gödesborg congress the German SPD broke with Marxism by accepting the market and a role for private ownership. The Dutch SDAP's conversion to the mixed economy and an electoral strategy that incorporated the middle classes happened as early as the 1930s. The Dutch PvdA (founded in the 1940s) shares a remarkable number of features with New Labour in the UK: the rejection of traditional welfarism and Keynesianism, and of planning and egalitarianism; an emphasis on combining economic efficiency with social justice; low taxation policies; competitiveness based on technological innovation; government intervention on social exclusion; a focus on labour and work as the basis for participation; partnership with the private sector; flexibility in worklife; and the importance of education and training (van den Anker 2001). While Sweden has been noted for its high taxation and large universal welfare system, several of the characteristics of present-day modernization were also exhibited by Swedish social democracy long before Blair had his day. And many of the criticisms of modernizing social democracy in the Netherlands are also comparable to those made of New Labour in Britain: too much emphasis on work as a solution to social exclusion and on opportunities at the expense of equality and redistribution, for example (van den Anker 2001).

Third-Way Economics and Welfare beyond Britain

While Thatcherism left New Labour with a neo-liberal inheritance, Maastricht and budget deficits were key factors that forced fiscal conservatism on other European social democrats. Social democratic parties across Europe were talking in the 1980s about the combination of social justice with economic efficiency and individual entrepreneurialism. In the 1980s and 1990s low inflation and stability replaced Keynesianism and full employment as the main goals, leading to the rethinking of economic, employment and welfare policies. Many European social democrats were well ahead of the British in their moves in these directions. Before Tony Blair became Labour leader, the Dutch social democrats were adopting their pragmatic approach to the market and regulation, and promoting deregulation, privatization and internal markets. They were practising sound public finances, implementing tax reductions and promoting the work ethic, flexibility and training initiatives in the labour market and reallocations of funding from social security to other areas, such as education. The Dutch social democrats have argued for and seemingly achieved what Blair aspires to: the combination of many of these liberal economic reforms on one hand with social cohesion and social justice on the other (De

Beus 1999). Others, such as the Spanish PSOE, put inflation above unemployment as an economic policy priority (Clift 2001).

Across European social democracy, nationalization has generally been discarded. Many social democratic governments talk of constructive partnership between business and government and are pursuing more ambitious privatization programmes than Blair or their own conservative predecessors (Sassoon 1999). An openness to private enterprise and a non-dogmatic attitude to state ownership has long been part of Swedish social democracy. As a small country dependent on exports, Sweden has accommodated itself to free trade and international competition for some time (Lindgren 1999). Well beyond Britain, social democrats propose active government, rather than the direct state intervention or laissez-faire of the first and second ways; business-friendly practices, such as lower business taxes, and increasing labour-market flexibility are pursued; and restraints on public expenditure are being widely implemented in response to pressures such as EU convergence and the perceived globalization of capital. Keeping inflation down is generally accepted as a prime target across Europe. Fiscal stability and curbing tax-and-spend policies are general commitments, as are the use of supply-side measures, subsidies and incentives to tackle unemployment. It is not only in the UK that small businesses and industrial innovation in hi-tech sectors are being promoted as the cutting edge of future growth. All this sounds very much like Blair's third-way recipe for Britain.

The French socialists make the strongest noises about national uniqueness and a more traditional social democratic road. But beyond their policy for a 35-hour week some see differences from Blair in hard policies as often not fundamental (e.g., Sassoon 1999). From this point of view, Britain has moved, albeit more weakly, in the direction of restricting working hours. Negotiations on Jospin's reductions to the working week have actually led to agreements on greater labour-market flexibility. While the British are reluctant to increase income taxes, in Germany there is widespread feeling that tax rates are too high and there are concerns to restructure the tax system. The principle of central bank independence has been broadly accepted – implemented in Sweden at the same time as in the UK and part of the German scene for decades (Sassoon 1999). Across Europe, from Jospin to Blair, social democrats wish to pursue reforms to international financial organizations.

Although welfare problems vary from nation to nation, comparable agendas of welfare reform are being discussed by many European social democrats across national boundaries (Vandenbroucke 2001). The Swedes have for decades been at the forefront of developing 'workfare' and active labour-market policies based on education and training. While they remain attached to universalism, they are shifting away from the idea that the state should shoulder all the costs. The fiscal deficit and an increasing proportion of pensioners and students in the population have led Swedish social democrats to limit rises in social security (Lindgren 1999). Across Europe employment is seen as a key to welfare reform. It is perceived that welfare needs to be more responsive to changes in the family and gender roles and more attuned to balancing work and family life. Welfare is seen as being as much about investment in education as spending on benefits (Vandenbroucke 2001). It is not just in Britain that welfare reform imposes obligations on the unemployed: the German SPD, for instance, has also been thinking along such lines. The advocacy of tough crime measures, the tying of rights to responsibilities and the prioritization of education and training as routes to employment and fairer chances are defining features of New Labour that have also been rehearsed in the talk of other European social democratic parties.

Third Ways and National Paths

But the story is more complex than this. Despite globalization and European integration, national differences are important. A commentator such as Clift (2001) writes that 'European social democratic parties are more similar now than at any time this century' (p. 71). But he still makes the central aim of his essay on this topic to explain how the most notable feature of the European social democratic landscape remains difference along national lines. Vandenbroucke (2001) stresses 'theoretical convergence' among European social democratic parties in terms of the policy commonalities we have discussed, but also sees divergence in actual national models and policies: 'convergence of view on this level of thinking will not necessarily lead to convergence on practical measures between countries due to their very different starting points' (p. 163). (See also Kelly 1999; White 2001, part III; Lovecy 2000; Martell et al. 2001.)

For a large part of the 1980s the story was of Labour lagging behind its sister European social democratic parties in the march towards modernization. It was attached to nationalization, Keynesianism, unilateral nuclear disarmament, close links with the unions and a less than fulsome embrace of European integration. Yet in the 1990s Labour is seen as having leapfrogged European social democracy in the race to 'modernize'. For some Blair has taken the politics of catch-up a little too far. At meetings of European social democrats Blair and Gordon Brown have tried to promote the virtues of liberalization and free trade, labour-market flexibility, welfare reform and cuts in regulation of business in pursuit of productivity and employment. Blair is said to have irritated fellow European social democrats, who see him as lecturing them to adopt what is effectively just warmed-up Thatcherism. Blair's suggestions that the Socialist International be renamed the Centre-Left or Third Way International were, reportedly, not received warmly.

The British third way has often been seen to contrast with the politics of those, such as the French prime minister, Lionel Jospin, who are not so opposed to the virtues of labour-market regulation and public spending on job creation. Some social democrats among the Italians, French and Germans (but not many of their leaders) have argued for demand management (at a coordinated European level) to boost employment where British modernizers have focused more on advocating supply-side measures, arguing that the world has been changed so much by globalization that Keynesianism is dead (Clift 2001; Giddens 1994 and 1998; Vandenbroucke 2001). At the same time the European Central Bank, supported by most social democratic governments, has pursued a very tight and conservative monetary policy in recent years. It has been the Anglo-American central banks in the UK and the USA that have pursued a more active and growth-orientated monetary policy by aggressively cutting interest rates. In Britain inclusion in the job market is seen as occurring essentially through private-sector jobs, whereas other European social democrats, such as the French, have put greater emphasis on public-sector job creation. The French socialist policy has been to decrease the average working week to thirty-five hours, while the British have trouble legislating for anything lower than forty-eight hours. Jospin argues 'yes to the market economy, no to the market society', an approach within which he pursues widespread privatization and deregulation but also the shorter working week and continued state intervention in the economy (Bouvet and Michel 2001, Jospin 1999).

Meanwhile, the 'social' in Germany's social market seems to require goals that go beyond inclusion and equality of opportunity to more egalitarian values and beyond laissez-faire to a more collaborative approach (Meyer 1999). In France, Germany, Sweden and elsewhere partnerships with the unions remain important, while New Labour has attempted to divorce itself from any special relationship with the unions, who emerged much weakened from the Thatcher years. For the Dutch and Swedes, politics is embedded in a social democratic political culture, emphasizing consensus and continuity – the 'polder model' as it is known in the Netherlands – quite different to the competitive individualism and Conservative domination of the British context (van den Anker 2001).

Welfare problems vary across Europe: pensions dominate the debate in Italy, Sweden, Germany and France; health expenditure – too low in Britain, too high in Germany; disability benefits in the Netherlands; unemployment in Germany and France; and poverty and exclusion in the UK (Kelly 1999). In Sweden there remains a stronger attachment to universal welfare than in some other places (Lindgren 1999). In Germany issues of citizenship and immigration take a particular form. The emphasis in foreign policy and in attitudes to the EU varies by nation. Britain's response to economic globalization emphasizes national incentives to attract mobile capital and less so harmonization and proactive supra-national political coordination advocated elsewhere in Europe (on which more in the next chapter). Britain has tended to resist moves towards a European social model and places especial rhetorical emphasis on national interest in domestic arguments for EU integration. Like the Swedes, the British remain open to economic globalization but cautious about European political integration. Yet, at the level of rhetoric at least, Britain is more pro-American, which contrasts especially with the attitude of the French, who like to cultivate their own 'exceptionalism'. And Blair has been explicitly interventionist and active in military coordination, as evidenced by his leading role in the Kosovo war, European defence and the war against Afghanistan. Other social democrats in Europe have remained neutral, true to national traditions, or shown greater qualifications about pursuing international military intervention or alliances with the USA. We shall return in the next chapter to Europe, foreign policy and globalization.

Why National Third Ways? Models of Capitalism

Why do differences happen? Different countries have their own historically developed economies, social structures, political systems and cultures which will affect rhetoric and policy (Vandenbroucke 1998 and 2001; Martell et al. 2001). For some, Blair and the US Democrats find a lot in common because they share the same Anglo-American tradition of capitalism: individualistic, laissez-faire and with limited government; flexible, less regulated, with weak unions and a market-based and short-termist financial system. The Anglo-American model has relatively low unemployment but high inequality and poverty. This is seen to contrast with the 'Rheinland' model of capitalism predominant elsewhere in Europe, where economic and political culture is more collaborative and corporatist, unions and partnership are more important, finance is less market-based and longer term, and employment is more skilled, secure and better paid – in short, where there is more of a 'social market' approach (Albert 1993; Hutton 1995). In Germany and other European countries there are more statist or collaborative political cultures, reflected, for example, in the Blair–Schröder document by references to partnership with the trade unions. Such sentiments rarely feature in New Labour statements. France has a tradition of centralized government and state involvement in public services, much of this still intact despite the Jospin government's privatization programme. In Sweden and the Netherlands political culture is predominantly social democratic, consensual, solidaristic and mutual, in contrast to the relatively more conservative, competitive and individualist culture of Anglo-Americanism. Furthermore, language, image and concepts differ according to national traditions. The French are much happier talking the language of solidarity, regulation and the state and the Germans of partnership and neo-corporatism, for example, than the British.

Some of these national differences were exhibited in the strong reaction of German industry and politicians to the attempt by the British mobile-phone company Vodaphone to takeover its German counterpart Mannesman. A foreign hostile takeover, the meat and drink of British competitive capitalism, sent Germans into shock. The Blair–Schröder paper slipped by unnoticed in Britain but provoked controversy in Germany, leading Schröder to distance himself from some of its more free-market aspects. Similarly French politicians, workers and shoppers were startled by the way in which the British firm Marks & Spencer announced its decision to shut down stores in France with more or less no consultation with unions or workers. Again, quite normal in the UK but beyond the pale in France.

So while reform of the Labour Party in the late 1980s looked to European social democracy for ideas, with Blair's accession to the leadership in 1994 Clinton and the New Democrats in the USA became a bigger influence and closer partners – and such differences between Anglo-Americanism and European models were probably reinforced (Clift 2001). More recently, a key factor in national political differences has been the reconstruction of the economic and political landscape by Thatcherism. The USA, like Britain, went through a radical right-wing experience under the Republican government of Ronald Reagan. Throughout the 1980s Labour was forced to confront the reforms of Conservative governments: fiscal conservatism, anti-inflationary policies, trade-union legislation, privatization, deregulation of the labour market and reforms to health, education and housing. Blair's third way is a post-Thatcherite project, defined by inheritance of the Thatcherite legacy alongside a reaction against it in policies geared towards devolution and communitarian inclusion (Driver and Martell 1998). The context that has led to this configuration has not existed to the same extent in other European countries. There governments of the Right in the 1980s did not carry out experiments as radical as those in Britain and the USA. Blair's rhetoric is more pro-market and friendly to private business than, say, Jospin's, in part because of the economic and political landscape he has inherited and had to work upon. This landscape also makes Blair more left wing in the UK context than he would be in other European countries – reforms which may seem less notable in other European countries amount to a shift in a leftwards and pluralist direction in the UK compared to the Thatcherite past.

Third Ways and National Paths: Political Influences

Elsewhere in Europe there are other pressures on social democrats that do not exist to the same extent in Britain, and these may also affect the different emphases of political rhetoric between countries and the varying forms that common policy agendas may take in practice (Lovecy 2000). Because of the first-past-the-post British political system, Blair has an absolute majority of seats. Blair does not have to compromise with left-wing or green coalition partners, as is the case in France, Germany, Italy, Denmark and Sweden (in some places these are formal coalitions, in others minority governments with *ad hoc* cooperation). Moreover, coalitions or not, there are no significant parties to the Left of Labour in the UK. As such Blair can dictate his own agenda to a greater extent and is less constrained by left-wing or green inputs or competition for votes from the Left. Demand management and environmental concerns get a higher profile in the Blair–Schröder document, for example, than they would in most New Labour statements on the third way, in part a reflection of the greater strength of the Left and Greens in the German government. Jospin's rhetoric is, to some extent, an attempt to keep his five-party centre-left coalition on board. He needs to 'talk left' to appeal to his socialist, communist and green 'gauche plurielle' (Bouvet and Michel 2001).

Blair is also not held back from his 'modernization' programme by a significant left-wing faction in the Labour Party, and the political opposition – the Conservative Party – remains weak and ineffective. It should also be added that, in systems where proportional representation requires coalitions, the decline of a party to a small vote does not necessarily lead it into the sort of oblivion that often entails radical modernization, as happened with the UK Labour Party in the early 1980s. Small parties can still wield significant government influence in such coalitions. The Labour Party sank to 27.6 per cent of the vote in 1983, leading to fears of permanent electoral annihilation and the road to modernization. The French socialists came into government and held the prime ministership after having gained only 26.5 per cent of the vote in 1997 (Lovecy 2000). The pressure for modernization, because of electoral decline at least, was not as great.

Germany faces further complications beyond its coalitional system. The SPD is a decentralized and fragmented party, making it more complex for a leader to negotiate policy reforms of the sort carried out in Britain between 1987 and 1997. In Germany there are more points of potential hindrance. Once in power, governments in Germany face a federal decentralized system with the devolved Länder system of government and strong interest groups representing employers and unions, so that power is diffused and there are many potential obstacles to reform (Busch and Manow 2001). Similarly, the consensual culture we have mentioned in the Netherlands is embodied there in a system of politics that requires coalitions and negotiation with formally empowered non-state-organized interests. The politics of a 'grand design' is not possible. The PvdA is less autonomous when it comes to policy reform and is restrained by the need to pursue change in a negotiated way (Hemerijck and Visser 2001).

Blair's and Others' Third Ways

By Labour's 1997 election victory the Thatcherite ground had been laid and pushed the political agenda to the Right, based on already existing differences rooted in Anglo-American economic and political culture. This has shaped what the third way has come to mean in the UK. And Blair is in a strong position to push through his ideas domestically without the same degree of constraints social democrats face elsewhere. Different pressures elsewhere require support for the market to be expressed in a less explicit and evangelical way and affect the degree to which pro-market policies can be followed.

So, it appears today (and maybe the appearance is deceptive) that the British Labour Party is in the vanguard, if that is the right word, of modernizing social democracy. In other countries, such as Germany, the journey to modernized social democracy is a more difficult process, the government being subjected to a number of forces which affect what it can do. The need to combine moderate electoral appeal with more radical appeal to coalition partners, the social-market culture, and the devolved nature of the German political system and institutions lead to different outcomes there compared to other countries where institutional and cultural pressures diverge. In Britain there is a more centralized state, a political system which gives the modernizers greater control, and a laissez-faire market culture, for example (Lees 2001). Similarly, the Netherlands has embedded in its culture consensual norms that counteract or balance some of the more economically liberal developments in social democracy there and elsewhere. And the Dutch PvdA places more emphasis on individualization and liberalization and less on moral communitarianism than Blair, drawing on a greater social liberalism and less on conservative communitarianism than found in the UK (van den Anker 2001). In France, of course, the rhetoric is sometimes hostile to modernizing social democracy for reasons of national tradition (French exceptionalism and the statist and public-sector tradition, for instance, which transcend partisan boundaries) and politics (such as the need to hold together a coalition of the Left). The French have been more inclined to spending on job creation and regulation of the market.

For some, there are lessons that different countries can import from one another. There are those in Britain – Will Hutton (1995) is one – who would like to see Tony Blair adopting an approach that imports more from, say, the German situation – more of a *social market* approach. In fact, Blair himself once made short-lived noises about the desirability of a stakeholder model that could have been interpreted as going towards the German model (Driver and Martell 1998; Blair 1996d). Conversely, there are industrialists and SPD modernizers in Germany who would not be averse to a greater dose of competitive individualism to shake up economic life. But Hutton's words fall on deaf ears, and Schröder's collaboration with Blair had to be swiftly downplayed in Germany when it was published. Blair, meanwhile, became keener on exporting Anglo-Americanism to Europe than importing the German model.

Conclusion

Across Europe social democratic parties are discussing or implementing more flexible labour markets, privatization, welfare reform, cuts in business regulations and taxes, low inflation and macro-economic stability and supply-side policies alongside continuing social democratic concerns for social inclusion and minimum social standards. But the contexts in which such issues are being addressed vary, and so the outcomes of comparable theoretical agendas differ from nation to nation, dependent on factors such as the degree of centralized control or devolution in political systems; the extent to which modernizers monopolize power or have to share it with the Left or other parties; and historical traditions of statism, consensus or economic liberalism. So, even if different social democratic parties are all experimenting with third ways between neo-liberalism and old-style social democracy, these are third ways in the plural, there being different third ways rather than just one, varying by national background among other factors. As these instances show, the third way is diverse and contested. Between them, nationally specific factors lead to rhetorical and policy divergence – to third ways rather than a third way.

Hay argues that distinctions can be made between input convergence (in constraints on government policy), policy convergence and output convergence (in the effects or consequences of policy) in different countries (Hay 2000). Hay does not say this, but it could be said that policy convergence need not imply input convergence: commonalities in policy ideals could come about in response to varying inputs. A more neo-liberal model among social democratic parties may result from EU convergence in some countries, openness to the global economy in others, ideological choice or national traditions of laissez-faire in others. Furthermore, as we have seen, some degree of theoretical policy convergence need not imply output convergence. As we have just suggested, similar policies being held to in the social democratic parties of different countries can still end up with different outcomes because of the varying national institutions, cultures and political contexts through which they are mediated.

These distinctions also lead us on to some of the concerns of the next chapter. Input convergence need not imply policy convergence. As we shall reiterate shortly, national governments often pursue different policies in the face of what seem to be common pressures such as EU convergence or economic globalization. A common input constraint of globalization could lead to different policies. Our concern in the next chapter is how different social democracies and different third ways respond in varying ways to pressures such as globalization or to European, defence or foreign policy.

5

New Labour, Third Ways and Globalization

The variation of third ways across Europe is mirrored in responses to the challenges of European and global integration. In this chapter we will look at how there can be different third-way responses to globalization and how New Labour has reacted to the world beyond its own borders – in its approach to the European Union and its policies on foreign affairs and defence. Often, as we shall see, the approaches of government in these areas are marked by national history, culture and institutions. But before examining this in more detail, we shall outline the globalization thesis and examine the pressures it puts on social democrats.

Forms of Globalization

Globalization as an idea has been applied to many different contexts: economic, social, political, cultural and military, for example (the literature is enormous but see, for instance, Held et al. 1999). Some advocates of globalization theses, what Held and his colleagues call the 'hyperglobalists', argue that factors such as the growth of information technology and telecommunications as well as of the global economy have eroded national cultural and communicative boundaries, so that there is easier, faster and increased contact across national boundaries and cultural groups. This could be leading to greater cultural homogeneity or to the opposite – increasing appeals to the security of local or national identities. Or it could be leading to a combination of both processes. Militarily, some commentators argue that wars between nations have declined. Many wars now involve ethnic or religious groups within or across nations and international blocs comprising many nations or supra-national military organizations (see Kaldor 1999 on some of these themes).

Key concerns in relation to social democracy are with economic and political globalization. *Economically*, increases in global trade are said to have rendered national economies more vulnerable to international economic fluctuations, so making it difficult to control the national economy. Furthermore, with greater openness to global markets, competition is increased. Companies become more resistant than they already were to social democratic impositions that hinder their competitiveness, such as corporate taxes and social regulations. For many social democrats the key aspect of globalization which leads to modernization is the increasing mobility of capital. National governments, it is argued, can no longer control their own economies or regulate capital for the fear of doing anything that will lead to capital leaving the country. Government policy – e.g., on public spending, taxation and regulation of business – has to be tailored to attracting and retaining investment. All this is particularly problematic for social democrats because it is said to force them to accommodate to business interests and neo-liberal policies.

Along with this comes a concern with the growth of transnational *political* organizations. These include the United Nations and the European Union, not to mention global financial regimes such as the IMF, G7, World Bank and World Trade Organization, or international law, to extend even further. Because of such institutions many decisions which affect nation-states are said now to be taken above the level of those states. Some of these may be on matters previously the preserve of nation-states, such as legal prescriptions on human rights, or social or environmental policy. Many may have arisen because of the growing consciousness of problems that transcend national boundaries and so require international collaboration to be resolved, such as ecological problems, crime or terrorism.

For advocates of globalization theses the growth of economic and political globalization poses a challenge to social democrats to rethink the way they have traditionally operated at a national level. Social democrats have to engage with processes and institutions which extend beyond the borders of the nation-state and confound the abilities of nation-states alone to deal with them. In particular, they have to deal with processes which seem to push the political agenda in a rightwards direction. Yet so far social democracy has been weak at conceptualizing itself beyond the nation-state and is, as such, poorly equipped to respond to fundamentally transformatory processes of globalization.

There are sceptics (see, for instance, Hirst and Thompson 1996; Dearlove 2000). There are those who see globalization as a tool used by politicians to justify electoral or ideological preferences, rather than as a real constraint. Or social democracy is seen as constrained by the perception or discourse of globalization rather than its reality (e.g., see Hay 2000; Watson 1999). The extent of globalization also varies according to the level at which you deal with it. Because, for example, there may be global capital mobility, it not does necessarily follow that companies do not have national allegiances or that production and trade are as globalized as capital is. Insofar as global capital mobility is possible, it is not always as easy as it may be portrayed. It can require relocation of businesses, offices and workshops, reorganization, re-employment of new workers and adaptation to new cultural and political institutions – a lot more than just a click on a mouse, as it is sometimes presented by globalization theorists. Nor if there is economic globalization does it necessarily follow that there is cultural globalization. Alternatively globalization may be more a feature of developments in media or consumption than of developments in other spheres. Some commentators argue that the extent to which nation-states are vulnerable to globalization may vary from nation to nation, dependent on balances of global power. Vandenbroucke (1998), for example, suggests that the idea of globalization explains better what has happened in culture, media and responses to ecological problems than in the economy. Insofar as it does describe this last, it does so more for the US experience (in which, furthermore, the USA is a more powerful and autonomous actor than other states) than for Europe, which he says has seen regionalization rather than than globalization.

For some commentators globalization is nothing new (e.g., Hirst and Thompson 1996): analyses of a new global era exaggerate the power of nation-states in the past and play down the fact that globalization has long been around. Furthermore, there are questions raised over the extent to which nation-states remain autonomous actors. On one level, they actually play a key part in global structures themselves, constituting and influencing them in the pursuit of national interest as much as being constituted and constrained by them (the 'transformationalist' perspective of Held et al. 1999). On another, they still retain significant powers within their own boundaries, for instance over education, welfare and defence, not to mention the fact that there remains much that they do to keep a hold on capital even in an open global economy (Dearlove 2000). This claim has been supported by much evidence of policy variations across national boundaries, often diverging from the neo-liberalism that economic globalization is seen to require (Vandenbroucke 1998; Dearlove 2000). This evidence may dispel false images of globalization, or at least that, if there is globalization, it acts with the effect of a structurally determining force. Globalization may be mediated nationally and leave open to nation-states some autonomy. Neo-liberal policies could be more a matter of ideological choice than of structural determination (Hay 2000).

Neo-Liberalism, Interventionism, Globalism: Social Democratic Responses

We wish to outline three main possible social democratic responses to globalization: 1) a bias to neo-liberalism which accepts the case that economic globalization severely restricts the power of national governments and has to be adapted to; 2) nation-state interventionism which may accept that we live in some sort of globalized economy but which argues for more space for national governments to pursue social democratic ends within it; and 3) political globalism which accepts the case for economic globalization, but not as something to be adapted to through neo-liberal policies or just at the level of nation-state responses, but says that social democrats can achieve their ends and exert control over the global economy through global democratic forms. Of course these are analytic categories. No social democracy fits neatly or completely into any one of them. But social democrats may have biases towards some of these responses more than others.

So, there are three main social democratic responses to globalization: 1) neo-liberalism; 2) active nation-state interventionism; and 3) political globalism.

Neo-liberalism

Neo-liberal adaptation is, to some extent, the road that modernizing social democracy is going down, especially in the case of

New Labour. In this approach macro-economic policy is designed to reduce obstacles to the competitiveness of domestic capital, such as taxation or costs imposed by social regulations. It aims to attract investment and deter capital from leaving the country. In such a context laissez-faire Anglo-American capitalism seems to have an advantage over other forms of capitalism which have higher taxes, regulation and corporatist constraints. Policy is based on national competitiveness and the pursuit of pro-grammes which are seen to favour private business. They may include low business taxes, labour-market flexibility, macro-economic stability, an emphasis on fiscal prudence and restrictions on public spending and business regulations. Of course, this leads to policy convergence between social democratic parties and parties of the Right. Where this is the response to globalization, the social democratic consensus of the post-war period from the 1990s onwards appears to have been replaced by a neo-liberal consensus.

This is not to say that such policies are always forced on social democrats externally, as some of them claim, or just passively acquiesced to as critics might say; they may well be an active chosen response to globalization. And they could be based on the perception as much as the reality of globalization. Furthermore, they need not involve completely giving in to business desires or neo-liberalism. They could involve the government introducing measures regarded as favourable to a healthy business environment, which some in the business world may not favour, e.g., measures to protect competition and prevent monopolies. As we have argued in this book, modernizing social democracy in practice includes policies on social inclusion and minimum opportunities, and a commitment to spending on education and health. This demonstrates that national governments can continue with moderately social democratic policies within the context of perceived economic globalization. Furthermore while New Labour may adapt to globalization in one sphere it is determined to be more proactive in shaping it in others. While adaptive to economic globalization it has, for example, been at the forefront of attempts to create cross-national military alliances which can intervene in instances of perceived significant humanitarian crises or terrorist threats, so trying to create new forms of global intervention.

The active nation-state

This leads us to the second form of social democrat response to economic globalization: using autonomy and choice at the national level despite globalization. A number of possible policy spaces for national social democracy have been highlighted by authors such as Garrett (1998), Vandenbroucke (1998), Wickham-Jones (2000) and Hay (2000). From this perspective, globalization may exist but need not determine national government policy. The business-friendly approach gives too much determining and constraining power to globalization and underplays the extent to which restraints on social democracy have been as much domestic and internal as external. It ignores possibilities for political choice. Hay, for example, argues that globalization has been less of a constraint on the pursuit of social democratic policies in the UK than political will or the internalization of the *idea* of globalization. He maintains that the British Labour Party could choose to follow a different path – one which was less neo-liberal and instead attempted to foster an indigenous investment ethic through a more dirigiste, developmental supply-side approach, more favourable to industrial than financial capital.

For Vandenbroucke, it is internal domestic constraints that have affected possibilities for social democratic policies more than external constraints. He is dubious of the claims of those such as Giddens (1994, 1998) that Keynesianism is dead. Furthermore, countries such as the Netherlands, which are very exposed to the global economy, have managed to maintain redistributive policies. More neo-liberal paths taken elsewhere have suffered from internal constraints not shared by the Netherlands – such as the lack of a culture of consensus or of strong unions integrated into politics. It seems policy choice is as much a matter of domestic circumstances as global pressures. Welfare states have remained larger in small countries most open to the global economy. This shows that in actual fact governments have not converged and there remain significant differences between national economies and welfare states. Garrett argues (perhaps overoptimistically) that economic globalization positively favours social democracy because it leads to feelings of insecurity and vulnerability among voters, who may then become sympathetic to interventionism and redistribution. Businesses, meanwhile, can be persuaded that social democratic economic policy could actually be in their interests.

A number of possibilities are put forward by authors such as these for ways in which governments can pursue social democratic ends while not leading to exit by capital. First, national governments have a great deal of national autonomy outside the realm of the economy narrowly defined. Whatever the fact of economic globalization, they can pursue reforms to welfare, education, health, defence, and law and order which may be different to right-wing preferences without necessarily frightening off capital. Obviously these are areas where Labour has followed policies and where policy variation is possible between national parties or across nations despite globalization.

Second, Garrett, Vandenbroucke and Wickham-Jones argue that a social democratic government in a country where trade unions cover a range of the workforce, are united and strong and can command the obedience of their memberships can make deals with capital, promising moderation in wage demands in return for agreement to redistributive, Keynesian or other social democratic ends. Countries such as the Netherlands may be in a better position to succeed with this approach than others such as the UK. In the UK broad union membership and centralized conformity in the union movement does not exist, and conflict or the exclusion of unions is historically more characteristic of industrial relations than consensus. This path is not much of a possibility for the Labour government, but more because of internal constraints than on account of the external power of globalization.

Wickham-Jones is more optimistic than Garrett about the prospects for transplanting such structures into the UK. He favours a shift in the British Labour Party back to its approach of the 1980s when attempts were made to align more with mainstream European social democracy. However, if more corporatist structures that involve unions and employers cannot be developed, there is a third active national possibility identified by Wickham-Jones. This is that social democratic governments can promise moderate wage demands on the basis of maintaining a weak role for trade unions and a tough public-sector pay policy, again in exchange for agreement to social democratic ends. This is not very social democratic on the trade-union side of things but still perhaps capable of delivering social democratic ends in exchange for the maintenance of such a balance of power. This would certainly seem to be more applicable to UK circumstances. It is also a third-way response offering something to both sides – wage restraint to employers (economic efficiency) and social concessions to the unions (social justice).

Fourth, there may be other more moderate things that social democratic governments can offer business which would make it worth while sticking around and agreeing to concessions to social democracy: collective goods in the form of, say, supply-side interventions in infrastructure, research and development or training and education – things the market alone will not supply adequately – or policies which deliver economic, political and social stability. Clearly some social democratic governments, New Labour included, have tried a moderate form of this supply-side and stability approach and have managed to pursue modest social goals. But it is unclear whether such strategies, which put a heavy emphasis on human capital, can provide the sort of economic prosperity and stability employers require for them to tolerate social democratic advances in other areas. Economic success is based on wider factors – some of which are out of the hands of national governments. Furthermore, supply-side strategies may be insufficient to deliver significant social democratic goals. For that, Vandenbroucke (1998) argues, citing the support of the US economists Paul Krugman and Robert Reich for his position, more directly redistributional and Keynesian approaches are needed.

Globalizing social democracy

However, another perspective is that, while governments may be able to do things within their own boundaries, the approach just outlined stays too much at a national level. Whether national concessions can be won for social democracy or not, such an approach by itself leaves out the necessity for engagement with international organizations and the possibilities that could be pursued at a supra-national level by social democratic governments. In addition it can pitch one national social democratic government against another, each pursuing their own national interest and competitiveness rather than common cross-national social interests.

This leads to the third response to globalization – globalist social democracy. This envisages social democracy organizing politically at supra-national levels in response to the globalization of the economy, politics, and the military. It is globalization of a proactive sort, with social democrats trying to carve a politically chosen route for world order, rather than one determined by market forces or the priorities of global capital or merely national interests. For its advocates, social democracy needs to take global-ization not just as an economic given to be accommodated to, but also as a political possibility, where global regimes can regulate globalized capitalism, explore new modes of redistribution and protect those excluded from the labour market internationally. It is about creating supra-national political institutions where social democrats can argue the case for and hopefully implement social democratic policies and objectives.

As we have seen, social democracy across Europe has been marked by a shift to modernized forms and liberal economic pri-orities. This is partly to do with liberal constraints imposed via the EU in forms such as the Maastricht criteria and the single market rules. In part it is because of the economic liberal inherit-ance of places such as the UK where the free-trade system is positively embraced for the benefits it is seen to deliver. It is also to do with the desire of governments to attract capital and so adapt themselves to business priorities. However, this desire results from their fear of losing investment to other nation-states in a globalized marketplace. But, for globalist social democrats, there is an alternative to this response. Nations, which together have a monopoly on the workforces and consumer markets that capital needs, can collaborate to enforce common standards and regulations on businesses and common social and redistributive programmes. Then capital will be left with nowhere realistic to go and will need to reconcile itself to such norms. To put it another way, a proactive, combined, political globalization might allow for a more social and egalitarian agenda of a traditional social demo-cratic sort which the passive focus of modernizing social democ-racy on economic globalization does not.

David Held is a prominent advocate of globalist democracy, and his proposals have an implicitly social democratic slant (see Held 1995 and 2000; Archibugi et al. 1998; Archibugi and Held 1995; McGrew 1997. See also Giddens 1998; Shaw 2001). His argu-ments are both empirical and normative, referring to real develop-ing processes of political globalization and pleading for their extension. Held does not claim that the nation-state has lost its role. His prescriptions are compatible with the active nation-state social democracy outlined above. In fact he argues that states have initiated many of the global changes, are active participants in them and may even be more powerful today than their prede-cessors. But he does hold that politics has been globalized and that nation-state powers are being reconfigured. The development of human rights regimes undermines state sovereignty; security and defence are international industries sometimes organized into international military alliances; environmental problems, drugs, crime and terrorism are global and increasingly require international collaboration to solve them; and the deregulation of capital markets has increased the power of capital in relation to states and labour. Nation-states have to share power with a myriad of other agencies at all levels, and nations cannot, therefore, be said to be self-determining collectivities. The fate of nations is determined partly by forces beyond the national level, both political and otherwise, and so nation-states have to build political forms at wider levels to control their fates. Communities' fates are increasingly bound together so that, if they want to make decisions concerning themselves, and be accountable to those affected, they have to extend democracy and representation to broader transnational levels. Held argues that new global forms of democracy, therefore, require citizens to be 'cosmopolitan', to mediate between different national traditions, communities and cultures. Institutions developing in such a global cosmopolitan direction, he says, already exist. They include the UN, which delivers important international public goods (in air traffic control, telecommunications, disease control, refugee aid, peacekeeping and environmental protection, for instance), and the EU, which pools national sovereignty in some areas of common concern (including social rights and the (de)regulation of markets). Furthermore, international law – on war crimes, environmental issues and human rights – limits the power of nation-states.

Writers such as Held suggest that this globalization of democracy can be deepened by immediate steps such as increasing common international regulations on markets (on child labour, union and workers' rights and participation, health and safety and social rights). New forms of economic coordination could be introduced to overcome fragmentation between bodies such as the IMF, World Bank, OECD and G7, stave off financial emergencies, and steer international capital markets and investment and spending priorities. Measures to regulate the volatility of capital markets and speculation can be introduced – via taxes on turnover in foreign exchange markets and currency speculation, capital controls and regulations to ensure the transparency of bank accounting. Held proposes a new 'Bretton Woods', introducing greater accountability and regulation into institutions for the coordination of investment, production and trade, and greater responsiveness to the needs of less developed countries. All this requires the reform and extension of transnational forms of democracy, such as found in the EU, the UN, international financial organizations and human-rights regimes. And already there are social democratic parties pushing in such directions – for example, within the EU to greater integration, inclusion and democratization in policies on, for instance, monetary union and enlargement.

New Labour shows characteristics of the neo-liberal approach. Some of its left-wing critics say that this is about all there is to New Labour, a passive submission to global capital. They have a point. But there is more to New Labour than this. New Labour's neo-liberalism may be as much active choice as passive acquiescence. Furthermore, Labour has, as we have seen, pursued active nation-state interventions, sometimes with a social democratic tinge to them. And elements of political globalism can also be seen in New Labour, albeit fairly moderate ones which fall short of the whole of Held's wish-list (Held 1998). The government has, for instance, promoted the reform of international financial institutions, with greater transparency and accountability to make them work more efficiently (although less is said of regulation to make them more social democratic in their orientation than of reforms to make international finance work better). Blair has supported the extension of global trade to reduce global inequalities and to include less developed countries (much to the ire of anti-capitalist protestors, who see the expansion of capitalism as furthering the interests of rich nations and deepening such inequalities). New Labour has been prominent in promoting international military alliances and, after initial opposition, transnational military initiatives such as the European Rapid Reaction Force. It has also supported global human rights regimes, such as international war crimes trials. It has been a leading actor (although sometimes with limited success) in international environmental negotiations and campaigns for internationally coordinated debt relief, and Brown has advocated the idea of a global 'New Deal'. Blair has been actively involved in EU attempts to harmonize liberalization, although there has not been that much that is social democratic about this latter role. And New Labour has tried to obstruct social harmonization or economic liberalization where it is perceived these will impose restrictions on business or affect British national interests. It has opposed, for instance, proposals from France and Germany about the Tobin tax on currency speculation. This is probably partly ideological (it goes against the drive to liberalization) but it is also out of national interest (a desire to protect the City).

Problems for Globalist Social Democracy

There are four main areas of possible criticism of globalist social democracy (see, for instance, McGrew 1997): 1) that it engages too far with capitalism and will reproduce rather than overcome global inequalities; 2) that it merely involves the imposition of Western values on other parts of the world; 3) that there is no sociological basis for world politics; and 4) that global democracy is just a recipe for conflict and disagreement. One attempt to pursue social democracy transnationally – through the EU – seems to reinforce some of these criticisms.

The first criticism is that globalist social democracy is about the incorporation of the whole world into structures of global capitalism and trade rather than anything social or democratic. This is a point made vociferously by anti-capitalist protestors. Social democrats such as Blair and New Labour's international development minister, Clare Short, argue that opening up world markets to less developed countries will enable them to grow and develop by selling goods on such markets. When less developed countries are excluded from global capitalism, they are merely kept excluded from chances for development and incorporation into the world order. Critics suggest that participation in such markets will only reproduce divisions and serve the interests of richer countries. Participation in global trade would occur on the basis of already existing deep inequalities in resources and power which favour the richer, industrialized North. The participation of poorer countries will provide cheap labour and goods for the markets of the North without touching unequal power relations between North and South.

This links with criticisms that globalist social democracy is merely an ethnocentric attempt to impose Western norms and ideas on the rest of the world. Global democracy's proponents might think twice about their proposals were global democracy likely to lead to a different set of values achieving hegemony through global institutions. What if such values were to be anti-democratic or illiberal? The possibility of global politics being dominated by such values suddenly makes it seem less desirable.

And if Western values were not to retain hegemony or to be shifted in a leftwards direction, what realistic possibility is there that global democracy would be accepted by powerful Western interests, Western alliances or multi-national corporations?

Another criticism is that globalist politics tries to establish democracy at levels for which there is no established political community. It lacks a social or cultural basis to give it legitimacy and support. The social bases for global democracy are ones of conflicting and diverging identities and interests who do not share any common global identity or sense of political citizenship. 'Agreed' values can be secured only by some actors dominating and imposing them on global entities. For communitarian critics, politics should be aligned with political forms where there are real cultural and political identities, maybe nation-states or other more devolved forms of territorial or functional representation. Furthermore, and relatedly, it is assumed in globalist democracy that the meeting of conflicting interests will bring about harmony and consensus when in fact it may actually exacerbate conflict and disagreement. Politics cannot solve disharmony which rests at more economic and cultural levels. This has been demonstrated by the record of global forums in failing to reconcile conflicting interests or solve common global problems, such as war, ethnic or religious conflict, ecology or development. Again, the obvious solution to such conflicts is more powerful actors imposing their own values.

These are complex problems, and some of the responses global social democrats could make can only be touched on here. Anticapitalist criticisms probably stick best to the approach of New Labour (which responds that there is no feasible alternative to the opening up of global trade and that to fail to do so only locks less developed countries out) than to that of social democrats such as Held, who would see the necessity for any such economic inclusion being accompanied by political incorporation and the negotiation of better terms of trade for less developed countries. But critics may doubt how much Held's *political* approach is equipped to deal with inequalities which are based primarily on *economic* power.

As far as Western dominance goes, three points can be made. First, global social democrats have to plead guilty to signing up to the promotion of Western values. They support the idea that Western values – such as liberalism and democracy – should be generalized across the world. Social democrats are also reconciled to capitalism and even see its virtues, albeit in a regulated and reformed form. Second, however, for more left-wing forms of global social democracy there are problems with Western liberalism and democracy. These include the need to extend them further (to a wider range of spheres and a broader range of actors – the economy and the empowerment of poorer countries, for instance) to realize their own logic more adequately. The problem is the failure of the West to apply its values consistently and the need for them to be further enforced and extended into deeper, more post-liberal forms of democracy – rather than their undesirability as the basis for global political forums. The alternative is a failure to establish such norms at global levels, so allowing democratic accountability to remain limited, and giving illiberal and undemocratic practices and beliefs within and beyond the West one less obstacle in their way.

Similarly social democracy may be reconciled to capitalism, but not to imposing it on unwilling recipients or, in all cases, to a laissez-faire version. For the more left-wing among global social democrats, the capitalist road has to be chosen democratically and voluntarily and ideally in a reformed and regulated version. Third, global democrats advocate forms that institutionally qualify as much as advance the promotion of Western power. Power relations at present are based on factors, economic and military for example, other than political enfranchisement. Any move to entrench power relations in more political equality – including economic democracy and the democratization of international military alliances – would, done in the true spirit of global democracy, actually reduce Western dominance. So the extension of liberal democracy itself – a Western value – limits the ability of the West to *impose* Western values through global democracy although not to pursue them democratically.

Global social democracy is an empirical as much as a normative project. This is clear from many of its advocacies, which analyse as much what *is* going on in the global transformation of politics and other spheres – for example the growth of supra-national political forums, social movements and human rights legislation – as what it is thought ideally *should* be going on. Furthermore, many problems are widely seen as requiring the extension of existing international institutions and agreements – environmental problems, crime, peace and security, development and debt, for example. And global democracy is also envisaged as transformatory, building on existing changes in the economic, political and cultural world but also advancing or reconstituting them. So, from this point of view it may seem slightly less utopian than at first sight for political forums at a global level to find common bases and problems upon which productive democratic negotiations can take place. Transformatory possibilities are grounded in institutions and dynamics which already exist. Furthermore, if you look at the historical shifting foci of political institutions over time you find that the social basis of citizenship is a complex and dynamic process and that both historical and now legitimate political institutions often have a social basis which is as diverse and complex as it is united. Many nation-states, for example, could barely be said to be based on anything much less complex than diverse ethnic, national and cultural mixes yet still remain legitimate and accepted.

However, as McGowan (2001) has argued, global social democracy is a long way off if the difficulties of establishing regional social democracy are any guide. Where supra-national proactive social democratic organization is possible – via the EU, for example – the liberal orientation of this institution and national differences between parties have made any social democratic reconfiguration of the EU unlikely for the time being. This is the case even in the most propitious of scenarios for social democrats, where most of the members of the EU around the turn of the twenty-first century were governed by social democratic governments and where social democrats are well organized in the European parliament.

For a start, there are reasons for doubting whether European social democratic parties can overcome differences across national traditions to forge common policies at a European level. For supra-national coordination to develop, various traditions of European social democracy that, as we have seen, have cultures and institutions which pull in different directions would have to combine and coordinate more. There are differences that divide social democratic parties, including British New Labour from others. These include traditions of consensus and collaboration and corporatism versus more Anglo-American individualism; Euro-reluctance as against enthusiasm for European integration; countries where the state and public sector involvement are more valued as against those where privatization and deregulation have so far been embraced more enthusiastically; those who have been through a neo-liberal experiment and those that have not;

and those with centralized systems with one-party government as opposed to those with complex decentralized systems and coalition governments, often of very many parties. These stand in the way of common social democratic policies being pursued. Sometimes parties on the Left and Right within the same nation may appear to share more in common with each other than with their sister parties abroad.

Optimists such as Robert Ladrech (2000) point to the record of social democrats in overcoming such differences and forging real commonalities. Yet there is a problem here also, as many of the common agreements that have been secured have been around economically liberal rather than social democratic goals. The EU has more and more been defined as a liberal project, with social democratic inputs more of a minor part, few and far between and with a moderate impact. The EU is more concerned with negative integration, about removing barriers to free trade, with Labour a key actor in pursuing this orientation. It is less concerned with positive integration, agreeing common policies to coordinate government and business behaviour and to pursue mitigation of the effects of the market or even redistribution. EMU convergence criteria have gone against the achievement of social democratic ends through macro-economic measures such as borrowing and running deficits. And, while the EU may currently offer more immediately realistic possibilities for coordination than as yet relatively less developed global regimes, it is also regionally focused, concerned with the interests of Europe in rivalry with other regional blocs in the world, rather than with global solidarity and overcoming inequality on a more universal human scale.

Many of the problems of using the EU in a positive social democratic way lie not just with the liberalism of the EU and such national differences, but with national social democratic parties themselves, such as New Labour, who have chosen to shift away from their more traditional agendas and constituencies to more economically liberal approaches and middle-class bases. Social democratic parties have never really been as internationalist in their practice as in their rhetoric. Their attitude to the EU is often constrained by the need to tailor it to domestic political consumption. How negative or positive they can be about the EU is affected by what they feel they need to say to domestic audiences – such as the electorate, business interests and coalition partners.

Blair beyond Britain: a New Attitude to Europe?

Old Labour, Conservatives and New Labour

The Labour Party has moved quite a way in its approach to the European Union from the days of Labour past, as well as the years of Conservative government in the 1980s and 1990s (Deighton 2001; Bulmer 2000). Britain, and that includes Labour, has long been slow to build up enthusiasm for participation in European institutions. As we have argued, Britishness matters in the explanation of national politics. Many reasons have been given for Britain's lack of eagerness for Europe. It is an island, consequently not quite connected to Europe, with a history of political stability and democracy, unbroken for centuries by invasion, revolution or coup. Greater integration involves more of an unusual reconstitution of stable democracy for Britain than for other European countries. It is a country still not ready to throw away the legacy of leading the world rather than being a junior partner in a regional club and is Atlanticist as well as European in its allegiances. Connected to this it has, as we have seen earlier, an individualist Anglo-American form of capitalism which some may see as in conflict with greater European integration. Britain is not one of the first leading members of the EU, able to determine the shape it takes as much as some others can, but neither is it one of the poorest members set to benefit most from inclusion within it. These are reasons for Britain's Euro-reluctance and so affect Labour specifically. And in the 1980s Labour, at some of its most left-wing moments, saw the European Union as merely a capitalist club intended to promote free trade and assert Europe's position in global capitalism at the expense of real internationalism. In addition the Labour Left argued that EU membership undermined democracy, making the British unable to hold accountable decision-makers who formulate policy affecting Britain (Benn 1981). The 1983 manifesto promised withdrawal from the EC.

Throughout Mrs Thatcher's terms in office, and to some extent John Major's, the British government was an especially reluctant member of the European Union. British ministers and civil servants engaged in debates about the future of the European Community, including the 1987 Single European Act that paved the way for the single currency. Leading Conservatives such as Geoffrey Howe, Nigel Lawson and Douglas Hurd were more pro-European than Mrs Thatcher. John Major's own Euro-reluctance was forced on him partly by divisions within his party rather than his own personal inclinations. But the British government was repeatedly a destructive actor within the EU, one who often saw integration as a threat to be resisted rather than as an opportunity for Britain. It secured opt-outs from the social chapter and monetary union and resisted post-Maastricht developments. In 1992 it was forced out of the Exchange Rate Mechanism, and later it came into conflict with European partners over BSE (something that continued under Tony Blair). The Conservatives became increasingly divided over Europe, between Euro-enthusiasts and Euro-sceptics plotting against Prime Minister John Major. Other European leaders began to envisage a two-tier Europe in which Britain, reluctant to participate, was left behind while those who were keen could forge ahead with integration. Some British Conservatives also proposed a version of Europe where some countries could integrate more than others, a view many strong advocates of European integration were not happy with.

Neil Kinnock's reforms to Labour Party policy in the late 1980s began to shift things back in a more pro-European direction within the Labour Party, and Blair promised a different attitude to Europe to Thatcher's and Major's. By 1997 national interest would still be the key motivation in participation, Blair argued, but this was seen as best served through constructive engagement within the EU rather than destructive opposition. There were three options, according to New Labour: withdrawal (desired by a small number of Conservatives during the Blair era), staying in but on the sidelines (perceived to be the Thatcher approach) and staying in in a leading role (what Blair saw as his approach). Staying in and playing a constructive line has prevailed. But there have been tensions within the New Labour camp. One-time Euro-sceptic Robin Cook became one of the government's keenest supporters of greater European integration and membership of the single currency. The government has tried to make its line on policy appear firm and consistent – when set conditions are met the government will recommend the public to vote for membership of the single currency in a referendum. Yet there have been notable differences of tone among ministers, Gordon Brown remaining much more cautious in speeches than Cook. Cook was Blair's first foreign secretary but, to the surprise of many, including probably Cook himself, was demoted after the 2001 election.

Blair himself has trodden a wary line of expressing support for the single currency and plans to join it, interspersed with long periods of silence on the issue.

1997 and after: a new approach?

Labour was committed to the completion of the single market and reform of the common agricultural policy, continuations of Conservative policies. Since 1997 Blair has been one of the leading advocates among EU leaders of enlargement. Britain ratified the December 2000 Nice treaty which committed the EU to enlargement from fifteen members to almost double that. It supported reforms of the EU which this required.

Signing up to the social chapter was a clear break with the Conservatives. In the 1997 manifesto Labour also committed itself to reform of the EU, including proportional representation for EU elections, also a shift away from the Conservative approach. Labour's introduction of PR for European elections is impossible to separate from its wider constitutional agenda: it has introduced PR elsewhere too, in elections to the new devolved assemblies, and one of the consequences of devolution may well be on UK–EU relations – assemblies, such as that in Scotland, perhaps developing closer links with the EU than the UK government does.

The government has continued to argue for political reform of the EU, allowing it to position itself as both positive and constructive about Europe but also as critical of its political weaknesses. A former Labour leader turned EU commissioner, Neil Kinnock, was given the job of leading EU reform, allowing Labour's link with positive change from a position of commitment to the EU to be strengthened. Blair has argued for a Europe of nation-states with power vested in the council of ministers representing the member states, something less integrative than the more federalist proposals of those such as the German foreign minister, Joscka Fischer. He has opposed extension of the European parliament's powers, favouring a second chamber made up of representatives of national parliaments. This chamber would look at possibilities for implementation of commission proposals at national levels. Unlike others such as the Belgians and the EC president, Romani Prodi, Blair has opposed a directly elected president. Also unlike other leaders in the EU the Labour government has opposed a written constitution for the EU or a legally enforceable charter of rights. Some of this involves opposition within the EU, and at other times positive proposals which try to preserve national powers. Some of it also involves a constructive role in European institutions, even if not always in line with other key leaders.

Labour remained committed at Nice to keeping the national veto in some areas such as taxation and social security, where national interests are seen to be negatively affected by convergence, but with an extension of qualified majority voting to a range of new policy areas previously subject to unanimity. This involves a clear step away from the Conservatives' resistance to integration. To accommodate to reforms required by enlargement, Blair agreed to the loss of one of Britain's two European commissioners in exchange for greater voting power in European councils.

In its election manifesto Labour promised a referendum on membership of the single currency, membership being backed by key members of the government such as Brown and Blair 'if the conditions are right'. While this was in the 1997 manifesto but not carried out by the 1997 government, it still proposed a position different to the Conservatives' opposition to the single currency. An early move in 1997 was granting independence to the Bank of England to set interest rates. This was portrayed as a domestic change aimed at taking the politics out of interest rates and so underpinning greater economic stability. But it also paved the way towards meeting the requirements for European Monetary Union. In effect it allowed Britain to meet one of the conditions for changing to EMU without actively campaigning on it. This has been Labour's strategy on the single currency generally. Blair has expressed his desire to sign Britain up to the single currency and even set up a national changeover plan in early 1999 based on the supposition of entry in 2002. Yet through the 1997 government and in the early days of his 2001 government he did not campaign actively on membership of the single currency. This left in place a solid majority of the British public against membership, unmoved by any significant attempt at shifting their views on the part of the government. The economic tests that Labour set for membership of the single currency were vague – that there should be convergence with single currency economies but with sufficient flexibility, and that membership should have a positive effect on investment, financial services and employment. They seemed in part more of a ploy to delay entry for political reasons, until a majority of the public came around to its merits.

Thatcherism Mark 2 on Europe?

Some have argued that Labour's approach to Europe has not been as different from that of the Tories as some may think (Bulmer 2000; Deighton 2001). Mrs Thatcher was obstructive but hardly herself on the sidelines. Her position compared to Labour's within the EU many not be as different as Labour likes to make out in trying to carve out its own distinctive image. New Labour has made it clear that it sees Europe as an alliance of independent states rather than as a European federal super-state, arguing, as we have said, for an emphasis on the council of ministers and a second chamber of national representatives to reflect this position. Like other leaders in Europe, Blair has opposed a written constitution for the EU. While accepting some extension of the national veto, Labour has resisted the loss of the national veto on areas such as tax matters and social security. National interest and autonomy rather than European cooperation sometimes still seem to form the principle guiding Britain's participation. How much convergence, and of what type, is judged very much according to national interest rather than in line with an ethos of European cooperation.

Britain has been keen on some European agreements on liberalization, such as energy (resisted by France), electricity and labour markets, or other forms of integration, but not on others. Integration on tax harmonization and the witholding tax has been resisted. These, it is seen, might reduce the UK's competitive advantage, leading to Eurobonds traded in the City to flee out of the EU. On issues such as tax harmonization Britain has remained, in its opposition, out of step with leaders such as Jospin, Schröder, and the commission president, Romani Prodi. In short in some areas of national interest and autonomy there seem to be continuities with New Labour's Conservative predecessors, alongside areas of difference (although how far the emphasis on national interest – and sometimes national autonomy – differs in reality from other European countries could be questioned).

Furthermore, Labour's approach to the EU has been geared around its benefits for business and the market economy through an economically liberal approach, rather than around a social democratic agenda in the more traditional sense. Completion of the single market has been a primary goal of the government, as has economic liberalization. Large sections of the business community in Britain are keen on European economic integration, including the single currency. The social agenda of the EU, such as the social chapter, is less of a significant a part of the EU agenda or of Britain's plans for the EU. Signing up to the social chapter was as much an expression of Euro-enthusiasm on Britain's part as of enthusiasm for a social agenda in Europe. The social chapter itself is as yet not a particularly significant set of commitments in real practical terms. At the Amsterdam summit of EU states in 1997, for instance, Blair succeeded in arguing against French employment plans based on extra investment managed by the European Investment Bank. Blair, with the support of the German chancellor, Helmut Kohl, argued instead for deregulation and flexibility to create an adaptable workforce more able to attract investment. As we have seen, Britain has urged economic liberalization in areas such as energy, on the basis that competition, flexibility and deregulation are the keys to economic competitiveness and employment. This is hardly the stuff of Old Labour social democracy.

Leaders in Europe?

Blair's attempt to be a leader in Europe, rather than a mere member or a reluctant or destructive presence, has not always been as successful as planned. Britain's more constructive attitude to Europe has certainly been welcomed by other members of the EU, albeit with some qualifications and disappointments – over the emphasis on liberalization for example, or Britain's continuing self-exclusion from the single currency. Tony Blair has certainly been a significant European figure on the world stage, especially when it comes to military interventions and relations between European nations and the USA. But Blair's desired leadership role *within the EU* has been held back by some important factors.

First, his rhetoric of economic liberalization, a programme to which he insisted other European leaders must conform – 'modernise or die' (Blair 1997a) – has jarred with the approaches of some others. As we saw in the last chapter, countries such as Germany and France, while going down the road of liberalization, are more qualified and restrained about this because of national cultures and institutions, and more sceptical about the British enthusiasm for individualistic capitalism. They are not convinced that the Anglo-American model fits with their circumstances, as Blair seems to believe it should. Nor are they convinced that it is all that desirable anyway, especially from a social democratic point of view. So Blair's attempt to lead by liberalization has not always been as successful in mobilizing support as he may have hoped, which is not to say that in many cases he has not found himself with allies (such as Spain and Portugal) able to secure support for such an approach.

Second, exclusion from the single currency has also sometimes made it difficult for Britain to claim a leadership role in the EU. During the 1998 British presidency, for instance, a summit on the single currency had to be chaired by Austria, damaging Britain's ambitions to be a leader in the EU. For reasons such as this, Britain's desire to muscle in with France and Germany has not always been that successful. Britain has often adopted a strategy of forming alliances on EU votes with whoever can be mobilized on that particular vote, often with smaller members, and often not on matters Britain itself has initiated. Much of the agenda of European reform was in place well before Blair came to power or has been led by other European countries. While Britain has led on issues such as a stronger European defence identity (something which it was initially reluctant about but came around to as an area where it could exercise a leadership role), it has eventually found itself, knowingly or not, having to adapt to its status as at most a third rather than as a first or second leading power in Europe. Defence and relations with the USA on the global stage have been where Britain has played more of a leading role, and we shall return to these shortly.

Nevertheless Britain under New Labour has, as we have seen, played a more constructive role in Europe than the Conservatives did. Despite many continuities with the Conservatives over issues such as liberalization and the desire on some occasions to preserve a national veto or resist reform in defence of national interests (not the exclusive preserve of the British anyway), there have been discontinuities too. Britain under Blair has signed the social chapter and been more positive about the single currency. It has agreed to significant extensions of qualified majority voting. Overall Labour's attitude has been to see the EU as an opportunity, not a threat, marking out a key difference in attitude and tone from the Conservatives (Bulmer 2000). Such differences in tone can play a part in shifting political culture and so make the mood underpinning future decisions on Europe different.

New Labour and Defence after the Cold War

But one area in which Britain has been able to exercise more of a leading role in world affairs is defence and international military intervention (Freedman 2001; Buller 2001; Gummett 2000; Little and Wickham-Jones 2000). While defence was being reformed and rolled back at home, Britain's attempt to expand its global leadership role was pursued in military interventions, and the government promised a different sort of approach in foreign affairs generally, more responsive to human rights and ethical considerations than in the past.

At home the strategic defence review placed an emphasis on defensive diplomacy and a downgrading of the nuclear deterrent, seen as more appropriate to conditions after the cold war. It faced little opposition from the armed services. But for some it did not signal as much of a shift away from Britain's hankering after its old imperial military role as could have been hoped (Gummett 2000). It did not question Britain's idea of itself as a major military power, or the Atlantic alliance, or nuclear deterrence. In 1983 Labour had been committed to unilateral nuclear disarmament and its leader, Michael Foot, was a member of the Campaign for Nuclear Disarmament. But this was an exception to Labour and Britain's otherwise historical aspirations to be a strong military power, from which New Labour has diverged less. To some Labour has overseen a shift to different forms of military action as much as a downgrading of Britain's military role. Greater emphasis is put on mobility, cross-forces coordination and rapid reaction forces, in line with Blair's emphasis on fast action to deal with humanitarian crises, as in Kosovo. This requires more joint rapid reaction forces, with a greater emphasis on long range transport. Meanwhile the Eurofighter order was continued and Britain remained committed to Trident. The Defence Diversification Agency, once supposed to deal with reductions in defence employment, became an agency concerned more with the transfer of technology between military and civilian spheres (Gummett 2000). In the Kosovo war Blair was a key leader. The USA and France may have provided more military muscle, but Blair was said to be the one who built the coalition that carried out the war and dragged along a hesitant Bill Clinton. In the war on Afghanistan Blair also seemed to be a key coalition builder, acting as an ambassador between the USA on one hand and Europe and Russia, Arab and Muslim nations on the other.

As we have seen, Britain's orientation towards rapid reaction led to its reversal of initial opposition to a European rapid reaction force to an alliance with Europe's other big military power, France, in positively pursuing such a project. This allowed Britain to exercise leadership on the European stage. It put telling strains on Britain's relationship with the USA, which were played down by both sides, and exemplified Britain's attempt to juggle ties with both the USA and NATO on one hand and Europe on the other. Britain was also at odds with France on the details of the new force and its relationship with the NATO command structure.

What has been questioned during Blair's period in power is the nature of military action. In a post-cold war world Blair saw the British military capability less as one for national defence and more as a force for international good where ethnic and religious conflicts led to mass bloodshed. War seemed to shift to involve international military alliances or intra-national or cross-national groups, such as ethnic or religious groups. The old days of war between states seemed to be in decline, despite the USA's continuing concern to build a defence system based on the assumption of military strikes by 'rogue' hostile states. The 1999 Kosovo war showed a commitment to war without casualties on the allied side, waged from the skies and without ground troops, other than special forces, in action. However, it also showed the limits of such a war: Milosevic's troops did not flee from the planes as quickly as they had been supposed to and, while the coalition bombed from on high, many undetected ethnic killings continued on the ground. Kosovo did not after all appear to be the last nail in the coffin of Western allies waging war with land forces. It also only encouraged Blair in his conviction that rapid reaction forces responding to humanitarian crises were important and that Europe needed to be able to provide these for itself rather than necessarily rely on the USA and NATO.

The attacks on the USA in September 2001 reinforced a shift towards a concept of war not against states but against cross-national terrorist networks, to do with intelligence and policing allied to military attacks of various different sorts, from air strikes to special forces. At the centre of all these shifts has been Blair as a leading builder of military coalitions, trying to straddle Europe and the USA, seeing military action as about international intervention as much as domestic defence and fought in a variety of new and some quite old ways.

Ethics and Internationalism:
a New Approach to Foreign Policy?

At the centre of Blair's military leadership has been his advocacy of international intervention for good in the name of human rights and humanitarianism (Blair 2001). This was signalled in a much-quoted speech in Chicago given during the Kosovo crisis on the 'doctrine of the international community' (Blair 1999a). The speech argued for something different from an isolationist foreign policy and for the ethical duties of countries beyond their own borders. There was nothing new to his argument in itself – just war and the grounds for intervening in others' affairs is an age-old problem that has been much picked over. But it was applied to a context of allegedly greater globalization than before, and it did mark some differences from previous Labour and Conservative approaches. Blair advocated reforms to international financial institutions, the UN Security Council, third-world debt and environmental agreements and argued for a shift away from a bias towards non-interference. International intervention beyond a state's own borders is justified, argued Blair, in cases of genocide, refugee crises and regimes based on minority rule. In practice genocide and refugee crises have come to be the key justifications for intervention. (To have taken on minority rule as a basis for international intervention may have led to Britain's later having to invade even some of its closest and most powerful allies, or even itself!) The international 'community', for Blair, should act when there is a humanitarian catastrophe that the government concerned will not or cannot address. Further possible conditions for intervention were added by Blair: that it should have a strong case for it, and that it should follow only when diplomatic solutions have failed, when military intervention is practical, with contingency plans and where national interest is involved.

Robin Cook (1997; Foreign and Commonwealth Office 1997), meanwhile, had promised an 'ethical content' to foreign policy (simplified in much commentary to the more radical commitment of an 'ethical foreign policy'). New Labour promised not to leave political values behind when making decisions about foreign policy: in other words, it would base foreign policy more around priorities such as human rights and ethics than was the case in the past. Wider human interests and not just domestic ones were to guide foreign policy; and there was to be some sort of principled approach and not just a continued pragmatism (on New Labour's foreign policy, see Hill 2001; Little and Wickham-Jones 2000; Buller 2001; Lawler 2000).

The government promoted the Department for International Development (DfID) to independent ministry status, with the international development minister, Clare Short, in the cabinet (Young 2000). This enabled her approach to be focused more directly on solving poverty and tied less to wider foreign policy goals. In the 1998 comprehensive spending review international development got more money, an average annual increase of 8.8 per cent, aid provision was expanded and the numbers of staff were increased. Britain rejoined UNESCO and stopped pulling out of UNIDO. Aid was refocused on Africa and low-income countries. Gordon Brown led the political initiative to cancel debt in some less developed countries, in part under pressure from high-profile 'drop the debt' campaigners. Personnel were exchanged between the Foreign Office and NGOs.

The government promised that arms sales would be linked more strongly with human-rights considerations: arms would not be sold to regimes wishing to use them for internal repression or external aggression. Britain backed an EU Arms Export Code of Conduct and banned the export of landmines. Britain and France were the first two nuclear powers to ratify the Comprehensive Test Ban Treaty. The Foreign Office and DfID introduced annual reports on the government's record in promoting human rights. It has supported an International Criminal Court. Robin Cook promised to increase recruitment of ethnic minorities, women and entrants from state education into the Foreign Office. The choice of ministers in the FO and DfID must have stirred some of the stuffier of Foreign Office feathers. Aside from the left-wing and outspoken Short, Robin Cook himself came originally from the Left. Peter Hain was a prominent former anti-apartheid direct activist. John Battle was from the Left and had opposed the Gulf War and nuclear weapons. Baroness Scotland of Adsthal became Britain's first black minister.

One of the symbolically most significant acts of the British government was the detention in Britain of the Chilean former dictator General Pinochet while Spain tried to pursue extradition for the torture and murder of Spanish and Chilean citizens during his rule. The detention was something it was difficult to imagine any previous government undertaking. In fact prominent Conservatives lined up at the time to adopt Pinochet as a dear friend. In the end, however, he was allowed home on medical grounds. This was an incident that rested very much in the hands of the then home secretary, Jack Straw.

But it is interesting that Labour's first foreign secretary and Tony Blair adopted different styles that could be seen possibly to have clashed (Lawler 2000). Blair increasingly became involved in foreign policy as time progressed, for instance on Iraq and Serbia. He was seen as more hawkish than Cook or even Bill Clinton. His approach showed more certitude, stressing leadership and bilateral relations with the USA. Cook's approach, on the other hand, was based more on multilateralism and dialogue, something which brought him great popularity abroad, and less irritation overseas than Blair attracted. After the 2001 election Cook found himself the subject of a demotion, although whether this was due to a clash of foreign-affairs style with Blair, Cook's growing enthusiasm for the Euro or other reasons is not clear.

Of course there have been criticisms of the government's approach. Many of these have questioned how much ethical content there is in Labour's foreign policy. Blair and Short have had to field criticisms from anti-capitalist protestors that their development policy is tied too much to free trade and is too little aware of political and economic power relations that might be seen to block third-world development. The hand of the Treasury and the DTI was detected behind some of the caution in the DfID's plans, on reducing tied aid for instance. Aid has increased, but not by much, and it remains well behind that of nations such as France and Japan and less than half of the UN target of 0.7 per cent of GNP. Debt cancellation is less impressive than it at first sounds when it is realized that much of the debt was beyond reclaiming anyway. The government disappointed many on arms sales. Britain continued to be one of the world's leading arms manufacturers. Arms sales continued to Indonesia during that country's repression in East Timor and to other places where the internal repression and external aggression criteria seemed to have been transgressed. Indonesia attracted the most attention, but arms exports to countries such as Turkey, Zimbabwe, India, Pakistan and Chinese-controlled Hong Kong among others raised the question of whether possible use for internal repression or external aggression had been that strictly interpreted. In 1998 the government broke a UN embargo on selling arms in Sierra Leone, although investigations of 'Arms to Africa' suggested that ministers were not behind it.

The new ethical criteria were not applied to arms exports approved by the previous government (the explanation for the Indonesian exports). Taking into account the effect of arms orders, or their cancellation, on British economic, financial and commercial interests and on UK relations with recipient countries heavily compromised the human-rights considerations. The problem is that there is insufficient separation of functions when the agency that promotes arms exports, the DTI, is also that which licenses them. Landmine parts continued to be sold to the USA, and the government pulled back from parliamentary monitoring of arms exports. In fact it issued gagging orders in the arms to Iraq affair, having criticized the Conservatives for the same thing. Labour has also been criticized for taking its friendliness towards the USA too far in endorsing President Bush's missile defence system.

For economic and political reasons the government felt restrained from stronger criticism of China's human-rights record or punitive action against it. Similarly the government was too quiet for some on internal problems within Nigeria and Russian attacks on Chechnya. The policy of enforcing no-fly zones and sanctions in Iraq, the latter widely alleged to be responsible for many thousands of deaths, cast a cloud over the government's alleged humanitarian approach. As we argued earlier, whether the Kosovo intervention could have been carried out differently to save lives more effectively is a criticism also raised. But the Kosovo action was condemned in addition for being a NATO intervention, even primarily a British-American led one, that ignored calls to involve the 'international community' by going through the UN, which NATO knew would be unlikely to endorse the action because of opposition on the security council. While of symbolic importance, and obviously intended to underpin interventions such as the Kosovo war, Blair's doctrine of humanitarian community has, therefore, been followed inconsistently to say the least.

There do seem to have been some changes in the government's approach to foreign policy, albeit alongside many continuities and even if they are sometimes as much symbolic as practical. The language of ethics and rights has been brought in, even if this is not completely novel. Foreign policy has been seen as not just about pursuing domestic interests but also as involving judgements about the international good and international human rights. Of course, the government has fallen short of such values, and critics would see such professed commitments as no more than an attempt to dress up what still remains foreign policy aimed at pursuing primarily domestic interests. For the critics the rhetoric sounds high and mighty, but the practice is all too frequently in contradiction to it.

New Labour is about more than New Britain. Blair has tried to establish a more constructive attitude to Europe, including a desire to encourage other European social democrats to take on board some of the features of the Anglo-American model. The Labour government has tried to revise its approach to defence, and to take a more interventionist and ethical role in affairs beyond the boundaries of the UK. We have also seen that New Labour's participation in affairs beyond its own border is affected by the institutions and culture within those boundaries. Labour's relationship with other European social democratic parties and with the EU is, in part, affected by British history and the culture of Anglo-American capitalism. And Labour policy on defence and foreign affairs cannot be separated from Britain's imperial history and its historical role as a major military power.

Part III

New Labour, New Britain

6

Blair and Britishness

Today I want to set an ambitious course for the country. To be
nothing less than the model twenty-first century nation, a beacon
to the world. It means drawing deep into the richness of the British
character. Creative. Compassionate. Outward-looking. Old British
values, but a new British confidence. (Blair 1997b)

New Labour, New Britain

The Labour Party led by Tony Blair was elected to government in
May 1997 promising to create a 'New Britain'. The slogan, unveiled
at Blair's first party conference as leader in 1994, sought to portray
'New Labour' as a political force in tune with modern times. New
Labour would complete the modernization of the Labour Party;
and then in government it would modernize Britain: 'The party
renewed, the country reborn', as Blair closed his speech to
Labour's party conference in 1995 (Blair 1994 and 1995c).

Appeals to national identity are normally associated with Conservative politics – whether the 'putting the Great back into Britain'
variety of Margaret Thatcher in the 1980s or the Baldwinesque
images of village cricket and warm beer from John Major in the
early 1990s. Former Tory leader William Hague staked his party's
future to the 'common sense' values of the British people, including personal liberty and defence of private property (Hague
1999a).

To Labour modernizers, these recent Conservative appeals to
Britishness are seen as exclusive, nostalgic and nationalistic, as

well as being attached to traditional institutions, such as the House of Lords, that have had their day. By contrast, Labour's modernization programme has been projected as being more in tune with what it really is to be British and with what 'New Britain' might be. Labour modernizers claim that Britain's national identity at home and abroad is stuck in the past; and in a version of the past that plays on the identity of the British as insular and conservative rather than as free traders open to new ideas and new ways of living (Dodd 1995; Leonard 1997). If Britain is to be modernized – *New Britain* – its identity needs renewing as part of the process of modernization. What Blair calls the 'forces of conservatism' include those who persist in remembering the glories of British times past. Moreover, for Labour modernizers, moral and cultural renewal is required to underpin the economic and social renewal of a divided nation (Blair 1995c). The task of government is to rebuild the moral basis for a more cohesive society by identifying the values and identities around which people can unite. Social exclusion, the central metaphor for the Labour government, is as much about culture – values and identities – as it is about economics.

The Labour government's devolution programmes for Scotland, Wales and Northern Ireland, as well as Britain's membership of the European Union, have brought the question of national identity to the foreground of contemporary politics. Blair has spoken of the Conservatives' 'false promise' of 'narrow nationalism', and prefers to equate New Labour's sense of Britishness with tolerance, openness and internationalism – especially regarding Europe. 'Enlightened patriotism', Blair calls it (Blair 1998b). As we saw in the last chapter, Blair wants Britain to be a 'beacon to the world': a leader in European Union politics; and an active – and ethical – player in world affairs.

In this chapter we shall focus on what Blair thinks Britain and being British is. What are the attitudes, values and ways of life that *New* Labour is promoting in its *New* Britain? What identity does it envisage for the British nation in the twenty-first century? We shall then explore whether these notions of Britishness are in tension with the Labour government's inclusionary politics and with the diversity of local identities in Britain and the pluralism of its political reforms, and whether Blair's ambition to modernize Britain sits uneasily with the government's emphasis on traditional values and institutions.

Patriots and populists in the 'giving age'?

The Labour Party's second political broadcast during the 1997 general election campaign starred Tony Blair and a fifteen-month-old pedigree bulldog called Fitz. During the broadcast, a listless Fitz is roused from his slumber by Blair talking about New Labour's plans for New Britain. As Blair announces that he is 'a British patriot' and that he wants 'the best out of Europe for Britain', Fitz breaks free of his leash and bounds off! Peter Mandelson, one of the main architects of Labour's media strategy, said: 'The Labour Party is the patriotic party. *New Labour is the party of one nation and the bulldog is a way of saying this.* It is an animal with a strong sense of history and tradition'(*The Times*, 15 April 1997; our emphasis).

New Labour's one-nation politics has involved the search for inclusive symbols of national identity – images that reach beyond Labour's traditional working-class support and which are seen as more in touch with popular opinion. Blair has cast himself as a 'new patriot' who identifies with, and understands, modern British people and their everyday lives. 'I love my country', 'I am a patriot', and 'enlightened patriotism' are among the sentiments he evokes in speeches. Blair perceives that the decline in community can be reversed with a renewal of pride in the shared identity of being British – 'one nation, one community', as he suggests. A strong sense of British identity underpins the collective values and institutions, such as social justice and the National Health Service, which bind the community – the nation – together. Devolution of government to Scotland, Wales and Northern Ireland has been paralleled by a reassertion by leading Labour modernizers of the shared political and cultural state that, it is argued, is the United Kingdom (Blair 1998b; Brown 2000a).

Blair's speeches, then, are an attempt to inspire a sense of community by appealing to national pride. Labour modernizers also project New Labour as the 'People's party'. Blair's sense of being British – just as Thatcher, Major and Hague have emphasized in turn – seeks to evoke the 'real' values of 'the People'. The almost ubiquitous use of 'people' as a prefix to government policies ('the people's budget', the 'people's parliament', etc.) involves a kind of populism that attempts to identify Labour with the British people and what it means to be British. As Blair puts it: 'New Labour is the political arm of none other than the British people as a whole. Our values are the same: the equal worth of all, with no one cast aside; fairness and justice within strong communities' (Labour Party 1997a).

Politically, as we saw in chapter 1, Labour's populism under Blair is a response to the party's contracting social base and its declining electoral fortunes. Since the 'Labour listens' events after the party's 1987 general election defeat, Labour has spent a lot of time with focus groups and opinion polling trying to regain a broad social basis of support and swing its values more into line with public opinion. The populist appeal to Labour's values and conception of national identity as those of the people is part of this process of reidentifying with voters and making the party electable.

Blair's ability to strike a chord with popular sentiments was forcibly illustrated in 1997, as the news broke of the death of Diana, Princess of Wales. Blair spoke with apparent emotion, *prefiguring* widespread displays of public grief. He called her 'the People's Princess' and negotiated a public funeral incorporating members of the charities she represented. The widespread emotion at her death was said by Blair to be partly a result of identification among people with her compassion and humanitarian values. In his first Labour conference speech as prime minister, weeks after Diana's death, Blair claimed that New Labour was expressing a more 'giving age'. He described the crowds that greeted his journey to Buckingham Palace on 2 May: 'Theirs were the smiles of tolerant, broad-minded, outward-looking, compassionate people... And with them I could see confidence returning to the British people, compassion to the British soul, unity to the British nation' (Blair 1997b). The implication was that New Labour, like Diana and the British people, shared the same 'compassionate agenda'. As MP Chris Smith put it: 'No-one who has lived through the last tragic weeks here in Britain [following the death of Diana, Princess of Wales] can doubt, either, that there is such a thing as a national cultural sense... of compassion and commitment to those who are marginalised and disadvantaged.... What a change this represents from the go-getting, me-first, thrusting Thatcherite world of 1980s values' (Smith 1998, 36–7).

'Creative Britain'

The use of Fitz as a symbol by Labour may seem incongruous. The bulldog, a traditional symbol of British national identity dating back to the early eighteenth century, is hardly an image of a party in tune with modern times. Nonetheless, New Labour has embraced what it sees as the modernity and youth in British national identity. Labour modernizers offer the British as an inherently creative people. As Blair put it: 'We are one of the great innovative peoples. From the Magna Carta to the first Parliament to the industrial revolution to an empire that covered the world; most of the great inventions of modern times have Britain stamped on them...Even today we lead the world in design, pharmaceuticals, financial services, telecommunications' (Blair 1997b; see also Labour Party 1997b; Smith 1998). So New Britain is 'creative Britain' in tune with the developments of a post-industrial information society. It has particular strengths in creative work and innovation, whether in science or in the cultural industries, industries that are crucial to a post-industrial economy dominated by services and the new information and communication technologies – an economy which New Labour aspires for New Britain (see Leadbeater 1999).

The symbol of creative Britain, the Millennium Dome in Greenwich, London, was intended to celebrate British achievements in innovation in science and technology. The dome was to be, Labour hoped, a symbol of a creative and confident New Britain, as Blair suggested when he unveiled the models of the building. It would, he said, be the 'envy of the world' and would 'bring the nation together in common purpose'. The dome was to be the Labour government's 'grand projet', combining a sense of national unity with that of modernization. Instead, its critical and commercial failure left 're-branded Britain' with a brand that didn't work (see Bayley 1999).

The 'young country'

The creative aspect of New Britain is one feature of what Blair has called many times 'a young country' (Blair 1996c). Many of the qualities New Labour wishes to promote as part of New Britain's identity are often associated, rightly or wrongly, with youth – creative, inventive, dynamic, forward-looking. To New Labour, the attraction of the icons of 'cool Britannia' – such as Britpop and Damien Hirst (a print of whose adorns the cover of Chris Smith's *Creative Britain*) – is their association with youthfulness, creativity and self-confidence. Blair himself is a young prime minister: born in 1953, the first PM to have grown up in the 1960s and the first to be young enough to play rock guitar (Wilkinson 1996). Similarly, many of the areas of cultural concern for Labour are those in which young people are perceived to be the key producers and consumers, such as film, broadcasting, pop music, fashion and the new media. The Labour government has made better access for young people a priority in arts policy – for example, free entry to museums and art galleries and proposals for a national endowment for science, technology and the arts (NESTA) aimed at young talent. This appeal to the interests of the young is seen by some modernizers as important because it is they who are thought to be disproportionately alienated from politics.

The 'young country' is an attempt by New Labour to be *modern* and focus on contemporary culture and the industries of the post-industrial information society, with a corresponding downplaying of culture as heritage. Thus, the Department of National Heritage became under Labour the Department for Culture, Media and Sport, not, the former culture minister Chris Smith argued, 'because heritage is unimportant...but because we wanted to capture something more forward-looking, a name which captured more accurately the new spirit of modern Britain' (Smith 1998, 2). So, while traditional cultural institutions such as museums, art galleries, opera and theatre all have their place in current Labour thinking on the arts (and Labour argues that access to such institutions must be 'for the many not the few'), there is greater excitement than in the past about modern cultural industries, such as film, broadcasting and the new media, seen to be undergoing rapid change, largely because of innovations in digital technology.

Blair's Britain

Let's build a new and young country that can lay aside the old prejudices that dominated our land for a generation. A nation for all the people, built by the people, where old divisions are cast out. A new spirit in the nation based on working together, unity, solidarity, partnership. One Britain. That is the patriotism of the future. Where never again do we fight our politics by appealing to one section of the nation at the expense of another (Blair 1995c).

This extract from Tony Blair's speech to the 1995 Labour Party conference illustrates, Philip Gould tells us, the link in New

Labour thinking between the values of community and the 'necessity for renewal' (Gould 1999, 252). Blair's sense of being British – of being part of 'one nation' – is embedded in a sense of community rooted in a communitarian understanding of the individual's relationship to society. If accounts are accurate, the prime minister genuinely believes that an appeal to 'enlightened patriotism' can bring people together in the pursuit of progressive causes. A new sense of being British can, then, be part of a process of modernization of British institutions and British society.

But does Blair's sense of Britishness provide an opportunity for drawing the country together? To what extent does Labour offer the basis for reconstruction of community around a new sense of British identity? In the rest of the chapter, we shall raise two concerns, concerns that will be explored in greater detail in the final chapters of the book. First, to what extent is Blair's Britain – and Blair's sense of Britishness – inclusive? Is there a danger that, in emphasizing the positive qualities of British identity, Labour is in danger of fuelling the kind of 'narrow nationalism' of which it accuses others? Second, is Labour's programme of modernization shackled by its attachment to traditional values and institutions?

Playing with fire?

Labour's interest in promoting national virtues and symbols of national pride will cause many concern. The Left in particular has tended to support the view that the nation – both as a polity and an identity – is a construction of the modern historical period. As such the nation overlays those economic and social relations which the Left views as the fundamental building blocks of society – primarily class but also gender and ethnicity. For the Left, nationalist politics endangers the 'real' politics of class by cutting across the lines of working-class community and solidarity. This perspective challenges the core theory of nationalism: that the nation is the 'natural' unit for social, political and cultural life. It also presents patriotism – the love of country – as irrational, dependent on romantic and often racist notions of people, place and ethnicity. By giving weight to the significance of national identity – of being British – is Blair in danger of being sucked into the arena of nationalist politics that he so often accuses others of indulging in? In attempting to 'reclaim the flag' from the Right, do

Labour modernizers create one Britain for insiders and another for outsiders, such as asylum seekers?

Recent attempts, for example, by David Miller, to link nation and community to progressive politics have tried to make the case that national territories – and the 'common sense of national-ity' (Miller 1989 and 1995) – provide a framework for citizenship within which social justice is possible: in particular, because the national community offers a set of already existing shared mean-ings which give people a sense of communal identity. If the Left wants to foster greater community feeling, the national commu-nity is the one we can most easily identify with. Anthony Giddens shares this view that national identity can provide the basis for rebuilding community. Giddens argues that: 'people who feel themselves members of a national community are likely to ac-knowledge a commitment to others within it' (Giddens 1998). Both Giddens and Miller are anxious to steer clear of charges of nationalism. Giddens supports the notion of a 'cosmopolitan nation'. Miller believes that questions of national identity can be separated from nationalist politics: identity is simply a question of shared beliefs rooted in history – not a set of objective characteris-tics; and what is shared in common need not preclude other forms of identity. Indeed, Miller believes that nationality provides a balance to the diversity characteristic of modern society – pro-viding the 'essential background' to citizenship in a pluralist soci-ety.

Labour modernizers, then, are not alone in thinking that the nation might be used for progressive ends. Blair's Britishness is meant to be different from, say, the Tories' 'narrow nationalism' because it is tolerant and outward-looking. There is, to be sure, some hazy thinking in New Labour's conception of 'New Britain'. It might be seen as essentialist: are national virtues such as cre-ativity and compassion natural or products of history? Rhetoric-ally, at least, New Labour promises that 'New Britain' will be inclusive, pluralist and internationalist. But can an aspiration to patriotic pride, national strengths and identifications really avoid racist and discriminatory possibilities towards 'outsiders'? Home Secretary Jack Straw's tough stance on asylum seekers suggests that New Britain isn't always as compassionate and cosmopolitan as we are led to believe by New Labour. The problem, in the end, is that Labour's sense of Britishness remains ill-defined. To be sure, the notion of 'one nation' serves the political interests of Labour well. It provides a rich heritage of inclusive politics. But it does little to address the roots of identity and the many ways people attach loyalties to nations and communities.

Which nation? Whose community?

So can Labour articulate a sense of Britishness that is sensitive to the pluralist character of British society, as well as to the regional and national identities of the United Kingdom (Thompson 1995)? Labour's vision of a creative, young country within a post-industrial economy is unlikely to apply evenly across the United Kingdom. It reflects a rather narrow view of British society and of being British. It is hardly representative of the British economy, British society – or even British demographics. Indeed, it plays to the view, skilfully put forward by the Countryside Alliance (and taken up less successfully by Hague's 'common sense' Tories), that New Labour is elitist, exclusive and metropolitan and not reflective of the people of the British Isles more widely. As such, Blair's sense of Britishness – at least his 'creative Britain' version – is unlikely to carry the same resonance in other parts of the United Kingdom and across British society as a whole.

But if 'creative Britain' has failed to embrace British farmers and manufacturers, among others, New Labour appears equally ill at ease with identity politics and with more pluralist conceptions of British society. Where many on the Left have sought to celebrate the 'expressive revolution' and what are seen as the multiple identities of post-modern society, Labour modernizers reject the resulting 'rainbow' politics, worried about the erosion of the institutions and values which, they argue, provide the bedrock for social cohesion. As we shall see in chapter 9, New Labour's response to the perception of fragmentation has been less to celebrate it and more to appeal to institutions (the nation, the family) and values (work, duty, obligation) that it is hoped can provide the basis for greater social cohesion in 'strong communities'. But concerns have been raised that New Labour is too traditional, too conservative, too white, too male, paying lip-service to the cultural diversity of Britain (see Parekh 1998; Wilkinson 1998a; Alibhai-Brown 1998). In the pursuit of middle-English votes, New Labour has forgotten that middle England is not England, let alone Britain; and in its search for legitimacy it has exchanged pluralism for populism.

However, it is worth adding that one of Labour's first acts in government was to establish an inquiry into the death of the black

London teenager Stephen Lawrence. The resulting Macpherson Report led not only to Labour extending the coverage of the Commission on Racial Equality to many parts of the public sector, but also to new targets for police and public sector recruitment and procedure becoming commonplace. As we saw in chapter 2, Labour's 1998 Criminal Justice Act introduced a new offence of racial aggravation. Having noted these developments in policy, leading Labour modernizers were quick to jump on claims in a Runnymede Trust report in 2000 that the word 'British' had racist connotations. Home Secretary Jack Straw – one of New Labour's leading patriots – would have none of it.

Labour modernizers clearly hope, then, that 'New Britain' will offer an inclusive sense of community which acknowledges diversity and which matches the notion of Britain as a hybrid, multinational state (Kelly 1997). But the dilemma Labour faces is that, if it tries to project a more pluralist identity that is sensitive to the many different voices of the United Kingdom (which is what some on the progressive Left would like it to do), it could miss out on genuine bases of common identity. This is especially true if its pluralism is simply pragmatic in the sense that it talks to different parts of Britain in different ways (Hassan 1995). In response to the centrifugal political forces unleashed by devolution, as we shall examine in chapter 7, Labour has, for example, responded in Scotland to the challenge from the Scottish Nationalist Party by asserting a sense of Britishness rooted in values and institutions such as social justice and the welfare state, likely to go down well with a Scottish audience (see Blair 1998b). But as political pluralism becomes embedded in the political culture post-devolution, there are already signs that such pluralism is reinforcing regional and national identities within the UK (see *The Scotsman*, 22 February 2000). This is likely to make New Labour's designs for a New Britain all the more difficult. It is certainly the case that constitutional devolution is provoking national and regional questions (such as the identity and representation of England and English regions) that play into the hands of Labour's political opponents (see, for example, Hague 1999b).

The Traditional and the Modern

Labour modernizers insist that renewing British identity will be on the basis of 'old values' (Blair 1997b). But does New Labour's attachment to traditional values and institutions constrain its ambitions to create a modern New Britain? Stuart Hall, for example, has written: 'On crime, on family values, on one-parent families, on questions of sexuality, on the particular variant of communitarianism which he [Blair] espouses, one can find no echo at all of the underlying sociological analysis that one would expect of a so-called "moderniser".' Hall added that New Labour's 'commitment to the monogamous nuclear family as the only credible and stable family form gives "modernity" such a deeply conservative inflection that it hardly deserves the name' (Hall 1995, 31; see also Driver and Martell 1999).

Certainly there is much to the view that Labour's modernization programme has strong socially conservative elements in terms of the family, education and law and order, as well as more broadly the 'Westminster model' of government. So there is substance to the argument that New Labour's commitment to traditional values and institutions shapes and limits modernization. But sometimes the policy doesn't actually match the rhetoric, as we shall see in chapter 9 on the government's family policies (see also Driver and Martell 2000a). Indeed, New Labour could just as easily be accused of playing fast and loose with traditional values and institutions as it sends New Britain hurtling into a global post-industrial age. The Labour government's policies are, if anything, undermining of traditional structures and identities, embracing as they do economic globalization and e-commerce.

On these two charges – that New Labour is too traditional and that it is not traditional enough – some care is needed. As we argued in part I of this book, New Labour, like Thatcherism before it, is a heterogeneous political formation. The 'project' does encompass more liberal and progressive stances, concerning, for example, the gay age of consent, the Human Rights Act, early years childcare and education provision, and wider constitutional reforms. In these policy areas it is not obvious that Labour's modernization programme is traditional in any real sense or constrained by conservatism. In other public-policy areas, notably education (especially pedagogy and the curriculum) and law and order, New Labour is more conservative and traditional.

Tony Blair is not the first prime minister – or the first Labour leader – to appeal to the distinctive qualities of the British nation, and he is unlikely to be the last. And, just as Margaret Thatcher wrapped her policies of market modernization in the Union Jack – they would make Britain great again! – so Blair has made

Labour's programme of modernization one of national renewal and patriotic pride: 'New Labour, New Britain'. In New Labour's identity politics, there is clearly an attempt to offer a range of images about what it means to be British. There is 'creative Britain'; the hard-working family Britain; and the socially just Britain supported by the welfare state. Blair's Britain is a series of audiences that require different messages: what goes down well in middle England may not touch Labour's heartlands. And each New Britain reflects different parts of the Blair project. But there are dangers in all of this – not least the lack of any coherent narrative to Blair's Britain. In particular, post-devolution, the appeal to Britishness will become increasingly problematical, as we shall see in the next chapter. Certainly, the latent (and sometimes not so latent) nationalist forces in the devolution settlement will make such appeals so.

7

The New United Kingdom: Reshaping the Constitution

Reshaping the Constitution

Over the past century, most British politics has taken the constitution for granted. What really mattered was what governments did in power. Not any more. Tony Blair is leaving his mark on the British constitution. The Labour government is shaping a new United Kingdom, not least by devolution to Scotland, Wales and Northern Ireland. In constitutional terms at least, Blair's Britain appears very different to Thatcher's (and Major's) before him.

Since coming to office in 1997, the Labour government has embarked on a major programme of constitutional reform. For a party that in the past has shown little interest in such matters, this constitutional turn is quite new (Marquand 1997). Devolution is central to Labour's constitutional programme. By the end of 1999, devolved governments were up and running in Scotland, Wales and Northern Ireland. By the 2001 general election, it felt like devolved government was a standard fixture of British politics. In a country famous for its unwritten constitution, devolution has swapped codification for convention – the constitutions for the three devolved governments are written in statute. Devolution has established proportional representation on the British mainland. In Scotland and Wales this has brought about coalition government. In a country equally famous for the authority of parliament (the doctrine of 'parliamentary sovereignty') and the centralization of executive power within a unitary state, devolution has created what some are calling a 'quasi-federal state'. Devolution raises important questions about the state of the Union.

What powers should be devolved and should all devolved governments have the same powers? How is the devolved constitution to be managed? And will devolution strengthen or hasten the dissolution of the Union?

Opinion remains divided over this programme of constitutional reforms. *The Economist* calls the cumulative impact 'nothing less than revolutionary. They will eventually change not only the way in which Britain is governed but also the meaning of "Britain" itself' (*The Economist* 1999). A study by the Constitutional Unit at University College London argues that the government's programme 'amounts to a new constitutional settlement, which will be looked back on as the major achievement of the new Blair government' (Hazell 1999; see also Hazell 2001). To the Conservative opposition in Britain, however, the Blair government's reforms 'represent a fundamental threat to the unity of the United Kingdom and to the democratic accountability of our government' (Hague 1999b).

These debates are breathing new life into British politics – not just in London but in Edinburgh, Cardiff and Belfast. The Conservative opposition has seized the Union standard. Nationalists in Scotland and Wales are in positions of power and influence. The Liberal Democrats (in Scotland) and Plaid Cymru even find themselves with a share in government. But what of Labour – and, in particular, *New* Labour shaped by Tony Blair in the 1990s? Constitutional reform goes to the heart of the political character of the Blair government: is it being run by pluralists or control freaks?

Pluralists or Control Freaks?

Labour's new constitutional politics developed in opposition to the Conservatives' centralization of government in the 1980s. The Thatcherites may have been committed to rolling back the frontiers of the state, but eighteen years of Conservative government saw Britain's centralized system of government become even more so. The former editor of *The Times* Simon Jenkins memorably called this extension of control by the Whitehall executive in London, especially over local government and in particular by the Treasury, the 'Tory nationalisation of Britain' (Jenkins 1995; see also Beetham and Weir 1999).

As we saw in chapter 1, Labour's defeat in the 1987 general election saw the establishment of a wide-ranging policy review by the party leader, Neil Kinnock. Over the next five years, Labour's economic policies embraced the market; and its politics took a constitutional turn. By the time of the 1992 election the party was campaigning for elected assemblies for Scotland and Wales (something that Kinnock had fought against in the 1970s), regional government for England, as well as a charter of rights, a Freedom of Information Act and reform of the House of Lords. Labour also set up a commission to study the merits of proportional representation.

The current crop of Labour leaders, unlike many of their predecessors, display sensitivity to the centralization of executive and legislative power in Britain. Where previous Labour governments sought to strengthen the power of the centre, the Labour government today is creating a plurality of institutions that share these powers. The 1997 manifesto promised devolution for Scotland and Wales and regional government for England; greater powers for local government; and elected mayors for London and other major cities. The manifesto also displayed a radical liberal streak, promising to reform parliament, introduce a freedom of information bill and, crucially, write into domestic law the European Convention on Human Rights (thereby creating, *de facto*, a British bill of rights). Furthermore, Labour's pre-election commitment to offering a referendum on electoral reform suggested an interest in creating a more pluralist system of politics where power is shared within – not just between – institutions. Devolution itself has altered the dynamics of British politics by empowering regional political parties and creating new centres of government. Blair frequently invokes the spirit of the British social liberals in the early part of the twentieth century. He often talks of creating a radical coalition of the Centre-Left against the 'forces of conservatism' (a phrase introduced by Blair at the 1999 party conference and covering, for example, both 'conservative' trade unionists on the Left and Conservative constitutionalists on the Right). Before the last election, Labour joined the Liberal Democrats in producing a joint constitutional statement. Once in power, Blair offered the Liberal Democrats places on a cabinet committee on constitutional reform. Blair has sought to bring into government figures from business and elsewhere, and to appoint individuals from the Conservatives and Liberal Democrats to chair special commissions. Many senior Liberal Democrats, such as Paddy Ashdown, held out the hope that Blair would make good on his commitment to voting reform and that Labour and the Lib-Dems would enter into some form of coalition government (with

Ashdown, perhaps, as foreign secretary) (Ashdown 2001). These hopes have largely been dashed: in Blair's Britain, the 'radical coalition' of the Centre-Left has been constructed predominantly on Labour's terms.

So, if the members of Blair's government might, in one light, be drawn as political pluralists, in another they might be seen as 'control freaks' whose commitment to pluralism and the decentralization of the British constitution is skin deep. Cast in this way, the Blair government is centralizing an already overcentralized constitution. The former Labour MP David Marquand argues that Labour displays a 'disciplinarian paternalism' quite out of touch with modern pluralistic social democratic thinking. Another supporter of radical reform, Anthony Barnett, says that Labour is failing to dismantle 'Thatcher's authoritarian approach... Instead the Blair government is updating her centralisation on corporate lines.' Blair's Britain, then, critics argue, is not that different from Thatcher's after all (Marquand 1999, 17; Barnett 1998, 46).

The charge sheet against the Blairites is growing. First, Labour is accused of creating a 'presidential' style of government around the prime minister that is undermining the pluralism of cabinet government. Second, the Blair government is accused of ignoring parliament and reinforcing what Lord Hailsham dubbed in the 1970s Britain's 'elective dictatorship'. Third, doubts remain over Blair's commitment to pluralist politics.

The 'Blair presidency'?

Tony Blair admits to admiring Margaret Thatcher's style of leadership. Not for Blair the 'weakness' of the Major years. It came as little surprise, then, that the highly centralized structure of Labour's political machine in opposition – a structure directly accountable to the leadership (Gould 1999) – was the model for the Blairites fresh into government. And it came as little surprise too that this style of government was quickly labelled 'presidential' by political commentators. Labour, they said, was undermining the pluralism of cabinet government. Britain was being run by Downing Street 'control freaks' (Riddell 1997 and 1998; Jenkins 1997). In particular, the incoming administration's new 'ministerial code' – what Peter Hennessy calls the 'highway code of government' – was seen as centralizing administrative power by the control it gave to Downing Street over government ministers.

Historians have been quick to point out that this trend away from cabinet government is long-term, and that the cabinet is still capable of reasserting its authority – as it did with Margaret Thatcher in 1990 (see Hennessy 1998 and 2000; Kavanagh and Seldon 1999). But there is little doubt that the Blair government has attempted to strengthen control of British government from the centre. Indeed, Labour modernizers such as Peter Mandelson, whose controversial appointment in 1997 to a job later called the 'government enforcer' helped spark the accusations of the 'Blair presidency', argue that the problem with British government is not that the centre is too strong but that it is too weak: turf wars rumble on between government departments; coordinated ('joined-up', as the Blairites say) public policy-making is difficult; and the weight of government business is now so great that the heart of government needs strengthening if anything is ever going to get done. Nowhere is this more evident, according to Mandelson, than in responses to complex policy areas such as social exclusion that demand 'joined-up thinking', as well as 'joined-up government'. 'Departmentalism', modernizers argue, should give way to a more 'holistic' approach to public policy-making and delivery (Mandelson 1997; Perri 6 1997).

Peter Mandelson's job as minister without portfolio in the Cabinet Office – a post held subsequently during Labour's first term by Jack Cunningham and Mo Mowlam – was as a kind of government cheer-leader cum head-basher. His job was not just to make sure that the presentation of government policy was 'joined-up', but to ensure that ministers were following government policy. This caused some concern, especially as the enforcer's role was seen as threatening the relative autonomy of ministers within the British system of government. Ministerial responsibility (to parliament) means that ministers should resign following policy failures but also that they should be responsible for those policies in the first place. If ministers lost that autonomy, some argued, then Britain's would in effect become a presidential rather than a cabinet system of government.

In fact, Mandelson's job as 'enforcer' was more revealing about a longer-term trend in the structure of British government and the function of the Cabinet Office – in particular, its relationship to the prime minister's own staff and to other government departments. The Cabinet Office acts as the secretariat for the cabinet, helping to coordinate policy across Whitehall, as well as overseeing the management of the civil service. As the demands on British public administration have risen, so the size of the Cabinet Office has grown, as has the range of functions it undertakes. These changes have been paralleled over the past thirty years by similar trends in the prime minister's own office in Downing Street, especially in terms of the size and powers of the Policy Unit and the Press Office. Over time, these two offices at the heart of British government have become increasingly integrated – in particular, concerning those functions seen as crossing traditional government departments. Under Blair, the setting up of two specialist units – the Social Exclusion Unit (1997) and the Performance and Innovation Unit (1998) – reflects concerns about 'departmentalism' and the need to give British government at the centre a stronger and more strategic role, especially over the management and delivery of public services.

Political commentators suggest that the reforms Blair has made to Number 10 and to the Cabinet Office make the heart of British government much more like the White House in Washington. With Jonathan Powell appointed to a newly created post of chief of staff, a job that allowed him to give orders to civil servants, it certainly felt more like life in the West Wing. Indeed, the creation of a new 'policy directorate' blurs the traditional distinctions between politically impartial civil servants and politically appointed policy advisors. The proposal to set up an office of the deputy prime minister, as well as a new policy delivery unit, in the Cabinet Office in spring 2001 reflected Labour's concern that British public administration needed a stronger central steerage if the government was going to deliver the much prized public service reforms it promised in its second term. But these changes are not new. In effect, political scientists argue, Blair has continued a trend that now sees Britain having an executive office 'in all but name': 'The Blair government, like its predecessors, has built on that trend to increase and integrate the advisory and strategic capacities of Number 10 and the Cabinet Office... these changes do not mark a break with the past but are the latest stage in the accretive development of the centre' (Burch and Holliday 1999, 44).

If recent studies of the 'core executive' are right, then Labour modernizers have every reason for concern: the problem with British government is not that the centre is too strong but that political and administrative power is held by a plurality of institutions and actors that potentially make policy-making and policy delivery hazardous (see M. J. Smith 1999). But whether Labour's response – giving the centre greater powers – is adequate remains to be seen. As we shall see in a moment, some political scientists argue that Labour's attachment to a traditional 'Westminster model' of government limits the radicalism of the government's modernization of British public administration (Richards and Smith 2001).

New Labour's new 'elective dictatorship'?

The second area of concern is the Blair government's relationship to parliament and its commitment to parliamentary reform. Labour is accused of ignoring the House of Commons, fudging reform of the Lords and reinforcing Britain's 'elective dictatorship'. Labour, with its huge majority in the House of Commons thanks to 'first past the post' plurality voting, can more or less do as it likes. Only the House of Lords has stood in the government's legislative way – notably over welfare reform, the right to jury trial and its own abolition – and this despite the 200-odd life peers appointed by Labour since 1997, part of a growing army of so-called Tony's cronies.

Labour's commitment to the reform of the House of Commons was the Blair government's weakest link in its first term. As Robert Hazell writes: 'Parliamentary reform started with a bang but has ended in a whimper' (Hazell 2001, 43). Pre-election promises to beef up Commons scrutiny of government legislation and ministerial accountability were lost. The speaker of the Commons, Betty Boothroyd, and many backbench MPs became increasingly frustrated as ministers briefed the media before parliament and used the familiar trick of the guillotine motion to hurry government business through the Westminster voting lobbies. Signs of a Commons revolt came shortly after the 2001 election, as MPs from all sides challenged the government over appointments to select committees. With Robin Cook moving from the Foreign Office to be leader of the Commons, the long-awaited 'modernization' of the lower house may gather momentum in Labour's second term.

Reform of the House of Lords was more of a success for the government – but the limits of first-term Blairism were still clearly evident. While few were willing to go public in their support for the hereditary principle, the government's approach to the reform of the upper chamber brought the accusation that Labour was lukewarm about serious reform to the Lords. The 1999 House of Lords Act abolished the right of hereditary peers to sit in the upper chamber. The problem many, including the peers themselves, saw was that the government would not give a clear indication of what 'stage 2' of the reform process would take. Many feared that the principle of birthright would simply be replaced by the principle of government appointment – and reform of the Lords would do little to address the fundamental questions of the powers and legitimacy of an upper chamber within a parliamentary democracy. These doubts caused the government to allow ninety-two hereditary peers to remain in the transitional House of Lords. At the same time, the government established a royal commission under the Conservative peer Lord Wakeham to make recommendations for the second stage of the reform process. The commission reported in January 2000, opting for a part-elected (from the nations and regions of the UK) and part-appointed upper chamber – appointments to be selected by an independent appointments commission. Labour's second term in office began with a commitment to legislate for a partially elected upper house and the removal of ninety-two hereditary peers. The resulting white paper, however, published in November 2001, offered a watered-down version of Wakeham: only a minority of members of the new upper chamber would be elected and the powers of government patronage remained largely in place. No serious attention was given to the powers of the upper chamber – and that, possibly, is what the Labour government wanted.

Taken together, the reform to the two chambers of parliament is unfinished business for Labour in its second term. The worry, according to one constitutional expert, is that the Labour government lacks 'any real desire to make Parliament more effective' (Hazell 2001, 48). Britain's 'elective dictatorship' may have life in it yet.

But if the Labour government has shown little political will for reform of parliament, its incorporation into domestic law of the European Convention on Human Rights is a significant constitutional reform. The Blair administration, despite the party's traditional hostility to what is seen as a conservative judiciary, has handed greater powers to the judges. Britain now has, in effect, a constitutional bill of rights. Conservative constitutionalists, among others, have accused Labour of undermining the sovereignty of parliament by handing judges the power of legislative judicial review. It is certainly true that judges can now declare laws 'incompatible' with the provisions of the 1998 Human Rights Act – a law that came fully into force in October 2000. But parliament retains its sovereignty over any legislative rewrites, though government, not parliament, controls the redrafting process. In many respects, the Human Rights Act reflects the view of many liberal lawyers that in an 'elective dictatorship', where parliament has become emasculated, the judiciary should take a more activist role within the British constitution and become the guardians of Britain's fundamental liberties. Indeed, some senior members of the judiciary favour even more radical reform, such as turning the Judicial Committee of the House of Lords into a permanent supreme court.

But if the Labour government delivered fully in its pledge on human rights, then its commitment to freedom of information legislation has been far weaker. A 1997 white paper out of the Cabinet Office set out robust proposals for the right to know. But responsibility for the legislation then shifted to the Home Office. A new draft bill appeared in 1999, but the government's original proposals had been considerably watered down: 'qualified persons', in particular, would retain a veto on the right to know information that would 'prejudice the effective conduct of public affairs'. A Freedom of Information Act became law in 2000.

Pluralist politics

Finally, doubts remain over Blair's commitment to pluralist politics. His obvious interest in building cross- (and non-)party coalitions, for example in support of the European single currency, does not sit easily with his preference for 'strong government' elected under some form of plurality voting. Proportional representation may have become established in elections for the devolved assemblies – and coalition government become the norm. But the issue of voting reform for the Westminster parliament was well and truly kicked into the political long grass by the Labour government, much to the relief of most of the Labour Party – and of a majority of the cabinet.

Blair himself is a confirmed supporter of 'strong government' – a euphemism for government by one party with an absolute majority in the House of Commons. Other Labour modernizers – the Institute for Public Policy Research for example – are more sympathetic towards voting reform, seeing it as a way of making national politics more pluralistic. Many such supporters also see it as a means of developing a more fluid pattern of party politics involving, in particular, closer links with the Liberal Democrats. The Labour Party's flirtation with voting reform in opposition (a commission under the Labour peer and academic Lord Plant reported for the party in 1993 – and ruled out most forms of proportional representation) led John Smith to commit the party to a referendum on the issue. Labour's thumping great majority in 1997 effectively sidelined the issue – and the Liberal Democrats for that matter.

In government, Blair established a commission on voting reform under the Liberal Democrat peer and former senior Labour cabinet minister Lord Jenkins. The commission's remit, to find an electoral system that was representative in single-member constituencies and delivered 'strong government', effectively ruled out any proportional system of voting, because the latter tends to deliver coalition (i.e., 'weak') government, often in multi-member constituencies. So the commission's elegantly written report (by Jenkins himself) proposed a non-proportional system whereby elections using the alternative vote method would be topped up to make the Commons more representative. According to some reports, Blair continues to leave his options open on reform to Westminster elections, certainly until after a review of elections to the devolved assemblies in 2003 (Webster 2001). Certainly Labour has fought shy of any firm date for a referendum even on the Jenkins Commission's limited proposals. This does not please those Labour modernizers who, like the Liberal Democrats, see voting reform as leading to a fundamentally different kind of politics – one that brings together progressive parties on the Centre-Left.

The Blairites have little time for party traditions and identifications. Blair, unlike his deputy prime minister, John Prescott, is no party political 'tribalist'. As we saw in earlier chapters, the political strategy of New Labour rests on reaching out beyond traditional Labour heartlands to Tory voters old and new in middle England. Blair appeals directly to 'the people' and has successfully stolen the Tory mantle of 'one nation'. But Labour has carried over its highly centralized election-winning organization into government. Labour did move quickly to deliver on devolution, but it is uneasy with the pluralist consequences. As result, Downing Street gets involved in political battles which it should keep out of. In the fight for the Labour candidate to stand for London mayor, Blair publicly backed the former health minister Frank Dobson over the left-wing MP and former leader of the

Greater London Council Ken Livingstone and the former trans-port minister Glenda Jackson. Dobson's narrow victory, thanks to an electoral college that gave London MPs a special vote, gave Blair the result he wanted. But, having won the battle, Downing Street promptly lost the war: Ken Livingstone stood as an inde-pendent candidate – and convincingly beat the official Labour candidate. Labour's mission to modernize Britain, in London as in Scotland, Wales and Northern Ireland, now faced opposition.

Labour and the Westminster model of government

Labour's first term in government for nearly two decades has given us some sense of its political character and its commitment to constitutional reform. In part, Labour is a radical reforming government. But it is also one that betrays some fairly traditional instincts. The political scientists David Richards and Martin Smith suggest that Labour's radical agenda for constitutional reform is trapped within the party's longstanding commitment to the West-minster model of government. This model is one that is found in all the textbooks about British government. It is characterized by political authority concentrated in a committee (the cabinet) of a sovereign parliament elected by a system of simple plurality. Public administration takes place through a departmental and hierarchical system, driven by commitments to the public good, and accountable to the people via parliament.

This model of government was subjected to eighteen years of 'almost continuous transformation' by the Conservatives. Power shifted up to the European Union; down to quangos, agencies and a whole host of new regulatory bodies; and out to the market and the private sector. The Labour government's attempts to reform this state, Richards and Smith argue, fail to address ad-equately the changes that have taken place to the 'core executive' (Westminster and Whitehall). As a result, the programme is 're-plete with contradictions'. In particular, the government wants radically to reform the constitution while keeping its key features, especially parliamentary sovereignty. It wants to devolve power while retaining the central powers of the British state. The govern-ment's attempts to address the problem of coordination within British public administration by increasing control from the centre has been undermined by the continued fragmentation of the state as a result of the creation of new institutions, and takes little account of the new devolution settlement. As a result, Labour's goal of 'joined-up government' remains as elusive as ever. 'New Labour', Richards and Smith conclude, 'is trying to reform the constitution and the state without surrendering the powers of the state' (Richards and Smith 2001, 166).

In many respects, Labour's programme of constitutional reform has been driven by a liberal agenda to which Labour modernizers signed up during the party's policy review. As Richards and Smith point out, this programme owed little to either Old Labour or Thatcherism. In opposition and in government, this agenda lost much, though not all, of its radical inheritance.

New Labour, new public management

But there is another side to the Blair government's reforms to the British state that betrays a marked continuity with the Thatcher and Major years. Under the Conservatives, British public administration was subject to a managerial revolution that saw the application of market models of governance applied to the civil service, local government and the delivery of public services (see Williams 2000). These reforms included the market-testing of civil service work, the creation of 'Next Step' agencies (such as the Benefits Agency), the compulsory tendering of local services to the private sector, and the introduction of internal markets into health and education. These reforms, known as the new public management, challenged the traditional bureaucratic and hierarchical model of public administration by focusing on local, 'flatter' management (of schools, for example), performance indicators (such as exam results) and the market allocation of resources (school funding according to bums on seats). This managerial revolution embraced the market, the manager and the private sector. Markets were preferred to hierarchies; the management of outcomes to the process of governing itself; and the private (and voluntary) sectors to the public sector as the delivery mechanism for services. This was a neo-liberal not a liberal revolution, driven by public-choice theories of individual behaviour (public servants are in the end just as self-interested as private sector actors), with entrepreneurs and the heads of (then) successful British companies such as Marks & Spencer (the late Lord Rayner) as heroes. This revolution was predicated on the idea that power should be taken away from public sector monopolies and their self-serving members and given to the consumers of public services. This, it was believed, would make the public services more efficient and accountable to individual people. This managerial revolution, it is suggested, has helped to weaken the foundations of the Westminster model of government by undermining the traditional lines of authority. And it has contributed to a more general shift from 'government' to 'governance' in public administration (see Rhodes 1996).

As Andrew Massey points out: 'As Prime Minister, Blair has embraced this inheritance' (Massey 2001, 19). New Labour likes the new public management just as much as the Tories do. Well, almost. As we saw in chapter 2, Labour's reforms to the NHS and education are far less dependent on market models of governance than were those of the Conservatives. And Labour modernizers are less ideological and more pragmatic about such reforms. But what Labour modernizers have embraced are private-sector techniques and private-sector actors ('partnership') in the management and delivery of public services. As the 1999 Cabinet Office paper *Performance Management: Civil Service Reform* put it, effective performance management required a 'well-functioning business planning system' (quoted in Bogdanor 2000). Indeed, the Labour Party under John Smith had come to terms with Conservative reforms such as the financial management initiative and the 'Next Steps' reforms. Labour's 1999 white paper, *Modernising Government*, published by the Cabinet Office, sought to develop the notion of 'joined-up government' – and, in doing so, the Blair government not only accepted the managerial reforms of the Conservative years but set out how they might be extended.

In this way, Labour shares with the Conservatives a view that the traditional structure and culture of the British public administration was inadequate for the management and delivery of reform, especially in the public sector. Like Margaret Thatcher and John Major before him, Tony Blair is attempting to reform Whitehall by introducing private-sector structures and cultures into the public sector. This, of course, is dangerous territory for the Labour Party, with its historical, cultural, ideological and financial links with trade unions, including those in the public sector. Many of the reforms the Labour government has developed for the reform of the public sector involve policies that directly challenge the interests of public service workers. The view of the Demos-based modernizer Charles Leadbeater, that 'we need to develop a new cadre of public-sector managers capable of acting entrepreneurially' (Leadbeater 1999, 216), a view whole-heartedly endorsed by Tony Blair and Gordon Brown, is not one that would go down very well at a Unison conference.

The debate over pluralists and control freaks, as we have seen, raises fundamental questions about the structure of the British state and Labour's programme of constitutional reform. The new United Kingdom the Blair government is shaping is marked by both decentralization and greater centralization. The strengthening of the prime minister's office does not, of course, preclude the devolution of government away from Westminster. What central government does, supporters say, it should do well. What it does less well, it should devolve. This programme of devolution, as we argued at the start of the chapter, is key to Labour's reshaping of the British system of government. In its first year of office alone, six of the twelve constitutional bills presented to parliament concerned devolution. It also raises, as David Richards and Martin Smith argue, important questions about the balance between different aspects of Labour's reform programme. Is the Blair government's commitment to decentralizing the British constitution marked by a residual centralism? It is this question that forms the main theme of the rest of the chapter.

Devolution and the 'Union State'

The British state has since Tudor times been highly centralized. Successive Acts of Union between England, Wales (1536 and 1543), Scotland (1707) and Ireland (1801) created a unitary state under the sovereignty of the Westminster parliament. In 1921, the Anglo-Irish Treaty led to the partition of Ireland, and the United Kingdom of Great Britain and Northern Ireland took its contemporary form. The UK is one of the largest democratic unitary states. Its 56.5 million people were, before devolution, governed through a single parliament. But the UK's population is concentrated in England: according to the 1991 census, 49.9 million live in England and Wales (Wales accounting for approximately 3 million); 5 million in Scotland; and 1.6 million in Northern Ireland.

The United Kingdom was always, however, more a 'union' than a unitary state – the point being that the old centralized British state was administered differently in different parts of the UK, and this reflected in part the underlying historical and cultural roots of the multi-national union. This asymmetrical character of the British state is clearly visible: Scotland has its own legal system, schools (as does Northern Ireland) and established church. Before devolution, Scotland, Wales and Northern Ireland had dedicated government departments with varying degrees of power. Between 1922 and 1972, Northern Ireland was governed by a devolved assembly in Belfast. Parliament also accommodated sub-national interests in its committee structure.

The current devolution programme builds on this. Power is being delegated in varying amounts to new representative institutions across the UK. But these institutions are legally subordinate to Westminster: parliament retains its sovereignty. So, the new United Kingdom is not a federal state, in the sense of a constitutionally entrenched division of powers across orders of government. But its federalist features – in particular, the formal division of legislative and executive power between two levels of government – lead British constitutionalists to call the new UK a 'quasi-federal' state. The politics of this quasi-federal state will make it tremendously hard to reverse devolution, whatever the legal supremacy of parliament. As the leading constitutional expert Vernon Bogdanor argues: 'Power devolved, far from being power retained ... will be power transferred, as dictated by political reality; and it will be impossible to recover that power except under pathological circumstances (Bogdanor 1999, 187). Such circumstances do of course still exist in Ulster, enabling the British government to suspend the Northern Ireland executive in February 2000 for three months following the failure of the IRA to start giving up its weapons. But, in Scotland and Wales, it is now almost inconceivable that devolution will be reversed. The Conservatives, who fought tooth and nail against devolution in the 1997 election, accept the new political reality.

Labour and devolution

Devolution was last on the Labour Party's political agenda in the 1970s. Faced with little in the way of a parliamentary majority, the Labour government after 1974 looked to the Scottish and Welsh nationalists in the Commons. Support for the Scottish Nationalist Party (SNP) and Plaid Cymru had risen since the early 1960s. This period also saw a decline in the two-party dominance of British national politics by Labour and the Conservatives and a revival of the fortunes of the Liberals. In the two 1974 general elections, the nationalists saw support turn into real electoral gains. Devolution Acts for Scotland and Wales became law in 1978 – and both required referendums with qualified majorities. This proved the stumbling block for Scottish devolution. In March 1979, on a turnout of 64 per cent, 52 per cent of Scottish voters voted yes – less than the required 40 per cent of the electorate. In Wales, 80 per cent voted against devolution.

There are a number of reasons for the failure of devolution in the 1970s. There was – and there remains – considerable hostility to devolution within the predominantly unionist-minded Labour Party. Moreover, the proposed model of devolution in the 1970s raised fears in non-Labour parts of Scotland and Wales, such as the Scottish Highlands and north Wales, that first-past-the-post voting would lead to Labour 'majority rule'. Furthermore, historically Wales was incorporated into the Union in the sixteenth century and the level of assimilation into British institutions and identifications is high. Wales has clear geographical divides that map onto cultural divisions especially between Welsh- and English-speaking communities. Welsh nationalist politics grew out of the cultural politics of language, and its core support remains Welsh speakers. As a result, Plaid Cymru has never attracted broad support in Wales for its politics: at the 1997 poll, it won 10 per cent of the Welsh vote; by contrast, the SNP won 22 per cent in Scotland.

The failure of devolution in the 1970s was not the end of the matter. Indeed, the alarming decline in Conservative support outside of England (Scotland and Wales became almost Tory-free zones on an MP head count) fuelled the perception in Scotland and Wales that Conservative governments were 'English'. The Conservatives' decision to pilot local government tax reform (the infamous 'poll tax') in Scotland, and its attempt to govern Wales through non-governmental organizations (quangos), only made matters worse.

New Labour and devolution:
Scotland, Northern Ireland and Wales

The experience of the devolution debacle in the 1970s has not been lost on New Labour. The Blair government sought pre-legislative mandates for Scottish and Welsh devolution with referendums using simply majorities. In Scotland the referendum showed a clear majority for a parliament with tax varying powers. But in Wales the 'yes' campaign scraped home with a majority of 0.6 per cent.

Under devolution, the government has set down the powers which Westminster will 'reserve', leaving the rest for devolution. In all cases, central government retains control of economic policy, social security, employment legislation, defence and foreign affairs, security and border control, ethical issues and the constitution. The devolved governments have particular authority over education, health, the environment, local government, transport, agriculture, sport and the arts. However, some of these devolved policy areas, in particular agriculture, fall under the remit of European Union legislation, leaving little scope for policy innovation.

Despite opposition from within the Labour Party, elections in Scotland and Wales have used the additional member system – constituency members are topped up from regional lists to give greater proportionality, thereby avoiding the prospect of Labour 'majority rule' – and throwing the Conservative parties in Scotland and Wales lifelines. In Northern Ireland, elections to the new assembly use the single transferable vote system of PR to deal with the particular circumstances of representation of the nationalist and unionist communities.

The new Scottish parliament has legislative and minor tax varying powers (by 3 pence up or down). Despite trailing the SNP in early opinion polls, Labour won the May 1999 election but without an overall majority. Donald Dewar, Labour leader in Scotland before his death in 2000, joined the Liberal Democrats in a coalition administration. Part of the deal between the two parties, the LibDems' commitment to the abolition of university tuition fees in Scotland, which had been introduced nationwide by the Labour government, was to provide the first test for the new UK's devolved constitution.

As in Scotland, the Northern Ireland assembly has legislative powers over devolved public policy. But it has no tax-varying powers. The Northern Irish government centres on a twelve-strong power-sharing cabinet. Membership of this executive committee reflects the strength of support in the assembly, and special safeguards are in place to ensure the representation of the minority community. Leadership of the executive is split between a first and deputy first minister from both communities. Both have identical powers, and their election by qualified majority vote ensures support from both unionist and nationalist politicians in the assembly.

The 1998 Government of Wales Act created a sixty-seat national assembly for Wales that has taken over the executive functions of the Welsh Office. The Welsh assembly has certain powers over secondary legislation – that is, the settling of the details of laws first passed by Westminster. But its main powers are over the allocation of the block grant from the Treasury to Wales (in 1997, around £7 billion).

England and the 'West Lothian question'

The legislative powers of the Scottish parliament and Northern Ireland assembly raise what in Britain is known as the West Lothian question – named after the former constituency of the veteran Scottish Labour MP Tam Dalyell, who has been one of the most persistent opponents of devolution for Scotland. The West Lothian question concerns the fact that MPs from Scotland and Northern Ireland at Westminster can vote on English bills but MPs representing English constituencies cannot vote on Scottish or Northern Irish affairs, which are dealt with by the Scottish parliament and the Northern Irish assembly. This anomaly led the former Tory leader William Hague to argue that Labour's devolution programme threatened the unity of the UK: 'The people of England now find themselves governed by political institutions that are manifestly unfair to them' (Hague 1999b).

The West Lothian question was in fact put to the test during the fifty years in which Ulster was governed from Stormont. Indeed, the West Belfast question is conspicuous by its absence from the largely bipartisan approach taken to Northern Ireland in recent years. Short of creating a federal state, there are two main ways of dealing with the West Lothian question within the existing constitution. The first is to reduce the number of Scottish MPs sitting at Westminster. Scottish voters are overrepresented in the House of Commons in terms of MPs per head of population. Under the 1998 Scotland Act, the number of Scottish MPs will be reduced in line with those in England (from seventy-two to around fifty-seven) in 2005. The second way of dealing with the West Lothian question is the one favoured by Hague: 'English votes on English law' in parliament. Despite the apparent simplicity of this idea, there are certain problems, not least the difficulty of deciding what is entirely English legislation at Westminster.

There is some support across the political spectrum for creating an English parliament. This would leave the Westminster parliament as the federal legislature for the UK. An English parliament would certainly bring an administrative symmetry to the new UK – albeit to an asymmetrical state. But would it actually address the problem that devolution set out to solve: namely the centralization of the British state? Given the position of England within the Union, not least in terms of population, its parliament would be hegemonic. And, in itself, an English parliament would do little to address regional inequalities within England.

Regional devolution

Since the early 1990s, Labour has developed two regionalist responses to the question of English governance. One was to create a 'rolling programme' of devolution to regional assemblies, the other to establish regional development agencies (RDAs). After consultation, Labour moved quickly in government to legislate for RDAs. Following the 1998 Regional Development Agencies Act, eight RDAs were set up by April 1999. John Prescott, in charge of the Department for the Environment, Transport and Regions and the leading Labour advocate for regional government, hoped that the RDAs would mark the beginning of a regional devolution in England. But the RDAs 'were born amid acrimony and uncertainty' (Tomaney and Hetherington 2000, 2). Few in the government supported Prescott's agenda; and turf wars raged between the new RDAs, government departments and the government offices in the regions over who ran the English regions. This wasn't exactly 'joined-up government' at its best! To the disappointment of supporters of regional government, the new RDAs are appointed by ministers, accountable to parliament and funded by Whitehall. This looked less like the development of regional governance and more like the extension of the quango state. Labour's ambitions for regional government were always dependent on there being popular demand in the regions for it. In the case of London, the Labour government did fulfil its commitment to the creation of a new city-wide authority. Following a referendum, the 1999 Greater London Act was followed in May 2000 by elections to the Greater London Authority and for the London mayor. The 2000 Local Government Act made provision for referendums on elected mayors in other cities. But whether the 'designation' by John Prescott of eight regional chambers in the summer of 1999 was a first step towards regional government – which would, in any case, first require the creation of unitary local authorities – remains to be seen.

Managing the 'Quasi-Federal' State

How is this new 'quasi-federal' state to be managed? Will the new devolved governments be able to go it alone on significant policy issues? How much political and policy diversity can be justified and tolerated within the new UK? And how are the many and varied relationships between devolved governments and national government to be mediated?

Money

The allocation of public funds across the UK is made on the basis of the Barnett formula. According to this, increases or decreases in public expenditure to Scotland, Wales and England are allocated on a ratio of the 1976 populations of the three nations: that is 10:5:85 respectively. In the late 1970s, the point of the formula was to allocate new expenditure. The hope was that, over time, the formula would lead to a convergence of spending levels across the UK. This has not happened. According to 1996–7 figures, which will become highly sensitive in post-devolution politics, public expenditure per head in Scotland was 19 per cent and in Wales 14 per cent above the UK average; spending in England was 4 per cent below that average. In short, England subsidizes the rest of the UK.

In a 1998 review of the formula, the fact that public expenditure is higher per head of population in Scotland and Wales was broadly accepted as necessary on the basis of need. However, questions were raised concerning the relative poverty of parts of England, such as the north-east and Merseyside, within the UK. The regional allocation of funds across the UK ignores differences of need within England – a fact that Labour MPs in the English regions view with disquiet. Any further moves towards regional government in England would likely demand such a disaggregation. Furthermore, the Barnett formula as it stands works against variations in policy across the United Kingdom – which is, after all, the point of devolution. The problem is that the allocation of funding within the UK is driven by policy initiatives in England, which take the lion's share of spending.

Local government lessons

The fiscal status of the new devolved governments finds parallels in that of local government across the UK. The years of Tory government between 1979 and 1997 saw a considerable diminution in the powers of local government. Conservative ministers in London, anxious to control public expenditure and believing, rightly or wrongly, that much of local government was in the hands of 'irresponsible' Labour councillors, created a financial strait-jacket for local policy-makers. By 1997, around 70 to 80 per cent of local council funding came from central government. The remaining finance raised in local taxes is limited by Whitehall under the Conservative 'capping regime' to check the increases in tax to local taxpayers. Moreover, local spending needs are determined by Whitehall standard spending assessments.

Labour opposed this centralization of British government and promised to reverse the Tory reforms. By the 1997 election, however, Labour was back-tracking, indicating, for example, that a Labour government would reserve powers to limit – in other words, 'cap' – 'excessive council tax rises' – that is, local tax increases. In government, Labour has shown ambivalence towards local government. Chancellor of the Exchequer Gordon Brown's first budget, for example, provided extra funds for hard-pressed local education authorities; but he also told them how to spend it – thus conforming to the dictum that 'the man in Whitehall knows best'. When John Prescott, minister in charge of local government, authorized a small easing of local government spending limits in December 1997, he lectured local politicians on the need for fiscal responsibility. But local authorities were allowed to spend some of the money sitting in their bank accounts from the sale of housing under the 'right to buy'.

The national Labour Party learnt the hard lessons of fiscal prudence at the feet of the tax-averse British electorate. In government, Labour argues that its reforms to local democracy, such as elected mayors and more frequent elections, will bring their own local fiscal disciplines to local politicians. In such a situation, many hope, national politicians will give local ones more fiscal freedom: by allowing councils to raise more tax locally; by abandoning the central assessment of local spending needs; and by limiting Whitehall powers to the total of all local government expenditure and borrowing. The 1999 Local Government Act did mark the beginning of the end of compulsory competitive tendering of local services, replacing it with a duty of 'best value'. In practice this meant that councils would have to demonstrate to an inspector from the Audit Commission why they were more expensive than another local council. But Labour has failed to return the right to levy rates on local businesses, a tax that the Conservatives brought under central government control.

Politics and policy-making after devolution

For all the warm words about local democracy, the Blair government is unable to kick the Whitehall control habit it inherited from the Conservatives. The Tories ensnared local government in a fiscal net. The Blair administration has cast another for the devolved governments in Edinburgh, Belfast and Cardiff. Politicians at Westminster are, of course, elected on a national mandate and have national concerns – such as the control of aggregate public expenditure and the degree of equity in taxation and the provision of public services across the country as a whole. But devolution in the new UK is meant to be about devolving politics and policy-making, not simply administrative systems. As Gordon Brown enthuses:

> In the new devolved framework, the whole of Britain can learn and benefit from the energy of each of its parts. Instead of people looking upwards to Whitehall for all their solutions, from locality to locality more and more people will themselves take more charge of the decisions that affect them. (Brown 2000a)

The ability of those in Scotland, Wales and Northern Ireland to do just this is set to become one of the main issues in the post-devolution politics of the United Kingdom. As Jeremy Mitchell and Ben Seyd argue:

> devolution will produce centrifugal pressures within the Westminster parties, and we will see more differentiation of policy within the parties in response to the particular needs of the regions. The

new legislatures will also represent alternative centres of power to that in Westminster. Distinct policy agendas will be followed and political careers fashioned well away from the House of Commons. (Mitchell and Seyd 1998, 109)

Already, these political pressures post-devolution are in evidence. Before the 1999 elections to the Welsh assembly, the more traditionally left-wing Welsh Labour Party fought with the New Labour party leadership over who should replace Ron Davies, who resigned from government in controversial circumstances, as party leader, and prospective first minister, in Wales. Alun Michael, Blair's preferred candidate, won. But Welsh voters returned only a minority Labour administration. By early 2000, the majority opposition parties in the Welsh assembly were gunning for Michael. The issue: money. Led by the nationalists, Plaid Cymru, the opposition argued that Michael had failed to secure European Union subsidies. To be triggered, these subsidies require matching national funding. Given that the Welsh assembly cannot raise taxes, this extra finance has to come from the Treasury. Michael was accused of not being tough enough in negotiations with London over money. Before an assembly vote of no confidence, Michael resigned. His successor as first minister was Rhodri Morgan, the man the Welsh Labour Party wanted in the first place. But will Morgan succeed where Michael failed? The devolution settlement for Wales makes the assembly dependent on a legislative process in which it has no direct involvement. Expectations rose in Wales with Morgan's appointment. But, given the terms of Welsh devolution, it is difficult to see how any government in Wales can deliver on such expectations. Like Alun Michael, Rhodri Morgan will be judged on the size of the slice of the national pie he wins from the Treasury. Morgan, like many others in Wales and London, doubts the long-term viability of the devolved set-up in its 1998 form and has proposed a review of that settlement.

The Scottish parliament, with its modest tax-varying powers, has the best chance of going it alone. But by comparison with Australia, a highly centralized federation where states still raise 20 per cent of their own revenue, Scotland can vary its budget by only 3 per cent. If the Scottish parliament was to raise income tax by 3 pence – the maximum allowed – it would bring in an extra £400 to 450 million – a drop in the fiscal ocean when compared with the £5 billion annual cost of the health service in Scotland.

As Robert Hazell and Richard Cornes argue: 'This seems little financial gain to set against the political pain' (Hazell and Cornes 1999, 207).

The almost total dependency of devolved governments on fiscal transfers from central government must weaken their autonomy. It may also threaten their democratic legitimacy. If voters in Scotland, Wales and Northern Ireland aren't getting what they voted for, then who is to blame: the pipers or the paymasters? Fiscal dependency, if not addressed, may play into the hands of nationalists in the devolved assemblies, who are already entrenched as the main opposition parties to Labour. According to a survey by *The Scotsman* newspaper (22 February 2000), most voters in Scotland and Wales were disappointed by the first eight months of devolved government. While there was a slight increase in support for Scottish independence, voters are making a clear distinction between the principle of devolution and its practice. A majority want more power, not less. In Wales this means an assembly with tax-raising powers.

The big issue may not, as Robert Hazell argues, be about the total level of finance raised by devolved governments locally, given the general trend towards, and the benefits of, centrally raised taxation – although Hazell believes that all the devolved governments must have some fiscal freedom. The real issue will be the detail of devolved budget allocations. As Hazell (1999, 9) argues: 'Significant decentralisation of both the provision and the supply of public services can be achieved without there necessarily being any increase in the proportion of finance raised locally.' But, for some, Whitehall must resist its natural inclination to meddle in how central government grants are spent.

These centrifugal pressures of post-devolution politics will demand new inter-governmental structures. As a result of the Northern Ireland peace process, the British–Irish Council, or Council of the Isles, was created to mediate devolution to the province. Formally, the task of resolving difficulties within the wider devolved settlement lies with the Judicial Committee of the Privy Council, although in practice ministers at Westminster will have the real powers (Beetham and Weir 1999, 138). The government also announced a joint ministerial committee to address devolution issues; and individual UK government departments have been drawing up concordats with devolved administrations to establish working relations. In December 1999, Gordon Brown announced a new framework for coordinating public policy across the UK. A system of committees has been set up involving ministers from Westminster and the devolved governments to draw up 'cross-border' public policy. Critics accuse the government of muscling in on devolved policy areas. But this is to conceive of devolution as a straight division, rather than a sharing, of powers and responsibilities. In the new UK, Westminster will legislate for England and Wales; the Treasury will retain fiscal control – even if it confines itself to aggregate numbers; and the British government will continue to be the point of negotiation with the European Union, even over those policy areas which have been devolved. If experience from federal states is anything to go by, inter-governmental mechanisms will be necessary post-devolution to avoid pointless duplication and ensure equity and common standards in public policy nationwide. These mechanisms will not be politics-free. As debates in federal states such as Canada on the constitutional responsibilities of federal and provincial governments show, finding a working model for devolutionary government touches on fundamental issues of sovereignty, identity and social justice. The future status of Scotland, in particular, will focus on how these issues are negotiated within the new devolved framework of the UK.

The New United Kingdom – or the Break-Up of Britain?

The Blair government's devolution programme, the creation of new representative institutions in Scotland, Wales and Northern Ireland, does represent a significant and lasting change to the British constitution. But this programme is marked by a residual centralism. In particular, the new devolved institutions are fiscally challenged. Moreover, the Blair government, in its efforts to 'get things done', is resorting, as did previous Tory administrations, to ministerial fiat. Local government is given money, for education, for example, with strings attached, or it is being bypassed altogether. These flaws, however, cannot hide the fact that pluralist democratic politics is taking hold in the new UK – however messy.

But where will this politics lead? The revival of nationalist politics in the UK in the 1970s led some, such as the radical historian Tom Nairn, to ask whether Britain as a nation was breaking up (Nairn 1977). Fifteen years on, Linda Colley's study of the emergence of the British nation in the eighteenth and nineteenth centuries questioned whether the traditional bonds of British national identity still held in the late twentieth century (Colley 1992). Any account of the Blair government's devolution programme must consider whether the creation of new representative institutions in Scotland, Wales and Northern Ireland will strengthen the union or hasten its dissolution. Labour insists that devolution will strengthen, not weaken, the Union. In reply to nationalists, especially in Scotland, demanding separation from the British state, Gordon Brown argues that 'Devolution does not create new identities but simply gives democratic expression to existing identities' (Brown 2000a). Britain, Brown suggests, has the potential to become the 'first successful multicultural, multiethnic and multinational country' (quoted in *The Times*, 2 December 1999).

Tom Nairn has his doubts. He believes that devolution might have worked in the late 1970s – the Union was then robust enough. Today he argues that 'a profounder identity-current', especially in Scotland, has been set in motion which is bound to 'take it [devolution] further' (Nairn 1998). Unionists in all parties share similar sentiments. The Labour MP Tam Dalyell said of Scottish devolution in 1997 that it was 'a motorway, without exit, to a separate Scottish state'. Conservatives in Britain have accused Labour of being constitutional vandals, arguing that the Blair government has little real sense of where its programme of constitutional reform is taking the United Kingdom; and that it is playing fast and loose with the institutional glue that binds the British nation and its people together (see Hague 1999b; Willetts 1998b; Redwood 1999). Even those sympathetic to devolution recognize that the current constitutional settlement is likely to lead to a looser federation of England, Scotland, Wales and Northern Ireland (Marr 2000).

There is much to be said for the view that devolution is a 'process, not an event': the current constitutional settlement is not an end state but something that will evolve over the next decade (see Hazell 1999). It is true, as we have seen, that dissatisfaction with the current settlement is creating pressures for more decentralization. But support for the 'break-up of Britain' is not growing significantly. There is evidence to suggest that the Scots and the Welsh identify with their own nations – not with Britain. Moreover, there is an expectation that the European Union, as well as the devolved governments, and not Westminster, will have the greater influence over people's lives in the future. Are these the cracks in the new constitutional settlement that can only widen? Or, as is more likely, is it a sign of a more decentralized political culture taking root again in Britain – a culture which had been dug up by successive post-war governments?

Supporters of British devolution point to Spain's rolling programme of devolution to the autonomous regions as a successful middle way between a centralized unitary state and separation. Whatever tensions undoubtedly exist in Spain, especially between rich and poor regions, devolution has drawn the sting of the separatist movements. Spain also provides evidence for the success of an asymmetrical model of devolution, in which some regions have more power than others. Such a model provokes heated debate in Canada regarding, in particular, the status of Quebec within the Canadian federation. British devolution will remain asymmetrical and will require careful management. An English parliament is an unlikely prospect. If regional government in England does develop – and this is by no means certain, given the absence of public support – it will not have, for example, the legislative powers of the Scottish parliament.

Whether the Blair government is being run by pluralists or control freaks is important for the future of devolution and for the mark Labour leaves on the British constitution. Bogdanor suggests that Blair is following in the footsteps of that nineteenth-century champion of Home Rule William Gladstone: 'The current Labour government's proposals for devolution lie in this pluralist and decentralist tradition. They are in essence liberal and not nationalist (Bogdanor 1999, 192). This may in part be true. But the success of Blair's devolutionary programme depends on addressing the centralist culture of British government. The new representative institutions are challenging this culture. But it remains to be seen whether the control freaks in Westminster and Whitehall can change their ways.

8

Ending Welfare as We Know it?

Since the early 1990s welfare reform has been at the heart of the Centre-Left's search for a new political middle way between post-war social democracy and Thatcherite conservatism (Commission on Social Justice 1994). For Tony Blair, welfare reform was key to establishing his *New* Labour credentials – just as it was for Bill Clinton and the *New* Democrats in the USA (see Teles 1996; Weaver 1998). Following Clinton's promise to 'end welfare as we know it', Blair demanded that New Labour 'think the unthinkable' on reform of the British welfare state.

In government, Labour's welfare-to-work programme, the New Deal, has been the centrepiece of this welfare-reform drive – and of Labour's attempt to mark out a new 'third way' for the Centre-Left. But some see New Labour's US-influenced welfare reforms as marking a consensus, not a break, with the New Right. In this chapter we shall examine whether the Labour government's welfare reforms are delivering on what social democrats and others on the Left want. In particular, can a policy strategy based on social exclusion and pushing 'work first' sustain a commitment to egalitarian social democratic values?

Social Exclusion, Social Justice and the Third Way

Social exclusion and social justice

The idea of social exclusion has its roots in European social policy debates. It addresses what are seen as the complex and multiple processes that result in some individuals becoming cut off from the rest of society – in particular, the labour market. In the UK, the core objective of the Labour government's social-exclusion strategy is to shift individuals from welfare to work using a mix of carrots and sticks. The aim is to get those capable but not working back into employment. Policies such as the working families' tax credit and the minimum wage to 'make work pay' are designed first and foremost to remove the disincentives for those on benefits to take jobs. Making low-paid work more attractive is key. The Labour government has also changed the rules of entitlement and introduced new time limits: after six months, there is no 'fifth option' of life on the dole for 18- to 24-year-olds on the New Deal for Young People. The social-exclusion strategy has the clear objective of promoting paid employment. Work is better than welfare because incomes rise, thereby reducing poverty; individuals and families become more independent of (and less dependent on) the welfare state; and the discipline of the labour market creates a virtuous circle of work and opportunity.

For the Labour government, tackling social exclusion is part of a broader strategy to promote social justice (see Oppenheim 1999). Thus New Labour's 'third way' on welfare reform is seen to be up-dating social democracy, not abandoning it. For the chancellor, Gordon Brown, this means government creating more equal opportunities over people's lifetimes (Brown 1997). Getting the unemployed back to work – social inclusion – is one thing. But the bigger picture is about equipping individuals ('education, education, education', as Tony Blair put it) with the tools to make the most of their lives. A more socially just society is about enhancing opportunities to work. Helping people become more employable – 'employability' – has both the short-term goal of getting the unemployed into the labour market and the longer term one of building the stocks of human capital that shape an individual's life chances, including earning capacities (HM Treasury 1999; Brown 2000b). As Geoff Mulgan, the founder of Demos and a key government policy advisor, put it:

> getting people into work has to be the priority and then we need to address the ways of making work become a career, having upward mobility, having access to skills etc. The second cannot come without the first. (Wilson et al. 1998, 44)

By and large, this supply-side strategy rejects fiscal means – at least in terms of higher income-tax rates and benefit levels for those out of work – to promote equality. Globalization, it is argued, has undermined the fiscal powers of the state to level incomes (Commission on Social Justice 1994). Instead, this strategy attempts to address egalitarian concerns by promising a range of policies to alter the supply of labour. These, it is hoped, will redistribute work (and life) opportunities to the benefit of those less well off in society. Policies such as the New Deal, the national childcare strategy, individual learning accounts and 'baby bonds' are about enhancing life chances, especially for the least well off, to find work and to increase earning capacities. This human-capital strategy is an attempt to influence the market-determined distribution of resources by giving poorer individuals more leverage in the labour market by enhancing their tradeable skills through greater provision of social capital, as well as providing them with individual assets (as with the 'baby bond'). In this way, opportunities are connected in New Labour thinking to outcomes.

So, for New Labour, welfare strategies to promote social justice and social inclusion overlap and complement one another. Social exclusion is not having a job. But it also encompasses the many ways in which individuals and families are cut off from the sources of social capital, especially education, which are seen as the main determinants of individual opportunity. The new egalitarians look to the stock of individual endowments (capital, as well as skills) that help shape individual lives – and the distribution of rewards in society (Kelly and Gamble 2000; Nissan and Le Grand 2000). For some Labour modernizers, the question of social exclusion is bound up with a wider debate about equality and distributive justice. Key to this is human capital. Including the socially excluded by way of the labour market can be part and parcel of a wider redistribution of opportunities – and even incomes – across society.

The concept of social exclusion does not, then, in itself exclude some more egalitarian understanding of social justice. It could well be part of a rethinking of social democracy rather than its abandonment. But some see New Labour's social-exclusion agenda crowding out the Left's traditional agenda on equality. Moreover, whatever the intentions, doubts remain whether the government's human-capital strategy can really deliver a more equal society.

The Price of the Third Way: Giving up on Equality?

The debate about Labour's welfare reforms – and the 'third way' more generally – has the question of equality at its core. Some on the Left accused the Commission on Social Justice of giving up on those egalitarian values that made the Left distinctively of the Left (see Cohen 1994). While Gordon Brown has robustly defended New Labour's position on equality (Brown 1997), critics have accused Labour modernizers of abandoning the Left's traditional concern with the distribution of wealth and income – and with equality of outcome. New Labour stands accused of embracing a meritocratic, as well as individualistic (see Phillips 2000), model of equality that is both spurious and not in itself of the Left. And in giving up on fiscal redistribution – in particular, higher rates of income tax and benefit levels – the Labour government has thrown away the central policy tools to redistribute resources across an unequal society. The notion of social justice has been stripped of its radical egalitarianism and replaced with a concern with minimum levels of opportunity that will never challenge entrenched inequalities of wealth and income. For many – even those in sympathy with New Labour – the danger of third-way ideas is that they can all too easily lead Labour away from social democracy and the values of the Left (White 1998). As Carey Oppenheim, IPPR social-policy expert and government advisor, insists, equality must be central to Labour's welfare reforms: 'At the very least, the traditional social democratic goal of improving the relative position of the worst off in relation to the average has to remain a crucial objective' (Oppenheim 1999, 5; Oppenheim 2001).

For many on the Left the debate about paid work and social inclusion in New Labour thinking ignores inequalities in the labour market more widely. As Ruth Lister argues: 'it is questionable how far genuine social inclusion can be achieved without addressing the inequalities which are the motor of social exclusion' (Lister 2000a). Both Lister and Ruth Levitas (Levitas 1998) suggest that the Labour government's social-exclusion strategy is too narrowly defined in terms of paid work. The socially excluded are to be included in society by their getting a job. This is crowding out the Left's traditional concern with equality and a notion of citizenship defined in egalitarian terms. Redistributive justice gets lost in worries about welfare dependency and social integration. Where the Left stands for more equal outcomes, New Labour believes in little more than minimum opportunities. In the hands of New Labour, then, social justice has lost its distinctively egalitarian – and socialist – value. As Lister argues:

> despite the continued espousal of the rhetoric of social justice, it is, arguably, primarily a social cohesion model of social inclusion to which New Labour subscribes. While the two are not necessarily incompatible, the promotion of a narrower social cohesion model, which ignores wider inequalities of resources and power, runs the risk of becoming detached from principles of social justice. (Lister 2000a, 14)

Much of the blame for this loss of critical edge has been put down to the American influence on British social policy – an influence first felt under the Conservatives and continued under Labour. In the rest of this chapter we shall examine whether the government's welfare-to-work programme is undermining Labour's commitment to social justice. Like most welfare reformers in the USA, the Labour government in Britain appears to be putting work, rather than education and training, first in its welfare-to-work programme (e.g., see Department of Social Security 1999). While Gordon Brown's 2000 comprehensive spending review (HM Treasury 2000a), as we saw in chapter 2, increased public spending, in particular on health and education, drawing the plaudits from old social democrats such as Roy Hattersley, the danger for the Left is clear. 'Work first' has no inherent interest in outcomes other than to increase work levels among those on welfare. Any job is better than no job because work is always better than welfare. But can the Labour government, as Geoff Mulgan suggests, combine a commitment to putting work first with a human-capital strategy that genuinely creates a more level playing field of opportunity – and which convinces critics, including the party's 'heartland' supporters, that New Labour remains committed to making society more equal?

From Welfare to Work

'Work not welfare' has broad support among Western leaders from all political sides. But important differences in approach remain: the spectrum of welfare-to-work programmes is wide (see

Finn 1999; Peck and Theodore 2000). On the one hand, there are active labour-market strategies – especially those rooted in European welfare regimes – that focus on education and training as a prerequisite for finding employment. On the other hand, there are strategies now prevalent in the USA that give priority to labour-force attachment: that is, to work as a necessary first step to developing the right kinds of skills and habits required for success in the labour market.

Between 1987 (the start of Labour's policy review) and the mid-1990s, the European – and European social democratic – influence on Labour thinking was obvious. Modernizers inside and outside the party were working with a model of political economy distinct from the neo-liberal/Anglo-American one. But sometime in the mid-1990s the tide of influence turned. A North Atlantic policy drift set in (see Driver and Martell 1998, chapter 2). US welfare reform under Bill Clinton had already left its mark on Labour modernizers – for example, the policy of tax credits to 'make work pay'. But by the 1997 general election, New Labour had ditched a continental European model of political economy for a North American one. Once in power, Tony Blair and Gordon Brown began to lecture fellow European Union leaders on the need to emulate the Americans on issues such as welfare and labour market reform. Despite Labour's attempts to build bridges with European social democrats, the third way – and the policy reforms that underpinned it – looked increasingly like an Anglo-American affair.

The American influence on British welfare reform, and, in particular, New Labour's social policies, has been widely commented on (see King and Wickham-Jones 1999). While Alan Deacon reminds us that 'Policy makers in Britain and the US operate in very different cultural, political and institutional contexts', he adds that these same policy-makers are 'seeking to achieve similar objectives and draw upon a similar range of policy instruments in order to do so.' In both countries, Deacon argues, welfare reformers have focused on welfare dependency and welfare obligations; and on both sides of the Atlantic, work requirements have been introduced and attempts made to 'make work pay'. These approaches are, Deacon maintains, 'integrative in that they draw upon and incorporate elements from quite different perspectives on the purpose of welfare' (Deacon 2000b, 16; see also Deacon 2000a).

But just how far – as King and Wickham-Jones put it – is the Labour government prepared to go down the American route?

There are two basic positions on what New Labour has learnt from the USA. The first is that New Labour has gone all New Democrat: that Blair and Brown are following in the footsteps of Clinton – especially the early Clinton (see interview with Robert Reich in the *Financial Times*, 13–14 May 2000) – and are marking out a new progressive agenda on welfare based on 'tough love'. This agenda is distinct from the conservative Right in its support for welfare entitlements, but also distinct from the liberal Left in insisting that these entitlements must be conditional: welfare rights must be matched by welfare responsibilities. This view of welfare reform sees the real possibility of tackling both social exclusion and social justice within the framework of a competitive free market economy (see also Jordan 1998 on the 'Blair–Clinton orthodoxy').

The second position is that New Labour has simply gone all New Right: that Blair and Brown have caved in to the Right's welfare agenda – just as Clinton did in the USA (see Lo and Schwartz 1998); and that all talk of a welfare 'third way' is so much hot air: the Anglo-American consensus is really a neo-liberal consensus. Labour has abandoned a human-capital model of welfare reform rooted in European social democracy and fundamental to the Commission on Social Justice. In its dash to learn lessons from the USA, the Labour government is importing a neo-liberal model of welfare reform – 'work first' – that is at odds with its commitments to social justice, because labour-force attachment strategies reinforce labour-market divisions, especially for the low paid (Peck and Theodore 2000). In the UK and USA – and elsewhere – the 'welfare state' is giving way to the 'workfare state'. Any possibility of the Labour government delivering on the traditional objectives of the Left has been lost.

Is 'work first' making it worse?

Has New Labour changed its mind on welfare reform? Has there, in particular, been a shift in emphasis from a human-capital model to a 'work first' one? And what are the implications of any change for Labour's fundamental objectives – and for those of the Left more broadly?

Welfare politics in the twentieth century on both sides of the Atlantic operated within a political and institutional culture that gave priority to managing social security and that neglected human capital (King 1995). In the 1980s, the Labour Party nailed its employment policy colours to education and training, commitments that have since been watered down (King and Wickham-Jones 1998). Certainly, 'work not welfare' became the central theme of New Labour's social policies in the mid-1990s, but this was tempered by the party's continuing commitment to education and training in supporting those looking for work (see Labour Party undated). Gordon Brown's announcement made in opposition that a Labour government would require young people after six months on its welfare-to-work programme to participate in one of the New Deal's four options is rightly considered a milestone in New Labour thinking on welfare reform. The compulsion and increased conditionality of the New Deal marks the reforms off from the post-war social democratic welfare paradigm, if not from an older ethical socialist tradition (see Deacon and Mann 1997 and 1999; Field 1995).

Jamie Peck suggests that Labour leaders squared the party and the trade unions on the introduction of compulsion by promising that the government would offer New Dealers 'a range of high quality options' backed by hard cash. The Labour government's New Deal would be just that – and not another Tory youth training scheme. For Peck, however, Labour in government has shifted ground. He accuses it of failing to deliver on its up-market version of welfare to work. Peck was open to the 'progressive possibilities' of Labour's New Deal (Peck 1999). And while Peck, writing with Nikolas Theodore, concedes that there is more to the New Deal than most US versions of welfare to work, they argue that the government has fallen for 'work first': 'While significantly more broadly based and service-rich than US-style "work first" programmes, the New Deal for 18–24-year-old unemployed people nevertheless places overriding emphasis on assisting transitions into paid employment' (Peck and Theodore 2000, 126).

The consequences of this new love affair with labour-force attachment are, according to Peck and Theodore, worrying, in particular, because 'work first' reinforces what they see as the neo-liberal policy orthodoxy on flexible labour markets. They support the arguments of New Labour's social policy critics that the government has given up on social justice for a narrow work-orientated social-exclusion agenda that we saw earlier in the chapter. Labour-force attachment marks a shift away from more service-rich and skills-based approaches to welfare to work – approaches that can be part of a more progressive agenda on welfare reform (see also Peck 1998). 'Work first' programmes erode rather than build the stock of human capital. The result of such programmes runs against the grain of traditional approaches to welfare provision: 'in contrast to the welfarist logic of providing temporary shelters outside the labour market for designated social groups, this workfarist logic dictates that targeted social groups are driven into the labour market, where they are expected to remain, notwithstanding systemic problems of under-employment, low pay and exploitative work relations.' Labour-force attachment is, according to Peck and Theodore, antithetical to progressive welfare reform: 'While there may be some progressive possibilities around the new orthodoxy of welfare-to-work, these will be extremely difficult to realise in circumstances where "work first" is the dominant principle' (Peck and Theodore 2000, 131–5).

The implication, then, is that, as the Labour government's New Deal becomes more orientated around 'work first', so its 'progressiveness' declines because it reinforces existing labour-market inequalities. As a result, New Labour has moved away from the left/liberal social agenda that addresses low-paid work, labour-market inequalities and the issues addressed by philosophical egalitarianism. The question, then, for the rest of the chapter is: has Labour shifted ground on welfare reform? Does it remain within the progressive tradition on welfare reform? Or has it, as it has sought to push public policy beyond Thatcherism, given in to the neo-liberal orthodoxy?

New Labour's New Deal

Building on a new welfare consensus?

In the 1980s, American conservatives such as Lawrence Mead argued that welfare must be made more conditional (Mead 1986). Progressives too were shifting ground. David Ellwood supported time-limited welfare alongside more training and efforts to 'make work pay' (Ellwood 1988). A measure of bipartisanship on welfare to work emerged in the USA. Democratic and Republican state governors alike – and Bill Clinton as chair of the state governors in the late 1980s was a leading figure – championed the new approach as welfare reform was increasingly devolved to states under the policy of federal waivers (see Weaver 1998 and 2000). By the mid-1990s, however, doubts were being raised on the means to deliver welfare to work. Support for labour-force attachment strategies grew. In states such as Wisconsin, this support crossed party lines. Labour-force attachment was seen as a better way of getting people back to work, especially those (the majority) who had recently become unemployed and who had the necessary skills to find another job quickly. Progressives continued to believe in active government. They agreed with the 'big government conservative' Mead that those on welfare needed to be hassled – and this meant making welfare conditional by introducing time limits. But they remained committed, unlike the libertarian Charles Murray (Murray 1984), to government help for those on welfare in the form of training, family and childcare support, and in-work benefits.

So, while many American progressives – and conservatives as well – became critical of human-capital strategies, what they were critical of was their ability to deliver welfare to work. For them, the problem was one of means. For many progressive supporters of 'work first', getting welfare recipients back into work quickly could be combined – notwithstanding administrative tensions between government agencies – with human-capital strategies that had broader objectives and progressive assumptions about the role of governments in providing welfare. Rather than one big 'race to the bottom', welfare reform in the USA, albeit in incredibly favourable economic times, has seen considerable investments in welfare-to-work programmes by state governments – including job search, short-term training, and family and childcare support. Those hoping that welfare reform – even on 'work first' principles – would simply save money have missed the point: welfare-to-work programmes are expensive (Wiseman 1996).

The essence, then, of the New Democrat position was to combine what were previously thought of as distinctively progressive or conservative political positions, by insisting that welfare reform could combine additional services for those on welfare, with strict expectations about their behaviour (Teles 1996). Bill Clinton's promise in 1992 'to end welfare as we know it' reflected a bipartisan consensus on welfare reform that had emerged in the USA in the late 1980s, especially at state level (Wiseman 1996). The package of reforms drawn up in Washington by Ellwood and Mary Jo Bane for President Clinton between 1992 and 1994 sought not, as the slogan suggested, to 'end welfare', but to insist that after a certain time period those on welfare would be expected to work in a subsidized job in a private firm, public agency or non-profit organization for their welfare cheques. This, essentially, is the welfare-reform strategy pursued by the Labour government in the UK. It marks the reform of the welfare state, not its demise.

What is happening to Labour's New Dealers?

In Britain, as in the USA, early studies of the government's New Deal have been broadly positive. These studies have attempted to assess the impact of the New Deal on falling unemployment rates, in particular, to quantify the deadweight loss – that is, the proportion that would have found jobs anyway. A study of the government's flagship programme, the New Deal for Young People, suggested that it had led to higher exit rates from unemployment for 18- to 24-year-olds. The deadweight was estimated at 50 per cent (Anderton, Riley and Young 1999; see also Institute for Fiscal Studies 2000, 101–6; *The Economist* 2000a).

After six months on job seeker's allowance, young people aged between eighteen and twenty-four are allocated a personal advisor whose job it is to provide assistance with intensive job search. This gateway period has been 'intensified' to boost 'soft skills', such as punctuality, appearance and communication. At the end of four months, those individuals who have not found jobs are offered one of four options: full-time education and training for twelve months without loss of benefit for those without basic education; a six-month voluntary-sector job; a job on an environmental task force; or a subsidized job (plus one day a week training). If an individual refuses one of these options, sanctions apply – including loss of benefits. It is important to note, however, that while the New Deal now covers most of the workless – including lone parents – the rules covering time limits, compulsion and sanctions differ from programme to programme. In 2000 the government announced the setting up of a new employment opportunities fund to finance the New Deal on a permanent footing. This included a new 'one-stop' benefits and employment agency, piloted in twelve areas in 2000 and launched in 2001. This agency integrates the work previously done by the Benefits Agency and the Employment Service. In 2000 the government also announced plans to extend the New Deal for the over 25s from April 2005. This will come into force for those unemployed for eighteen months, though plans are for a 'staged increase in provision and support' after six months (HM Treasury 2000a; Finn 2001).

Peck and Theodore argue that the structure and ethos of the New Deal for Young People is biased towards the employment options – either in the initial gateway period or in the choice of options after four months: the 'non-employment options are provided on a *de facto* remediation basis'. In fact, for those who joined the New Deal by the end of April 1999, 47.1 per cent were on the education and training option and 20.5 per cent on the employer option (Institute for Fiscal Studies 2000, 99). According to the House of Commons Select Committee on Education and Employment, by the end of April 2000, 470,000 young people had started the New Deal for Young People and approximately 330,000 had left the programme. Of these, just over 215,000 individuals had found work – and 139,000 in 'sustained and unsubsidised jobs' lasting more than thirteen weeks. 30 per cent of destinations are unknown – though some survey evidence suggests that more than half of these found work (Select Committee on Education and Employment 2000, 1–2, 5). There is also a very high (over 80 per cent) drop-out rate from the full-time education and training option. While the then minister for employment, Tessa Jowell, told the select committee that this option should not be 'an excuse for not getting a job', she insisted that there was no evidence that New Deal advisors were putting pressure on individuals to take jobs rather than complete education and training courses. Indeed, Conservative opposition to the government's New Deal is that too little pressure is put on individuals to find work rather than take what are seen as expensive and unnecessary training programmes (see Willetts 1998).

Notwithstanding these Conservative claims, the New Deal is orientated towards getting individuals back to work as quickly as possible and is supported by the working families' tax credit (including childcare support) and the minimum wage. The primary aim of these 'carrot and stick' policies is to reduce the disincentives to take work, especially low-paid work. In many cases, the unemployed have found work with or without the New Deal: the economy grew strongly during Labour's first term; there were vacancies nationwide; and, while a significant minority of young people in the New Deal have problems with basic numeracy and literacy, the majority clearly have the skills and ability to find work. The relative success of the New Deal has been such that it has faced a problem of recruitment: while the number of New

Deal programmes has risen, the size (and cost) of the main New Deal for Young people has decreased, due largely to lack of demand and the higher proportion of individuals leaving the programme (Select Committee on Education and Employment 2000).

In many respects, 'work first' is a product of good economic times: many of those on welfare are 'work ready', and since 1997 there have been jobs to be had in a buoyant labour market. As in the USA, the question remains whether such programmes will work as the economy turns down and unemployment rates creep back up. The challenge for social policy-makers is how welfare-to-work programmes deal with those who have very real problems in finding and holding down work, especially those in localities with deep-seated economic and social problems. The 2001 global economic downturn will test the limits of welfare-to-work programmes in the UK and across the rest of the world.

Attention in Britain is shifting from the front end of the New Deal – the 'Intensive Gateway' – to the myriad of programmes dealing with everything from community regeneration and family support to reforms to and investments in health and education. Whether all of these programmes actually work – and whether they work in a coordinated way – is a key practical consideration. The targeted and often local character of programmes such as Sure Start and the Health, Education and Employment Action Zones does weaken Labour's commitment to a universal welfare state. However, the government may be putting work first on its welfare-reform agenda, and it may be doing it in such a way that targets social policy provision, but this is neither the 'end of entitlement' nor the end of welfare.

Welfare Reform beyond Thatcherism

The debate about welfare reform in Britain is partly about means: what is the most effective way of reducing unemployment and poverty? On the one hand, there are those who insist that Labour's welfare reforms improve the chances of individuals finding work; and that these supply-side reforms will in the longer term expand the capacity of the economy to generate more jobs (see Boeri, Layard and Nickell 2000). On the other, there are those who are sceptical about the supply-side assumptions of these arguments and insist that the demand for labour, especially on a regional basis, needs much greater emphasis in government policy (Peck 1999). Equally there are those who argue that paid employment is the best means of dealing with poverty and those who dispute whether work always works (see HM Treasury 1998 and 1999; Walker 1998).

But the welfare reform debate is about ends too. Labour modernizers believe that a third way on welfare reform can deliver on old left goals such as social justice while sustaining an efficient market economy. New policies to enhance levels of human capital, especially of the poor, can bring a measure of social justice to society by promoting opportunities in the labour market. The Left, however, while acknowledging the Blair government's actions to promote social justice – on combating poverty and social inclusion – insists that Labour's commitment to egalitarian values has evaporated. In particular, the Left insists that Labour has given up on any attempt to make economic outcomes more equal.

The data on welfare-to-work transitions give some credence to the government's critics. The fact that the New Deal results in a relatively high level of unsustained jobs – about 25 per cent of those who enter employment through the New Deal for Young People do not last thirteen weeks – would appear to support Peck and Theodore's view that there is a 'revolving door' between welfare and contingent labour markets – that is, part-time, temporary and low-paid work. The US evidence on welfare-to-work destinations supports the view that those leaving welfare usually end up at the bottom of the labour market (see Brauner and Loprest 1998; US General Accounting Office 1999). Within the American political debate, this evidence tends to reinforce the liberal Left's view that welfare to work is about 'flipping hamburgers'; and that these 'McJobs', rather than leading on to something better, are more likely to be either 'McJobs for life' or a revolving door back onto welfare. In either case, welfare to work does little or nothing to address fundamental issues of inequality and poverty, especially among families with children. American egalitarians want more from welfare reform (see Jencks 1997; Lo and Schwartz 1998; Teles 1996).

The New Deal is meant in part to offer the unemployed across all age groups – including the long-term unemployed – the opportunity to enhance their human capital as a means not just of getting work but of increasing their chances of finding better paid, more secure work – and, in this way, enhancing the life chances of those who start with least in society. The fact that a quarter of young New Dealers enter employment that does not last thirteen weeks, or that the vast majority of young people on the education and training option fail to finish their course, suggests that something is wrong. We need to wait before we have sufficient information about the New Deal to determine whether the programme is enhancing the human capital of the unemployed and whether this is leading to better prospects in the labour market. But it would be wrong to suggest that these opportunities are not available – whether inside the New Deal or in the wider education system. The challenge for Labour in its second term and beyond is to provide the necessary support to those who do find work to keep it and to start building ladders to better jobs in the future.

But does the New Deal help New Labour pass the Oppenheim test – that is, improve the relative position of the worst-off relative to the average? Simply in terms of relative rates of wealth and income, the answer must be no. After a period of stabilization in levels of income inequality in the UK in the 1990s, the end of the decade saw the gap between rich and poor widen as the economy boomed and wages differentials opened (Office for National Statistics 2001). It is certainly true, as we say in chapter 2, that the government has pursued a fiscal policy that redistributes the fruits of a booming economy to poorer groups in society, especially those in low-paid work and those families with children. But even if in the longer-term the government's welfare-to-work programme and its wider reforms to education and training did boost the human capital of the poor, it is very unlikely that this would lead to a reduction in inequality, as average incomes are also likely to rise. Those already well stocked in human capital are always going to have the edge where education and training attracts a premium in the labour market, and where lower paid workers often find themselves in competition with workers in low-wage economies. As David Miller concedes, 'supply-side egalitarianism' may be 'an excellent approach, but it will probably work much more effectively as an anti-poverty device, preventing people from dropping out of the bottom of the labour market, than as a device for reducing inequality between top and bottom' (Miller 1997, 89).

For this reason, many egalitarians such as Miller remain committed to the kind of government interventions, both in terms of the ownership of property and the fiscal powers of the state, in the capitalist market economy explicitly ruled out by New Labour. Moreover, those who support a more modest 'asset egalitarianism' make very limited claims, insisting that the objective is to guarantee minimum starting points rather than equal starting points, let alone equal shares (Kelly and Gamble 2000). As Andrew Glyn and Stewart Wood argue, policies concerned with the absolute position of the least advantaged can coexist with policies that tolerate and even encourage the pursuit of wealth. As a result, society may become more inegalitarian, even if more meritocratic. According to Glyn and Wood: 'In this respect New Labour has disentangled the traditional social democratic aims of promoting equality and eliminating poverty in ways that many on the left find both unacceptable (in respect of greater inequality in the top half of the distribution) and unconvincing (in respect of the near-exclusive emphasis on the labour market)' (Glyn and Wood 2001, 64).

In the end, the government's critics on the Left have a point: the New Deal and its associated policies are primarily about a policy agenda narrowly focused on social exclusion and paid employment – a view readily conceded on the 'big government' Right (Mead 1997). As Raymond Plant argues, there is nothing inherently social democratic about the New Deal: enhancing the marketable skills of the poor still leaves the market as the final arbiter of the value of those skills. To this extent, New Labour's welfare-to-work programme is as much centre-right as it is centre-left. But, as Plant argues too, the New Deal may not be that social democratic but neither is it very neo-liberal (say of a Charles Murray vintage). There is something third-wayish about the New Deal in terms of how it conceives citizenship, the labour market and the role of the state.

For this reason, lumping the Labour government's welfare reforms into one big political pile with those of previous Tory governments – and the New Right generally – has limited value. In the end, New Labour is more than just Thatcherism Mark 2. Grover and Stewart (Grover and Stewart 1999), for example, are right to point to some of the continuities between Labour and Conservative 'workfare' schemes: both have set out to reform the tax-and-benefit system to encourage the unemployed to take jobs. The Tories tightened eligibility rules (as has Labour), introduced in-work income support (family credit – now working families' tax credit) and reduced the real value of some benefits (only reversed in part by Labour). But Grover and Stewart write off Labour's welfare reforms as 'symbolic differences and one disjunction'. While written in anticipation of Labour's welfare reforms,[1] this

---

1 Grover and Stewart's paper was accepted for publication in October 1997.

does little justice to the Labour government's national childcare strategy or the job and training guarantees in the New Deal – both dismissed as different from the policies of the Tories, though 'more at a symbolic level'. The 'one disjunction', the minimum wage, is dismissed in a final paragraph.

There is, to be sure, a degree of continuity between Labour and Conservative approaches to welfare (to work) over the past two decades. But there are some important social democratic elements in New Labour policy-making that betray a continued commitment to social justice – and which cast doubt on a straightforward 'neo-liberal convergence' thesis (Rhodes 2000; see also Crouch 2001). The 'symbolic differences' noted by Grover and Stewart are what set New Labour apart from previous Tory governments, as well as from the New Right more generally.

Central to the 'third-way' politics of New Labour – and to the New Democrats in the USA – is the notion that different policy approaches, whether from the Left or Right, can in some way be combined – if not actually reconciled (see Driver and Martell 2000b; Deacon 2000b). The welfare reforms of the Labour government reflect this political strategy. They combine policies on incentives, prevention and rehabilitation, as well as a new paternalism (see Weaver 1998). On incentives, New Labour, like Clinton's New Democrats, has moved to 'make work pay' by introducing in-work tax credits and a minimum wage, and to provide support (such as childcare) to enable individuals to take work, as well as subsidies to support low-paid employment (in the New Deal, for example). On prevention and rehabilitation, the Labour government has introduced policies to enhance the human capital of those on welfare and those in work. All of these policies fit, though not exclusively, a progressive social democratic agenda on welfare reform that is concerned with family poverty, labour-market opportunities and social inclusion – and, in sum, they mark out a substantial role for the state in providing welfare.

At the same time, New Labour, again like the New Democrats, has drawn on the 'new paternalism' of some (i.e., Mead), but by no means all, of the New Right. The Labour government has made the rights of citizens to welfare even more contingent on responsibilities – in particular, to find work. New Labour's welfare reforms demand, as the new paternalism requires, certain types of behavioural responses and sanction those forms of behaviour deemed as 'irresponsible'. Third-way politics is not neutral on the 'good citizen'. This element of new paternalism in New Labour and the New Democrats led to the policy of work require-ments and marks an obvious break with the old progressive agenda on both sides of the Atlantic that believed that rights to welfare should not be contingent on work requirements. But while New Labour and the New Democrats have broken with the post-war progressive Left, they have retained a distance from sections of the Right – in particular, that part of the New Right that advocates a deterrence strategy (i.e., Murray). This strategy believes that welfare entitlements should be withdrawn to prevent undesirable behavioural outcomes (such as teenage pregnancy). This is a strategy that seeks the end, not the reform, of the welfare state.

Pursuing such a welfare middle way, especially for progressive politicians, brings threats as well as opportunities. As Kent Weaver (Weaver 1998) argues, Bill Clinton's repositioning of the Democratic Party widened the policy options on poverty and wel-fare for a centre-left party. The 'modernization' of the Labour Party has done much the same. But these new opportunities bring with them dangers when the policy-making door is opened to reforms far more radical than those initially envisaged. In 1996, after having largely ceded the legislative initiative to congress, President Clinton signed the Republican welfare reform bill. Wel-fare politics in the USA took a giant leap to the Right. Crucially, the 1996 legislation ended federal entitlements and introduced a five-year time limit to the newly devolved state welfare support.

But must the ideological concessions made by New Labour and the New Democrats inevitably lead to further shifts to the Right, as Weaver warns is possible? As Steven Teles argues, the New Democrat position on welfare – after a certain time period, benefit claimants should work or study for their welfare – reflects con-temporary public opinion. Most Americans, Teles shows, want those on welfare to work, but they don't want the government to cast them adrift (Teles 1996). Such a view underpins Mead's 'new politics of poverty' (Mead 1992). This shift from welfare to work in public policy, as Mead concedes, might relegitimize the welfare state – and this is just as likely to promote a shift to the Left as it is to the Right. Once the voters know that those on welfare are going to be hassled to find jobs, they could be more happy to help them.

After four years in government, New Labour's attack on the so-called something for nothing welfare culture is starting to pay

political dividends. The flip side of getting tough on social security entitlements – always that part of the welfare budget least
popular with voters – is a series of budgets, as we saw in chapter
2, that have set the Blair government on a more traditional Labour
course to increase spending and investment on the public services, especially on education and health, as well as increasing the
incomes of the 'working poor', in particular those with children.

The fact that the Clinton presidency did not mark a liberal
counter-revolution after the Reagan/Bush years rather misses the
point about what being a New Democrat was all about (O'Connor
1998). By the same token, that Blair has not turned the welfare
clock back to a pre-Thatcher era – he never said he would – is to
miss what is really new about New Labour. Like those of the New
Democrats, New Labour's welfare reforms cross ideological lines.
But there remains, despite the overlaps, a distinctively progressive
and social democratic side to these reforms. This is not a government in thrall to the New Right. Yes, there are continuities between Labour's welfare-to-work programme – and its broader
political economy – and that of previous Conservative administrations. But putting 'work first' on its welfare-reform agenda is not
excluding more progressive policy reforms on family poverty, opportunities in the labour market and social inclusion.

9

New Labour, Work and the Family

New Labour has put support for the family at the core of its notion of the 'strong community'. 'Family life', wrote the former home secretary Jack Straw, 'is the foundation on which our communities, our society and our country are built. Families are central to this government's vision of a modern and decent country' (Ministerial Group on the Family 1998; Labour Party 2001). Across a range of areas – family support, childcare, fiscal redistribution, parental leave – the Labour government can be seen to be developing direct and explicit family policies. But what kind of community is the government trying to shape by these policies? On the one hand, Labour appears to support the family as the basis of a more moral, dutiful and cohesive community. On the other hand, the government has given weight to policies that support social inclusion in the community through paid work. Is there a tension here in Labour's social policies between its emphasis on the importance of stable family life and the primacy given to paid work? Critics such as Ruth Levitas argue that the government's emphasis on paid work devalues, and is unsupportive of, unpaid work, especially caring for children and other family members. Alternatively, this combination of communitarianisms – community as 'stable family' and community as 'paid work' – could be seen as marking out some 'third way' on the family – one perhaps that breaks with what Helen Wilkinson (1998b; 1999) from Demos often calls the 'tired and worn' debate between liberals and conservatives.

In this chapter we shall examine the coherence of the Labour government's policies on work and the family. We shall show that different aspects of its family policies reflect different perspectives and policy agendas within New Labour and third way thinking more broadly. And, while recognizing the tensions between work and the family, we shall suggest that they are often overstated and fail to give sufficient weight to the complementary aspects of Labour's welfare reforms.

The Family, Community and the Third Way

As we saw in chapter 3, New Labour's 'third way' is articulated as a reaction to both Thatcherism (the 'New Right') and post-war social democracy (the 'Old Left'). The key to Labour's embrace of family values lies in this dual critique of post-war social democracy and Thatcherite conservatism. Labour modernizers have cast those of the post-war Left as libertarians and social individualists whose neutrality on family forms had dire social consequences. The Thatcherites have been tarred as economic individualists whose only concern was the free market – an approach seen as destructive of forms of community such as the family. So New Labour has challenged what it perceives as Thatcherism's *economic* individualism and Old Labour's *social* individualism (Blair 1995a). Indeed, Blair and other Labour modernizers share the view of social conservatives on the Left and Right that the social individualism of the post-1960s Left was destructive of family life because of the libertarian values it promoted (Boseley and Wintour 1995; Wright 1997; Rowthorn and Ormerod 2001). This 'Old Left', New Labour claims, was too focused on rights-claiming at the expense of individual and collective responsibilities; and it stood back non-judgementally from a range of social problems where government intervention is now thought to be required.

To be sure, these caricatures distort the diversity and complexity of post-war politics. As David Marquand (1996) has pointed out, both Labour and the Tories have had their share of 'moralists' and 'hedonists' since 1945: those who see the 'good life' as one in which individuals follow their own preferences; and those that believe that the individual 'good life' is embedded in a developing moral entity that ranks some preferences over others. But these caricatures have served New Labour well. In particular, they have enabled Labour modernizers to construct a politics that prioritizes responsibilities and obligations that individuals owe in the community. And it is the family that above all else animates the notion of the dutiful community through parenthood. In policy terms, family forms matter because the family both requires and underpins individual responsibility in the community.

This dual critique of Thatcherism and post-war social democracy – 'beyond Old Left and New Right', as Blair puts it – is, then, the core of the contemporary third way view in Britain. As we have suggested, it offers a rationale for New Labour's activist family policies. But, as we saw earlier in the book, there are important debates *within* the third way about the characteristics of the contemporary social world and the kinds of social policy best suited to these 'New Times'. Some third ways between 'Old Left' and 'New Right' are more or less egalitarian; some are more liberal and others more communitarian; and some share a conservative edge with the 'New Right' while others have roots in the progressive thinking of the 'Old Left' (Driver and Martell 2000b; White 1998).

These debates raise important questions for current government policy on the family. Significantly in terms of the themes of this chapter, two of the major proponents of the third way, Anthony Giddens and Tony Blair, appear to have different takes on what constitutes 'New Times' and what, if anything, government can do about them. In particular, Giddens and Blair have a different view of individualism. Giddens sees the growing individualism in modern society not, as Blair tends to, as a product of Thatcherite economic egoism that needs to be counteracted by more community (Giddens 1998). For Giddens, individualism is a symptom of post-traditional modernization, where people have more choice, reflexivity and control – all of which are to be celebrated. Blair is more of a communitarian social moralist, Giddens a post-traditionalist celebrating a new era of individual choice (see Deacon and Mann 1997 and 1999).

These views are reflected in third-way thinking on the family. Blair's third way on the family is more socially moralist than that of Giddens, with a stronger emphasis on the two-parent family (the 'traditional family') and on the family as the basis for stability and strong moral foundations in society, albeit alongside a recognition that the family has changed (Blair 1996a). Giddens, however, argues that it is not feasible or desirable to reconstruct the traditional family. For Giddens, we live in a post-traditional era where the traditional family is now in a small minority and has been supplanted by other post-traditional social forms. As a result, Giddens believes, we should go with the flow of new forms of family, recognizing and acknowledging the social, cultural and moral diversity inherent in modern societies; encourage the flexibility, choice and affective individualism of the late modern era; and build on possibilities for greater democracy, equality and active participation in these circumstances. Rather than aspiring to a traditional family that can offer stability and security in a fast-moving world, Giddens argues that the family should be seen as part of that world, expressing flexibility and change instead of acting as a counter-balance to them.

This has parallels with Giddens's difference of emphasis from Blair on the third way in general that we saw in chapter 3: Blair emphasizes communitarian antidotes to individualism while Giddens locates individualism in profound social change rather than just the post-war politics of Thatcherism and social democracy, and calls for the promotion of individualism, choice and flexibility. What this means for the family in practice is not always that clear. Despite positive celebration of the post-traditional family, Giddens criticizes the desirability of lone-parent and separated families. One thing for which he does argue, though, is an emphasis on parenting contracts, in recognition of the fact that life-long partnerships are in decline and that the priority in the future has to be on maintaining committed parenting amid flux and change in the family (see Giddens 1998, 89–98).

A similar position has been taken by Helen Wilkinson. She argues that, when it comes to the family, 'diversity is king': '[Governments] should start by valuing today's families, rather than judging them. They should aim to strengthen and stabilise them in all their diverse shapes and sizes' (Wilkinson 1999, 23; see also Coote, Harman and Hewitt 1990; Hewitt 1996; Lloyd 1998; Giddens 1996; Smart and Neale 1999). Wilkinson's point is that neither conservative hand-wringing about the decline of the traditional family nor liberal celebration of individual choice adequately addresses the many problems faced by contemporary families: 'Family change has brought greater freedom and autonomy but this process has not been without costs, and these have been borne most clearly by children' (Wilkinson 1998b, 112). Such a post-traditionalist view of the family would, for example, accept that public policy should address the parenting position of fathers in the family. But it should do so in a way that accepts changing family structures (see Burgess and Ruxton 1996; for recent debates, see Wilkinson 2000).

What, then, is new about New Labour on the family is that issues of family form and structure are put on the table and become explicitly part of the government's agenda. This, as Hilary Land argues (Land 1999), marks a shift away from the family policies of previous Labour, and for that matter Conservative, governments, which were generally implicit in other economic and social policies. So, while families were to be supported by the state, the issue of the shape and form of the family was seen as a private matter in which governments had little or no role. As the feminist critique of gender inequalities in the family grew in influence, Labour neutrality on the structure of the family often turned to hostility towards arguments for its traditional form. The political and intellectual alliances made between feminism and socialism in the 1970s and 1980s consolidated the 'anti-family' view of the Left (e.g., Barrett and McIntosh 1982). These perspectives were further reinforced by Conservative government attacks on non-traditional family forms in the 1980s and the links made by neo-conservative intellectuals between welfare dependency and single parenthood (see Murray 1994).

So, by embracing the family, and by linking the family with wider questions of 'welfare dependency' – in particular, concerning lone parents – New Labour, some have suggested, has moved onto Conservative territory (S. Smith 1999). Indeed, its supposed advocacy of the 'traditional family' as the best means to support parenting and paid work has brought accusations of 'prescriptive conservatism' (see Barlow and Duncan 2001; Hall 1998). But what does the Labour government actually say on the family and what are its policies aimed at achieving? In the next section we want to suggest that accusations of conservatism miss the mark, not because they are entirely false, but because there are other more progressive agendas in play. Moreover, this combination of agendas should not be thought of as necessarily incoherent and contradictory, whatever tensions there may well be. Rather, it is this combination of agendas, pragmatically conceived, that is illustrative of the government's third-way politics.

New Labour and the Family: Prescriptive Conservatism?

New Labour, as we have argued, has drawn accusations of 'prescriptive conservatism'. But what, both rhetorically and in public policy, does New Labour have to say about the current state of the family? What is the Labour government trying to address and how? Is New Labour's approach a prescriptive one demanding adherence to particular conservative forms of family? Our argument is that New Labour has neither purely conservative nor solely progressive intentions for the family. It is neither simply prescriptive nor completely liberal. There is more than one agenda present in its proposals for the family. This does give rise to tensions in policy-making – for example, on parental leave. But it is not one that is completely contradictory.

New Labour's social conservatism on the family links the changing structure of the family with welfare dependency and what might be termed the problem of social order. Part of New Labour, especially that part close to ethical socialists such as Norman Dennis and A. H. Halsey, views the 'break-up' of the family with alarm (e.g., see Dennis 1993; Field 1996; see also Deacon and Mann 1997 and 1999 on the revival of interest in the relationship between welfare and behaviour on the Centre-Left). As we suggested earlier, New Labour's critique of the 'Old Left' – in particular, the social liberalism of the post-1960s Left – included an attack on the value of choice within the family, especially regarding parental responsibilities. Some Labour modernizers share with the neo-conservative wing of the New Right a concern that the decline in the 'traditional family' has contributed to greater welfare dependency, especially among young single mothers, and a wider problem of social order. Blair argues that the reassertion of strong collective values in the community requires the family (Blair 1996a and 1996b). Part of the New Labour discourse, then, in particular that associated with social exclusion and law and order, makes causal connections between changing family forms, growing welfare dependency, social exclusion, the decline in shared moral values, and the rising tide of criminal and anti-social behaviour.

As a consequence, New Labour appears to favour the 'traditional family' and insists that parents must accept the duties and responsibilities that come with parenthood – and that these override the principle of choice. Indeed, the 1999 Crime and Disorder Act provides the courts with parenting and child safety orders – with penalties attached – to enforce such duties and responsibilities. While a caveat is added that single parents or non-traditional couples can do a perfectly good job, the ideologically conservative side to New Labour supports the married two-parent family as the best environment in which to bring up children: work can be shared, children get more attention, the family income can be higher, children have role models of both sexes, and so on. Marriage is preferable to cohabitation, mostly because marriages seem to last longer and involve more commitment. Boys need fathers as role models; and without fathers they are liable to turnout to be irresponsible themselves, more likely to commit crime and to father children in whose parenting they themselves will not participate. Teenage pregnancies, usually leading to single-parent motherhood, are undesirable and relatively high in Britain (see, for example, Ministerial Group on the Family 1998, especially chapters 3 and 4; Social Exclusion Unit 1999).

This commitment to the 'traditional family' can certainly be detected in the rhetoric of New Labour – and it is no less important for being rhetorical (see Fairclough 2000). Labour modernizers have been engaged in a cultural politics that is both about discrediting the New Left and about sending messages to society about what is considered good and bad behaviour. For this reason, New Labour rhetoric has a symbolic, psychological and behavioural significance that gives cultural support to some sorts of families and can demoralize those in others who feel alienated from, and unsupported by, the government. Whatever the actual policies, and whatever other progressive agendas there are in Labour discourse, there is a cultural politics going on, of validation and disapproval. New Labour's often conservative rhetoric on the family is significant to the extent of constructing particular sorts of preferred subjects in society and demonizing others, and, in doing so, of promoting particular kinds of behaviour.

It is also the case that some Labour government *policies* are socially conservative. For example, a number of policies are about giving advice and support to protect marriage as a preferred form of family relationship. The government green paper *Supporting Families* proposes measures to improve couples' decision-making about getting married, and to enhance services which prevent marriage breakdown. Proposals include: an increased role for registrars in marriage guidance; a statement of the rights and responsibilities of marriage; a longer 'cooling off' period between giving notice of marriage and the ceremony; the restructuring of marriage counselling to place greater stress on saving marriages; and funding for marriage advice centres. One of the government's leading social conservatives, the former secretary of state for education and employment David Blunkett, insisted that marriage be taught in schools as part of sex education: 'pupils should be taught the importance of marriage, family life, love and stable relationships in bringing up children' – although Blunkett then added: 'the [government] guidance will also make clear that it is not the job of teachers to promote a particular sexual orientation' (Department for Education and Employment press release 046/00 February 2000). And while there are proposals to make divorce fairer, including tackling the pension rights of women, and to support cohabiting couples, there is a definite emphasis on 'strengthening marriage', as the relevant chapter in the green paper is titled. Marriage is set up as a more desirable form of family and one that it is worth giving special effort to protecting and shoring up.

For some critics these policies amount to an attack on, and a discouragement to, full-time lone parenting (S. Smith 1999). Such a view gained ground with the government's decision in 1997 to implement the previous Conservative government's reductions to lone-parent benefits. Labour's argument that its welfare-to-work programme would cover lone parents was taken by some as evidence not of the government's progressive intentions – women should be supported in the labour market – but of its 'prescriptive conservatism': New Labour had bought the New Right argument that lone parenthood and welfare dependency went hand in hand. Such critics argue that lone parents should not be put under pressure to find work but should be supported unconditionally by the state because of the contribution their childcaring work makes towards society (S. Smith 1999) – a policy rationale central to continental European welfare regimes, such as that in France. Certainly the reduction in the lone parent supplement lowers the income of lone parents while in full-time parenting. Doubts have also been raised about whether Labour's fiscal strategy to 'make work pay' benefits lone parents and other carers (Gray 2001). This may put pressure on lone parents to return to work earlier than they had intended, and it may provide a disincentive to becoming a lone parent in the first place – assuming that choosing to be a lone parent is a rational economic decision. Moreover, the New Deal for Lone Parents tries to encourage lone parents back into the labour market, something not directed at dependent childcaring parents in couples (i.e., partners or spouses not in paid work). However, the 2001 queen's speech included a new Welfare Reform Bill that will require women whose partners are unemployed to attend a job interview or face a loss of benefits.

The government's handling of the lone-parents issue has not helped its progressive supporters. New Labour's message appears to be: don't become a lone parent and, if you do, start supporting yourself as soon as possible. New Labour's agenda on women's independence – in particular, women's growing participation in the labour market – has tended, as a result, to get lost. This supports the right of women to make informed choices about balancing work, family life and childcare and seeks to expand the range of opportunities women, especially those with children, have in finding work. While the Labour government has clearly given priority to welfare to work – individuals should if at all possible support themselves through paid employment – the rules for claiming welfare for lone parents under the New Deal for Lone Parents, for example, are more relaxed than those for other groups of claimants. Under the social security minister Alistair Darling, the government has extended the requirement to attend a job search interview to lone parents. But the tougher welfare regime applicable to individuals – especially 18- to 24-year-olds – without dependent children does not apply to lone parents; and it is certainly less punitive than the welfare state in the USA.

It is this strand to New Labour that argues that welfare reform is necessary because the post-war welfare settlement was based on assumptions of work and family life that no longer hold: the majority of women are in paid employment; and family life exists in a variety of diverse and changing forms (see Commission on Social Justice 1994). This progressive strand comes out clearly in chapters 2 and 3 of the government's 1998 green paper on the family. The latter is in part pragmatic about these social changes: families now come in all shapes and sizes, and it is the job of public policy to deal with this diversity. There is also in part a positive celebration of the changing face of the family and the role of women in the labour market. Whether New Labour is progressive enough on the issue of balancing work and family – on parental leave, for example – is another issue. As we shall see later, Labour's welfare reforms have drawn the accusation that the government is much more interested in paid employment than in issues such as unpaid childcare in the home. Nevertheless, the fact that the government is supporting women with children in the labour market – for example, through measures in its national childcare strategy to provide free nursery places for three- and four-year-olds and a childcare allowance in the working families' tax credit (see McLaughlin, Trewsdale and McCay 2001) – is evidence of a liberal, progressive agenda in New Labour. Indeed, it is part of the agenda that New Labour has inherited from the progressive 'Old Left'.

Taken as a whole, *Supporting Families* – note: families, *not* the family – has a largely pragmatic view on the variety of forms that the modern family takes: what works should be supported, and in practice most families get by. Many of New Labour's proposals on the family in *Supporting Families* are relevant to a range of family forms and not just to the 'traditional family'. Many of the government's policies are about providing support in the form of finance, services and advice to families as they exist, whatever form they take. The new National Family and Parenting Institute, for instance, will provide services for all forms of family and parenting, as would health visitors in a new expanded role, the 'Sure Start' programme, and the childcare tax credits as part of the government's national childcare strategy. These policies are all aimed at families whether based on marriage or biological parenthood or not. Indeed, the home secretary, Jack Straw (often singled out as another of the government's leading social conservatives), when opening the new National Family and Parenting Institute, cautioned against the myth of the golden age of married family life: 'We need to remind ourselves of that so we don't get into a panic that in our society the foundations of the family are dissolving' (Frean 1999).

It is not only Chancellor Gordon Brown's budgets that have marked a significant shift away from public policy support for married couples with abolition of the married couples' allowance; Treasury policy has seen a shift of resources from childless families to families with dependent children with the increase to child benefit payable to all families with children, whatever their marital status. Children and child poverty are higher than marriage on the government's fiscal agenda. In the autumn of 1999, it was announced that the Lord Chancellor and the Law Commission were to review the law to give equal rights for cohabiting, including gay, couples (although plans to introduce 'no fault' divorces within eighteen months have been scrapped by the Lord Chancellor for administrative and cost reasons).

Indeed, it is this range of policy reforms by the Labour government that have drawn fire from what Jane Millar calls the 'family reactionaries' (Millar 1998). Viewed from a conservative perspective, whether on the Left or Right, the Labour government's family policies taken as a whole look dangerously liberal and progressive. Melanie Phillips argues that social policy must privilege marriage and the traditional family and not deal simply with the consequences of family breakdown. For Phillips, the 'problem' of lone parenting is not primarily an economic one that can be solved by making lone parents more economically self-sufficient – through welfare to work, for example. Rather, lone parenting is a moral and cultural issue that requires public policy to make judgements about different types of family units (Phillips 1999). Patricia Morgan is equally damning of the Labour government's family policy, arguing that *Supporting Families* undermines rather than supports the traditional family. Morgan claims that the government's policies, such as the abolition of the married couples' allowance, weakens the legal and financial status of the family. For Morgan, the tax and benefit system should give special privilege to one-earner married couples; and the Conservative Party is pledged to restoring the fiscal advantages of marriage (Morgan 1999; Hague 1999c; Webster 2001).

None of this marks New Labour out as a government in the grip of an unyielding conservative agenda. Interestingly, some responses to the government's family policy have put the question of family form to one side and focused instead on the effectiveness of many of the proposals and the lack of evidence in support of its plans. Questions have been raised about the effectiveness of telephone hot-lines for parents, the proposed expanded role for heath visitors, the changes to marriage notice periods, baby-naming ceremonies and pre-nuptial agreements. Concerns have also been raised that the government's commitment to closer family relations will be undermined by its childcare tax credit, which can only be claimed by parents using formal childcare arrangements.

Reading *Supporting Families*, as well as looking across the broad range of policies affecting the family, it is possible to identify different agendas in play – and also, very often, the sponsoring government department of each chapter: crudely put, where the Department of Education and Employment tends to emphasize work, the Home Office supports marriage and the family. Critics, such as Phillips and Morgan, who claim that the government's proposals will undermine marriage, will find evidence to support their view, as will those who suggest that the green paper puts too much emphasis on marriage as the most desirable family form (Barlow and Duncan 2001; Home Office 1999). The charge of 'prescriptive conservatism' levelled against New Labour misses the mark because support for the 'traditional family' by the government competes with, and is tempered by, a more progressive family-policy agenda that recognizes the diversity of contemporary family forms and that fits more comfortably with the social and cultural changes which have taken place in gender relations over the past decades. This agenda is interventionist but it is also pragmatic; and it is less prescriptive and more liberal than many critics give it credit for (see Harding 1999).

However, the government's commitment to supporting women in the labour market has drawn the criticism that New Labour is more interested in paid work – and in policy agendas on social exclusion limited to getting paid work – than unpaid work in the home. It is to this debate that we shall now turn.

Work and the Family: Two Communities in Conflict?

One central criticism of New Labour's family policy, repeated in a number of different forms, is that it comes into conflict with its welfare-to-work programme; and that paid work in the labour market is given precedence over unpaid work in the home. Ruth Levitas argues that the Left's traditional egalitarian agenda, what she calls RED (the redistributive discourse), has given way in New Labour thinking to a socially integrationist discourse (SID) and a moral underclass discourse (MUD) (Levitas 1998; see also Lister 1999 and 2000a; Hughes and Little 1999). SID's community, Levitas argues, is to be secured through the inclusion of a poor underclass breaking out of welfare dependency through paid work. Central to SID are the government's welfare-to-work programmes, including the New Deal for Lone Parents. There is also in New Labour elements of a discourse, Levitas suggests, that believes that there is a poor underclass, encouraged by the benefits system to remain dependent on welfare and with a lack of responsibility or adherence to society's moral values – the MUD discourse. MUD implies public policies that might promote a moral rejuvenation beyond simply helping individuals into paid work. This moral rejuvenation is seen as coming through strong families, who inculcate values, and provide role models and supportive stable underpinnings for later life. The MUD discourse implies that many social problems, such as crime, drug-taking, truancy, teenage parenthood and so on, are the result, at least in part, of a lack of community integration through the family. The solution is strong families, preferably biological two-parent families bound by marriage.

The three discourses – RED, SID and MUD – interplay to different degrees in New Labour and overlap with one another. But Levitas argues that the Labour government's emphasis on inclusion through paid work (SID) causes problems for the government's family policy. The latter, to some extent, stresses strong families as a basis for the moral inclusion of an underclass of teenage parents, absent fathers and criminals who at present are irresponsible and happy to live off benefits (MUD). But how, the government's critics ask, can the strong families of MUD be built if most of the emphasis in the government's social policies is on the paid work of SID rather than the unpaid labour of parenting – at the very least without falling back on the 'traditional family' where women do not work? Can the government really support a community based on work *and* one based on the family?

We agree that there are tensions between the Labour government's commitment to both work and the family. Increasing women's participation in the labour force would obviously put pressures on families with children – especially if women continued to do the bulk of domestic work. And there is another tension between the government's commitment to flexible labour markets, which requires fewer obligations on business, and 'family-friendly' employment practices, which require more. Moreover, is Labour so work-centred that it fails to recognize the value of the family and unpaid parenting? This accusation, we suggest, can go too far, at the very least when applied *beyond* lone parents.

In the rest of this chapter we suggest that the tensions in government policy can be exaggerated and that New Labour's commitment to work and the family can offer a plausible and coherent policy agenda. This third-way agenda draws on and mixes traditional ideological alternatives while not necessarily favouring one exclusively over the other. Such a pragmatic combination of agendas should not automatically be seen as incoherent and contradictory, whatever tensions there might be.

Levitas argues that, by stressing the importance of paid work, the dominant communitarianism undermines the importance of the unpaid work that props up the modern family. The emphasis on paid work as the route to the government's overriding objective of social inclusion devalues the unpaid work that they claim to value. Seeing paid work as the route to inclusion fails to provide routes for inclusion for unpaid workers and carers. For Levitas:

there is a profound contradiction between treating paid work as the defining factor in social inclusion, and recognising the value of unpaid work. How can Labour's claims to recognise the value of unpaid work be reconciled with their insistence on inclusion through paid work? (Levitas 1998, 145)

So, if New Labour says the priority is inclusion through paid work, can it really care that much about unpaid parenting as it claims to? Also:

non-market activities are looked at from a perspective which privileges paid work so that although unpaid work is visible, it is not consistently interpreted as work, or valorised as economic activity... This establishes a hierarchy of forms of work: the unpaid activity or 'responsibility' of parenting, the unpaid activity of volunteering, and paid work, with only the last constituting real work and delivering real social inclusion. (ibid., 146–7)

So something is recognized as work only if it is paid or economically useful, and parenting, therefore, goes unrecognized.

Ruth Lister (2000a, 12–13) has made similar points to Levitas. She argues that, seen through a gendered perspective, this clash between paid work and unpaid parenting can be understood as a preference by the Labour government for a universal breadwinner model, in which women become citizens in a man's world, rather than a universal caregiver model, in which men take on more of the unpaid parenting work currently done disproportionately by women (see also Lewis 1998, 12–13; Rake 2001). Concerns have also been raised that the effect of the working families' tax credit will not give women greater independence but will create incentives for second earners, mostly women, to leave work, thus reinstating the male breadwinner model (see Land 1999, drawing on work by the Institute of Fiscal Studies).

Jane Lewis (1998) argues that lone mothers are always treated in social policy as *either* mothers *or* paid workers. In the late 1980s they were treated as mothers and dealt with through the Child Support Act, which tried to get support for them, as mothers, from absent fathers. However, when this act failed, attention shifted back to lone parents as paid workers. They were seen as having an obligation at least to seek advice on getting back into work, facilitated by support from the state in the form of childcare and attempts to improve flexible employment. This is a shift that Labour has continued and which, Lewis argues, ignores the value of lone mothers' childcaring as work – a shift in policy that parallels welfare reforms in the USA on families with dependent children.

One of the assumptions behind these criticisms has to be that, if parents are to do more paid work, then unpaid parenting will be negatively affected. On the surface this seems to make sense. The more time and energy is devoted to paid work, the less is left for parenting, which means that the time left for parenting will be diminished in quality because the working parent will return home tired and distracted, with not only childcare but also all the domestic labour to do. Levitas argues explicitly that the paid work emphasis of the Labour government will just leave mothers with a double burden, simply adding on paid work to their already existing unpaid labour and, presumably, having a negative effect on their capacity to do the latter well. So there is a question here not just of valorization, but of the practical consequences of more women going out to work.

Conflict or Complementarity?

But does the emphasis on the inclusive, SID-based communitarianism really have to be so antagonistic to, and mutually exclusive of, unpaid parenting? There *is* a tension between the priority given to paid work, on the one hand, and unpaid parenting, on the other; between the communitarianism of inclusion through work and the moral communitarianism of strengthening family life. However, this does not necessarily lead to contradictions and antagonisms between the two in the way some critics seem to suggest. The two are not necessarily mutually exclusive. In fact, it is possible to see some ways in which they could positively benefit one another. The picture might be more rounded than the critics have painted. There may be more opportunities in Labour's family policies than critics suggest.

One of Levitas's criticisms, to recap, is that economic inclusion is the priority of the government and that paid work is valued as the route to inclusion. Unpaid parenting, as such, is devalued. However, this criticism does not work, because New Labour clearly does value unpaid work, but in terms which are not always economic and which focus on the inclusion of the child as much as the parent. Government policy, as we have seen, supports and values parenting and the family: as the basis for the development of individual and shared moral values; as a source of security and stability; and as a major contributor to children's opportunities in life. Lack of economic opportunities and social exclusion – for both parents *and* children – are linked by the government to problems of parenting and family effectiveness. Labour argues that family life is a key part of the explanation for why some people become part of an excluded underclass and for a range of social problems such as teenage parenthood, crime and poor educational attainment. Unpaid parenting, as such, is valued in non-economic terms to do with morality, responsibility, security and children's opportunities. And it is valued for the inclusion of the child as much as the parent.

In short, a focus on the lack of economic valorization of parenting fails to give recognition to the moral and cultural weight that Blair and his colleagues put on the family and its importance for the economic opportunities of children. The Labour government has advanced quite effectively a policy agenda on the family that addresses concerns about women and the labour market *and* the effectiveness of families in supporting and bringing up children. The weight given by critics to *economic* valorization leads to insufficient attention to the concerns with *moral* valorization, and the focus on *parenting* as a non-route for inclusion fails to bring out Labour's concerns for the family's functions in inclusion of *children*.

Furthermore, paid work can have practical benefits for parenting. For some, full-time childcare, for all its joys, can also be tiring, boring and unfulfilling. The hours are long and demanding and can leave little space or energy for the fulfilment of other capacities and needs, such as intellectual ones. As such, full-time childcare can make the parent less happy and fulfilled and, possibly, consequently, a worse parent. The opportunity to find periods away from childcare and to develop other capacities can allow for better parenthood. Of course this is by no means the case for all parents, but it can be for many. Furthermore, paid work brings in money and can provide children with the role model of a parent with paid-work status, both of which may be beneficial for the family and the child. So paid work may not necessarily clash with unpaid parenting. In fact there are some quite strong reasons to believe that it can enhance it, through providing resources, a working role model, and a more rounded, happier parent.

As Lister (1999) acknowledges, measures, especially on childcare, which give women the chance to get into paid work should not be dismissed. Increased possibilities for paid work for parents are in themselves to be welcomed. Furthermore, if women are to be able to get into paid work with the help of government, then that is one more step towards men being in a better position to play more of a parenting role.

This is not to say that increased male parenting is a top priority for Labour. There is a clear tension in the government's approaches towards flexible labour markets and light regulation of business and 'family-friendly' employment policies, such as paternal leave and the working time directive (see Department of Trade and Industry 1998; Employment Relations Act 1999; Byers 1999; Labour Party 2001). These family-friendly policies are, as Land (1999) suggests, 'modest'; and there have been calls by, among others, Harriet Harman to extend the support given to working mothers to provide them with greater choice, including the right to go back to work part time, and for working parents to be lent financial support to stay home and look after a child in the first three years of its life (Harman 1999; Childcare Commission 2001). Certainly more progress towards a culture that positively values male parenting is needed. There is at least some recognition by the government of the problems and some potential in its proposals for facilitating changes in family roles (see the government's green paper on work and parenting: Department of Trade and Industry 2000). Indeed, in the budget of March 2001 Gordon Brown announced a rise in statutory maternity pay and an increase in its length, as well as the introduction of two weeks' paternity leave from 2003.

Conclusion

So New Labour's approach to the family is a reaction to a number of factors: from social change in the family to perceived weaknesses in the family policy, or lack of it, of Thatcherism and social democracy. The third way draws on different discourses: from post-traditionalist, to social-integrationist to social moralist. And it is clear that the Labour government's policies on work and the family encompass different ideological and policy agendas: social conservatism on the family; inclusion and opportunities; a desire to cut the welfare bill and welfare dependency; and a progressive view on women's employment opportunities, for example. These varying influences are evident in differences between the third ways of figures such as Blair and Giddens and in the diversity of ambitions in Labour's own proposals, from the strengthening of marriage and the traditional family to more neutral support and services for all sorts of parenting and family forms.

A key problem is the extent to which Labour's emphasis on inclusion through paid work devalues family life and the committed parenting it wishes to promote. While there are real tensions here between the communitarianism of inclusion and that of the family, these two communitarianisms can also co-exist and need not undermine each other. In fact there are ways in which they could potentially be mutually supportive. The debate, we argue, should keep a balanced sense of the possibilities and opportunities in the Labour government's family policies.

Conclusion:
After Thatcherism: Blairism

After Thatcherism

What came after Thatcherism: more of the same or something different? Certainly John Major's Conservative government in the 1990s extended the Thatcherite legacy, especially into the public services, with more market-led reforms to health, education and the civil service. Major's style of government may have differed from Margaret Thatcher's, but his administration was in some ways just as radical. For Tony Blair, just as for John Smith and Neil Kinnock before him, the reform of the Labour Party was always going to be overshadowed by the Thatcher legacy, just as much as by Labour's own failure in government in the 1970s.

In our last book (Driver and Martell 1998) we argued that New Labour is 'post-Thatcherite': it is what it is partly because it came after Thatcherism. The ideological ground broken by radical Tory governments in the 1980s and 1990s helped to create a new political landscape. The Conservatives, especially after 1983, were confident in their own ideas and willing to tackle entrenched vested interests to put those ideas into practice. For much of the 1980s and 1990s, Thatcherism was hegemonic. Not that the public believed every line of Mrs Thatcher's. Public-attitude surveys have consistently shown how untouched the public are by many of the ideas of Thatcherism. Rather, Thatcherism was hegemonic in the sense that its ideas shaped the political debate and the policy-making process. After Thatcherism, no politician or any political party that had any ambition to power could ignore those core elements of Thatcherism: the fight against inflation and trade-union power, competition, the market and the size and role of the state. These helped to define Thatcherism – and came to define the 'modernization' of the Labour Party from Kinnock to Blair.

No doubt the reform of the Labour Party in the 1980s and 1990s would have happened anyway. And no doubt some of the ideological and policy turns taken since 1987 would have happened, Thatcherism or no Thatcherism. Labour, like other European social democratic parties, would have to some degree embraced the market and the virtues of sound money and come to terms with the forces of globalization and social change. Indeed, the British Labour Party was clearly behind the rest of Europe on these questions in the 1980s, while it rather overtook them in the 1990s. New Labour may have looked in Britain as being in the vanguard of a new social democracy, but that is not how it was viewed on the continent in the 1980s.

There is something different about the British experience. As we argued in chapter 4, the influence of different models of political economy and national institutions and cultures on the shape of social democratic politics across Europe should not be underestimated. Unlike most other European social democratic parties, the British Labour Party spent most of the 1980s in opposition to a radical conservative government. This was not a traditional conservative government, such as Helmut Kohl's Christian Democratic administration in Germany, but a government committed to a radical agenda of market-led reforms to the private and public sectors. This opposition shaped not only the reform of the Labour Party, but also the legacy Labour inherited when it came to power in 1997. In many respects, the parallels with the Democratic Party in the USA are closer than with social democracy in Europe.

All of this leaves open the question of how Labour was affected by Thatcherism. One argument, as we have seen, perceives New Labour as the culmination of an accommodation with Thatcherism started by Neil Kinnock as leader in the 1980s. This view sees that after Thatcherism is more of the same. The Blair government is little more than a pale imitation of the real thing. Others argue that, in the political battle against Thatcherism, Labour also won the ideological war. What emerged from the 'wilderness years' of opposition wasn't Thatcherism Mark 2 but a renewed and modernized form of social democracy ready to advance the cause of progressive politics in the twenty-first century.

There is something in both these arguments – and one does not necessarily exclude the other. If accommodating itself to Thatcherism means that the Labour Party accepted some of the key Conservative reforms – anti-inflationary economic policy, labour-market reforms, privatization – then Labour did just that. New Labour was not about to take public policy back to a time before Thatcherism. To an important degree, after Thatcherism is indeed more Thatcherism. Labour's fiscal and monetary reforms codify many Thatcherite themes; its welfare reforms extend the work-orientated policies of the Conservatives; and private-sector involvement in the provision of public services continued. There is, then, the basis for a new political consensus.

But we have some doubts about the Thatcherism Mark 2 thesis. On closer inspection, the new consensus falls apart. Many aspects of Labour's first term in government are quite un-Thatcherite. The most obvious example is the Blair government's programme on constitutional reform. This programme has been weakened by the continuing powers of central government, especially the Treasury, just as Labour's reforms to health and education are marked by the heavy hand of Whitehall. But Labour's constitutional reforms derive from a liberal pluralist tradition little in evidence during the Thatcher years. Furthermore, the Labour government's political economy may be pro-market, but its interventions such as the minimum wage and the New Deal offer a more progressive social democratic side to the Blair government. Chancellor Gordon Brown's 'prudence' may echo Thatcherism, but his 'purpose' – increased spending on the public services and modest redistributions to support social inclusion and to end child and pensioner poverty – does not.

What is Blairism?

What then is Blairism? Part of the problem in answering the question lies with the modernizers themselves, who, in attempting to distance themselves from Old Labour (usually defined as the worst aspects of post-war Labour governments) and the New Right (the worst aspects of Conservative governments in the 1980s and 1990s), have defined New Labour in negative terms. New Labour is neither Old Labour, nor the New Right. This attempt to articulate a 'third way', as we saw in chapter 3, creates all kinds of problems, not least exactly what 'Old Labour' and 'New Right' stand for. The use of concepts such as 'community' and 'social exclusion', and arguments about social justice and economic efficiency, have been useful in setting out some of the broad themes of Blairism. But the more positive attempts to define New Labour – 'social-ism', 'stakeholding' – have been vague and short-lived. The 'third way' itself never caught the public imagination.

Like Thatcherism, New Labour – and Blairism – is a political composite. There is a plurality of New Labours just, as we saw in chapter 3, there is a plurality of third ways. Some parts of this composite are more Thatcherite, others more progressive liberal and social democratic. The 'third way' was the most obvious attempt to bring coherence to this political composite. Its failure – or at least its failing lustre – was not a failure of the practice of fashioning compromises between competing political goals and values. In many respects, the Blair government proved highly successful in creating coherent policy narratives such as that around work, welfare and social exclusion. In this manner, the third way worked. But the problem with the third way stemmed not from its practice but from its theoretical hubris. It was hailed as a radical alternative to the discredited political ideologues of Left and Right. But it was nothing of the kind. Blair's third way was another episode of middle-way politics – and no worse for it for that.

So, if the Blairist third way is a middle way, what kind of middle way is it? The following features of Labour's first term help to define Blairism.

- Inflation matters, competition is good, high taxes undermine incentives and the financial books should balance.
- Work is better than welfare: it promotes social inclusion, it increases the income of the poor and it encourages independence.
- Collective public services such as health and education should be supported: they promote social justice and more equal opportunities, especially for those with least in society, and help to prevent the many problems associated with social exclusion.
- Money isn't everything: the public sector needs reforming.
- Delivery is all: it doesn't really matter who provides public services so long as they are delivered efficiently, to high standards, and are available free to all.
- Constitutional reform strengthens the United Kingdom.
- Britain should be an active player on the European and world stage, but the degree of European integration is limited by national interests.

Many of these features of Blairism are of course contested. Conservatives argue that the Blair government has undermined incentives for business, made the tax and benefit system too complex, spun a web of initiatives around the work of public-sector professionals, undermined the constitutional glue of the United Kingdom and failed to defend British interests in Europe. By contrast, radicals claim that Labour cares more about business than workers, that the welfare state is being eroded by privatization, that the government has failed to address the deep inequalities across British society, that its constitutional reforms are timid and piecemeal and that it has failed to take a lead on further European integration. And everyone from the prime minister down seems agreed that Labour has yet to deliver significantly better public services.

Do these features add up to a government of the Left? Certainly many reflect traditional social democratic and social liberal concerns: poverty, social justice, and the provision of collective public services in promoting opportunities and supporting individual freedom. Allied to these, however, are features that today are more commonly associated with the Right: fiscal and monetary conservatism; the positive value of free markets and low taxes; the priority accorded to wealth creation over equality of outcome; and the emphasis on managerial reforms to the public sector. In the end, the Labour government 1997–2001 – and Blairism – is defined not by any one of these but by the combination of these features in public policy.

Tony Blair's line has been that the Labour Party had to 'modernize or die'. Globalization, new technology and new social relations rendered Old Labour defunct. But did Labour have to modernize in quite the way it has? Blairism has the propensity to claim the social changes underlying the 'new politics' are as irrefutable as are the compelling political changes that have to be made in response. The 'third way' is not a choice but a sociological necessity. But the impact of globalization on government competences, the social and economic implications of the new information and communication technologies, the changes to household structures are, as we have seen, open to dispute. They are not social facts free from empirical dispute or value systems. And even where such facts are agreed, such as the pattern of world trade or new family structures, there remain deep divisions about the political and policy responses to such changes.

The strength of Blairism is its willingness to confront new times: the world is changing and political ideologies need to keep pace; what worked yesterday may not work today. Its weakness, however, has been to treat these changing times as a given: as something that is not open to interpretation and to a variety of policy responses contingent on political choices.

The Political Impact of Blairism

What has been the political impact of Blairism and what are likely to be the major challenges for Labour in its second term? Blairism has clearly breathed life into the Labour Party, which has become an election-winning machine. Three terms is not beyond the limit of credulity. Whether it has done the same for social democracy is open to dispute. Does Blairism offer a new model for social democracy or stretch to the very limits what might be classed as social democracy? The answer depends in large part on what you think social democracy is and what it can and should achieve. Certainly, in comparison with the Conservative governments of Margaret Thatcher and John Major, the Blair government does offer something different. But does it offer something different as far as social democracy is concerned to these administrations of the Right? For those who believe that governments of the Left should intervene far more substantially in the (global) market economy to control private enterprise, provide public services and redistribute resources to make society more equal, then Blairism is at best marginally social democratic. For those who believe that, given the constraints and opportunities offered by a market economy, the Blair government has supported (reformed) collective public services and targeted resources on those most in need, then the Blair government is reworking social democracy.

In terms of European social democracy a pattern of political development is well established. Since the 1980s, in the face of globalization, European social democratic parties have edged within the constraints of national traditions towards economic liberalization and welfare reform. New Labour is part of this trend. While Tony Blair has appeared a dominant figure (in the British media at least) within European social democracy, this may reflect more his domestic political success and the relative weight of Britain within European debates than any political hegemony. As such the direct political impact of Blairism on European social democracy is proving to be limited.

Back in Britain, the biggest loser of the success of Blairism is the Conservative Party. Two straight landslide defeats – if that were not enough – does not do justice to the impact of New Labour on the Conservatives. Blairism has stolen Thatcherism's thunder. It has snatched the banner of economic competence. It has relegitimized active government. It has delivered more resources to the public services – if not yet better public services. Its song sheet – community, social inclusion – chimes with popular sentiments – and conservative ones too. The Labour Party has come in from the cold and captured the all-important middle ground of politics. It shows no signs of giving it up.

Where do the Conservatives go? Under William Hague, the Tory party veered from 'compassionate conservatism' to 'common sense conservatism' to 'saving the pound'. The voters were hardly troubled. Inside the party, the 'mods' and 'rockers' fought over whether the party should embrace contemporary society and modernize or reassert traditional values in the face of new times. After Hague's resignation in the aftermath of the Tories' 2001 defeat, Michael Portillo carried the modernizers' standard into the party's leadership election. Ian Duncan Smith emerged with the traditionalist banner. And Ken Clarke was left holding the empty glasses – and nursing a political hangover – as he and Portillo were defeated by the ex-army officer from the Right. In victory, Duncan Smith leads a party divided over Europe and over modern times. Margaret Thatcher casts a deep shadow over the Conservatives. Her legacy is picked over and fought over. In many respects, however, the greatest challenge the Tories face is not after Thatcherism but after Blairism. In opposition, the Conservative Party has shown some signs of its Disraelian political nous. Hague drew a line under the party's opposition to devolution. Portillo, as shadow chancellor under Hague, completed an elegant U-turn on the minimum wage and an independent Bank of England. But still the Conservatives got themselves into a mess over taxing and spending. Like the Labour Party in opposition, the Conservatives will have to wait for the Blair government to slip up. But they will also have to come up with convincing arguments about how to improve funding and standards in the public services.

An enduring political legacy of Blairism is the British constitution. The devolution settlement challenges the centralist culture of British government and politics. It has introduced written constitutions for Scotland, Wales and Northern Ireland. Proportional representation and coalition politics has become a fact of political life in many parts of the United Kingdom. Moreover, the Human Rights Act creates, *de facto*, a legally entrenched bill of rights. It empowers the judiciary and brings into question the sovereignty of parliament. Labour's constitutional reforms have created their own political momentum. Devolved government and politics and the human-rights culture are only now bedding down and look set to deepen over the next decade. The irony is that the Blair government has not always looked comfortable with constitutional reform and its consequences. In many respects, the party's commitments to reform were formed under John Smith. Some of Labour's reforms have been lacklustre, even regressive – to parliament, to freedom of information – and the Blair style of government is notable for its 'presidentialism'. But the genie of constitutional reform has been let out of its bottle. It shows no sign of going back in. The test not just for Labour but for all parties is the decline of interest in government and politics among the electorate. The record low turnout in the 2001 general election weakens the credibility of government and opposition alike. This may of course be a temporary blip. But unless this is addressed seriously, we face the prospect of not too much politics but too little.

The second term: can Labour deliver?

Tony Blair made the 2001 election a vote on the future of the public services. William Hague made it a test on Europe. Labour, it turned out, had more common sense than the Tories. But Hague had a point. The question of Europe remains one of the big unanswered questions of Blairism and Labour's second term. There are genuine divides within New Labour on joining the European single currency and the degree of European integration on such issues as tax harmonization, an EU constitution and a common defence and foreign policy. For a party that promised a more positive engagement with Europe, the Blair government has proved remarkably pragmatic on the European question. It declared itself in favour *in principle* of joining the Euro, but laid down early on the economic tests that would need to be passed before any such membership could proceed. In the end, this 'prepare and decide' strategy is not a million miles away from the Major government's 'wait and see' approach. And we will have to do just that!

At the start of Labour's second term the big domestic test was the funding and reform of public services. On 2001 projections, the money runs out in 2003–4. After that, the chancellor will have to raise taxes or borrowing if current spending is to be maintained. Or services will have to be cut to meet the Treasury's fiscal rules. Labour's first term was by comparison fair-weather sailing – helped by Brown's adroit hand on the tiller. The economy was buoyant and tax takes high. As the economic cycle turns, not only will the chancellor's navigational skills be tested, but so too will Labour's commitment to the public sector.

Brown's 2002 budget, and the comprehensive spending review that followed, signalled the government's second-term intent. In stark contrast to the fiscal strait-jacket after 1997, the chancellor in 2002 set the Labour government on course to increase substantially public spending. Health and education were the big winners: Under Brown's spending plans, the proportion of national income devoted to public spending will rise from 39.8 per cent in 2002–3 to 41.8 per cent in 2005–6. These increases came with the standard New Labour strings – 'modernization' – although Brown rejected alternative forms of health financing, such as insurance, following the recommendations of the review of NHS finance by the banker Derek Wanless. But these increases to public spending also came with a whiff of good old Labour governments: from April 2003, national insurance rates for employers and employees were set to rise by 1 per cent. Gordon Brown may not have broken that New Labour golden rule – 'don't increase income taxes' – but this was sailing pretty close to the fiscal wind.

Brown's Treasury figures assume an underlying growth rate for the British economy of 2.75 per cent per year. These figures make the government's public spending promises prudent over the economic cycle. While a report from the Institute of Economic and Social Research shortly after Brown's 2002 budget suggested that these Treasury predictions were overoptimistic and that the Blair government was heading for a £15 billion fiscal hole – time, in the end, will tell – the big issue is delivery across all public services. Labour will not only have to deliver higher standards of care in the NHS and better results in the nation's classrooms, but it will also have to address those areas of public policy that loomed large on New Labour radars only after it was too late: transport, the environment and rural communities. This will be a huge political test for Blairism, one that the Conservative Party will be praying that it fails.

Bibliography

Albert, M. (1993) *Capitalism against Capitalism*. London: Whurr.

Alibhai-Brown, Y. (1998) Nations under a groove, *Marxism Today*, November/December, 47.

Anderson, P. and Mann, N. (1997) *Safety First: The Making of New Labour*. London: Granta Books.

Anderton, B., Riley, R. and Young, G. (1999) *The New Deal for Young People: Early Findings from the Pathfinder Areas*. Report ref. ESR34, Employment Service/National Institute of Economic and Social Research.

Andrews, L. (1995) New Labour, New England. In M. Perryman (ed.), *The Blair Agenda*, London: Lawrence & Wishart.

van den Anker, C. (2001) Dutch social democracy and the Poldermodel. In L. Martell et al., *Social Democracy*, Basingstoke: Palgrave.

Archibugi, D. and Held, D. (1995) *Cosmopolitan Democracy: An Agenda for a New World Order*. Cambridge: Polity.

Archibugi, D., Held, D. and Köhler, M. (eds) (1998) *Reimagining Political Community: Studies in Cosmopolitan Democracy*. Cambridge: Polity.

Ashdown, P. (2001) *The Ashdown Diaries, Volume 2: 1997–1999*. London: Allen Lane.

Bale, T. (1999) The logic of no alternative? Political scientists, historians and the politics of Labour's past. *British Journal of Politics and International Relations*, 1, 192–204.

Barlow, A. and Duncan, S. (2001) The rationality mistake: New Labour's communitarianism and 'supporting families'. In P. Taylor-Gooby, *Risk, Trust and Welfare*, Basingstoke: Palgrave.

Barnett, A. (1998) All power to the citizens. *Marxism Today*, November/December, 44–6.

Barrett, M. and McIntosh, M. (1982) *The Anti-Social Family*. London: Verso.

Bayley, S. (1999) *Labour Camp*. London: Pan.

Beer, S. (2001) New Labour: old liberalism. In S. White (ed.), *New Labour*, Basingstoke: Palgrave.

Beetham, D. and Weir, S. (1999) Auditing British democracy. *Political Quarterly*, 70, 128–38.

Benn, T. (1981) *Argument for Democracy*. Harmondsworth: Penguin.

Bevir, M. (2000) New Labour: a study in ideology. *British Journal of Politics and International Relations*, 2, 277–301.

Blair, T. (1994) *Speech to the 1994 Labour Party Conference*. London: Labour Party.

Blair, T. (1995a) The rights we enjoy reflect the duties we owe. *The Spectator* Lecture, 22 March.

Blair, T. (1995b) The Mais Lecture, City University, 22 May.

Blair, T. (1995c) *Speech to the 1995 Labour Party Conference*. London: Labour Party.

Blair, T. (1996a) My vision for Britain. In G. Radice, *What Needs to Change: New Visions for Britain*. London: HarperCollins.

Blair, T. (1996b) Speech to Commonwealth Press Union, Cape Town, South Africa, 14 October.

Blair, T. (1996c) *New Britain: My Vision of a Young Country*. London: Fourth Estate.

Blair, T. (1996d) Speech to the Singapore Business Community, 8 January.

Blair, T. (1997a) Speech to the Party of European Socialists' Congress, Malmö, Sweden, 6 June.

Blair, T. (1997b) *Speech to the 1997 Labour Party Conference*. London: Labour Party.

Blair, T. (1998a) Speech to the French National Assembly, 24 March.

Blair, T. (1998b) Speech on Scottish parliament, Strathclyde University, Glasgow, 12 November.

Blair, T. (1998c) *The Third Way: New Politics for the New Century*. London: Fabian Society.

Blair, T. (1999a) *Doctrine of the International Community*. Speech to the Economic Club of Chicago, 22 April. London: Foreign and Commonwealth Office.

Blair, T. (1999b) *Facing the modern challenge: the third way in Britain and South Africa*. Speech in Cape Town, South Africa.

Blair, T. (2001) Speech to the Labour Party Conference.

Blair, T. and Schröder, G. (1999) *Europe: The Third Way – Die Neue Mitte*. London: Labour Party.

Bobbio, N. (1996) *Left and Right: The Significance of a Political Distinction*. Cambridge: Polity.

Bochel, C. and Briggs, J. (2000) Do women make a difference? *Politics*, 20, 63–8.

Boeri, T., Layard, R. and Nickell, S. (2000) *Welfare-to-work and the fight against long-term unemployment*. Report to Prime Ministers Blair and D'Alema. London: London School of Economics.

Bogdanor, V. (1999) Devolution: decentralisation or disintegration? *Political Quarterly*, 70, 185–94.

Bogdanor, V. (2000) Whitehall falls prey to the time and motion men. *The Times*, 12 September.

Boseley, S. and Wintour, P. (1995) Blair backs stable two-parent families. *The Guardian*, 30 March.

Bouvet, L. and Michel, F. (2001) Pluralism and the future of the French left. In S. White (ed.), *New Labour*, Basingstoke: Palgrave.

Brauner, S. and Loprest, P. (1998) *Where Are They Now? What States' Studies of People who Left Welfare Tell Us*. Washington, DC: Urban Institute.

Brown, G. (1997) *The Anthony Crosland Memorial Lecture*. London: Labour Party.

Brown, G. (2000a) This is the time to start building a Greater Britain. *The Times*, 10 January.

Brown, G. (2000b) *The James Mead Memorial Lecture*. London: HM Treasury.

Buller, J. (2001) New Labour's foreign and defence policy: external support structures and domestic policies. In S. Ludlam and M. Smith (eds), *New Labour in Government*, Basingstoke: Macmillan.

Bulmer S. (2000) European policy: fresh start or false dawn? In D. Coates and P. Lawler (eds), *New Labour in Power*, Manchester: Manchester University Press.

Burch, M. and Holliday, I. (1999) The prime minister's and cabinet offices: an executive office in all but name. *Parliamentary Affairs*, 52, 32–45.

Burgess, A. and Ruxton, S. (1996) *Men and their Children: Proposals for Public Policy*. London: Institute for Public Policy Research.

Busch, A. and Manow, P. (2001) The SPD and the Neue Mitte in Germany. In S. White (ed.), *New Labour*, Basingstoke: Palgrave.

Butler, D. and Kavanagh, D. (1997) *The British General Election of 1997*. Basingstoke: Macmillan.

Byers, S. (1999) *Over a million to benefit from new family friendly package for working parents*. Department of Trade and Industry, 4 August [press release].

Cabinet Office (1998) *Bringing Britain Together: A National Strategy for Neighbourhood Renewal*. London: Cabinet Office.

Cabinet Office (2001) *A New Commitment to Neighbourhood Renewal: National Strategy Action Plan*. London: Cabinet Office.

Callinicos, A. (2001) *Against the Third Way: An Anti-Capitalist Critique*. Cambridge: Polity.

Childcare Commission (2001) *Looking to the Future for Children and Families*. London: Childcare Commission.

Childs, S. (2001) Attitudinally feminist? The New Labour women MPs and the substantive representation of women. *Politics*, 21, 178–85.

Clark, A. (1994) *Diaries*. London: Phoenix.

Clark, T., Myck, M. and Smith, Z. (2001) *Fiscal Reforms Affecting Households, 1997–2001*. London: Institute for Fiscal Studies [IFS election briefing note 5].

Clift, B. (2001) New Labour's third way and European social democracy. In S. Ludlam and M. Smith (eds), *New Labour in Government*, Basingstoke: Macmillan.

Coates, D. and Lawler, P. (eds) (2000) *New Labour in Power*. Manchester: Manchester University Press.

Cohen, G. A. (1994) Back to socialist basics. *New Left Review*, 207, 3–16.

Colley, L. (1992) *Britons: Forging the Nation, 1707–1837*. New Haven, CT: Yale University Press.

Commission on Public Private Partnerships (2001) *Building Better Partnerships*. London: Institute for Public Policy Research.

Commission on Social Justice (1994) *Social Justice: Strategies for National Renewal*. London: Vintage.

Cook, R. (1997) *Opening statement by the foreign secretary, Mr Robin Cook, at a press conference on the FCO mission statement*. London: Foreign and Commonwealth Office.

Coote, A. (1999) The helmsman and the cattle prod. In A. Gamble and T. Wright (eds), *The New Social Democracy*, Oxford: Political Quarterly/Blackwell.

Coote, A., Harman, H. and Hewitt, P. (1990) *The Family Way: A New Approach to Policy-Making*. London: Institute for Public Policy Research.

Crouch, C. (2001) A third way in industrial relations. In S. White (ed.), *New Labour*, Basingstoke: Palgrave.

Dahrendorf, R. (1999) Whatever happened to liberty? *New Statesman*, 6 September.

Deacon, A. (2000a) Learning from the US? The influence of American ideas on New Labour thinking on welfare reform. *Policy and Politics*, 28, 5–18.

Deacon, A. (2000b) Same ingredients, different recipes? Comparing the British and American approaches to welfare reform. Paper for APPAM fall research conference, Seattle, Washington, 4 November.

Deacon, A. and Mann, K. (1997) Moralism and modernity: the paradox of New Labour thinking on welfare. *Benefits*, September/October, 2–6.

Deacon, A. and Mann, K. (1999) Agency, modernity and social policy. *Journal of Social Policy*, 28, 413–36.

Dearlove, J. (2000) Globalisation and the study of British politics. *Politics*, 20, 111–18.

De Beus, J. (1999) The politics of consensual well-being: the Dutch left greets the twenty-first century. In G. Kelly (ed.), *The New European Left*, London: Fabian Society.

Deighton, A. (2001) European Union policy. In A. Seldon (ed.), *The Blair Effect*, London: Little, Brown.

Dennis, N. (1993) *Rising Crime and the Dismembered Family*. London: Institute of Economic Affairs.

Department for Education and Employment (1997) *Qualifying for Success.*
Department for Education and Employment (1999) *Learning to Succeed.* Cm 4392.
Department for Education and Employment (2001) *Schools: Building on Success: Raising Standards, Promoting Diversity, Achieving Results.* Cm 5050.
Department of Education and Skills (2001) *Schools Achieving Success.* Cm 5230.
Department of Social Security (1999) *A New Contract for Welfare: The Gateway to Work.* Cm 4102.
Department of Trade and Industry (1998a) *Fairness at Work.* Cm 3968.
Department of Trade and Industry (1998b) *Our Competitive Future: Building the Knowledge Driven Economy.* Cm 4176.
Department of Trade and Industry (2000) *Work & Parents: Competitiveness and Choice.* Cm 5005.
Department of Trade and Industry (2001) *A World Class Competition Regime.* Cm 5233.
Dilnot, A. and Emmerson, C. (2000) Ministers' challenge lies in delivery. *Financial Times*, 19 July.
Dionne, E. J. (1999) Construction boon: it's no accident that the GOP is being rebuilt by its governors. *Washington Post*, 14 March.
Dixon, J. (2001) Health care: modernising the leviathan. *Political Quarterly*, 72, 30–8.
Dodd, P. (1995) *The Battle over Britain.* London: Demos.
Downes, D. and Morgan, R. (1997) Dumping the 'hostages to fortune'? The politics of law and order in post-war Britain. In M. Maguire, R. Morgan and R. Reiner, *The Oxford Handbook of Criminology*, 2nd edn, Oxford: Clarendon Press.
Driver, S. and Martell, L. (1997) New Labour's communitarianisms. *Critical Social Policy*, 17(3), 27–46.
Driver, S. and Martell, L. (1998) *New Labour: Politics after Thatcherism.* Cambridge: Polity.
Driver, S. and Martell, L. (1999) New Labour: culture and economy. In L. Ray and A. Sayer (eds), *Culture and Economy after the Cultural Turn*, London: Sage, 246–69.
Driver, S. and Martell, L. (2000a) New Labour, work and the family. In H. Wilkinson, *The Family Business*, London: Demos.
Driver, S. and Martell, L. (2000b) Left, right and the third way. *Policy & Politics*, 147–61.
Dworkin, R. (2001) Does equality matter? In A. Giddens (ed.), *The Global Third Way Debate*, Cambridge: Polity.
Eagle, M. and Lovenduski, J. (1998) *High Time or High Tide for Labour Women.* London: Fabian Society.
The Economist (1999) Undoing Britain? 6 November, 15.
The Economist (2000a) The New Deal: killer facts. 15 July, 34–7.
The Economist (2000b) Waiting for the new economy. 14 October, 38–43.

Edwards, L., Regan, S. and Brooks, R. (2001) *Age Old Attitudes: Planning for Retirement, Means-Testing, Inheritance and Informal Care*. London: Institute for Public Policy Research.

Ellwood, D. (1998) *Poor Support: Poverty in the American Family*. New York: Basic Books.

Employment Relations Act (1999) London: HM Stationery Office. C26.

Evans, G. (ed.) (1999) *The End of Class Politics? Class Voting in Comparative Context*. Oxford: Oxford University Press.

Evans, G. and Norris, P. (1999) *Critical Elections: British Parties and Voters in Historical Perspective*. London: Sage.

Fairclough, N. (2000) *New Labour, New Language*. London: Routledge.

Field, F. (1995) *Making Welfare Work*. London: Institute of Community Studies.

Field, F. (1996) *Stakeholder Welfare*. London: Institute of Economic Affairs.

Finlayson, A. (1999) Third way theory. *Political Quarterly*, 70, 271–9.

Finn, D. (1999) Job guarantees for the unemployed: lessons from Australian welfare reform. *Journal of Social Policy*, 28, 53–71.

Finn, D. (2001) Welfare to work? New Labour and the unemployed. In S. Savage and R. Atkinson, *Public Policy Under Blair*, Basingstoke: Palgrave.

Foreign and Commonwealth Office (1997) Foreign secretary announces new criteria to ensure responsible arms trade. FCO daily bulletin, 28 July.

Frean, A. (1999) Idyll of family life 'is a myth'. *The Guardian*, 1 December.

Freeden, M. (1999) The ideology of New Labour. *Political Quarterly*, 70, 42–51.

Freedman, L. (2001) Defence. In A. Seldon (ed.), *The Blair Effect*, London: Little, Brown.

Gamble, A. and Kelly, G. (2001) Labour's new economics. In S. Ludlam and M. Smith (eds), *New Labour in Government*, Basingstoke: Macmillan.

Gamble, A. and Wright, T. (1997) Commentary: breakthrough? *Political Quarterly*, 68, 315–16.

Gamble, A. and Wright, T. (eds) (1999) *The New Social Democracy*. Oxford: Political Quarterly/Blackwell.

Gamble, A. and Wright, T. (2001) From Thatcher to Blair. *Political Quarterly*, 72, 1–4.

Garrett, G. (1998) *Partisan Politics in the Global Economy*. Cambridge: Cambridge University Press.

Giddens, A. (1994) *Beyond Left and Right*. Cambridge: Polity.

Giddens, A. (1996) There is a radical centre-ground. *New Statesman*, 29 November.

Giddens, A. (1998) *The Third Way: The Renewal of Social Democracy*. Cambridge: Polity.

Giddens, A. (ed.) (2001) *The Global Third Way Debate*. Cambridge: Polity.

Giddens, A. (2002) *What Next for New Labour?* Cambridge: Polity.

Gilmour, I. (1992) *Dancing with Dogma*. London: Simon & Schuster.

Glennerster, H. (1999) A third way? In H. Dean and R. Woods, *Social Policy Review 11*, Luton: Social Policy Association.

Glyn, A. and Wood, S. (2001) Economic policy under New Labour: how social democratic is the Blair government? *Political Quarterly*, 72, 50–66.

Goodman, A. (2001) *Inequality and Living Standards in Great Britain: Some Facts*. London: Institute for Fiscal Studies [Briefing note 19].

Gould, P. (1999) *The Unfinished Revolution: How Modernisers Saved the Labour Party*. London: Abacus.

Gray, A. (2001) Making work pay: devising the best strategy for lone parents in Britain. *Journal of Social Policy*, 30, 189–207.

Gray, J. (1993) *Beyond the New Right: Markets, Government and the Common Environment*. London: Routledge.

Gray, J. (1996) *After Social Democracy*. London: Demos.

Gray, J. (1997) Speech to the NEXUS/*Guardian* Conference, London, 1 March.

Grover, C. and Stewart, J. (1999) Market workfare: social security, social regulation and competitiveness in the 1990s. *Journal of Social Policy*, 28(1), 73–96.

Gummett, P. (2000) New Labour and defence. In D. Coates and P. Lawler (eds), *New Labour in Power*, Manchester: Manchester University Press.

Hague, W. (1999a) Identity and the British way. Speech to the Centre for Policy Studies, London, 19 January.

Hague, W. (1999b) Strengthening the Union after devolution. Speech to the Centre for Policy Studies, 15 July.

Hague, W. (1999c) *Freedom and the Family*. London: Centre for Policy Studies.

Hall, S. (1988) *The Hard Road to Renewal: Thatcherism and the Crisis of the Left*. London: Verso.

Hall, S. (1994) Son of Margaret. *New Statesman*, 6 October.

Hall, S. (1995) Parties on the verge of a nervous breakdown. *Soundings*, 1, 19–45.

Hall, S. (1998) The great moving nowhere show. *Marxism Today*, November/December, 9–14.

Hall, S. and Jacques, M. (eds) (1989) *New Times: The Changing Face of Politics in the 1990s*. London: Lawrence & Wishart.

Hall, S. and Jacques, M. (1997) Blair: is he the greatest Tory since Thatcher? *The Observer*, 13 April.

Halpern, D. and Mikosz, D. (1998) *The Third Way: Summary of the NEXUS 'Online' Discussion*. London: Nexus.

Harding, L. (1999) Family insecurity and family support: an analysis of Labour's *Supporting Families* 1998. Paper to Social Policy Association Conference, University of Surrey, Roehampton, London, 21 July.

Hargreaves, I. and Christie, I. (eds) (1998) *Tomorrow's Politics: The Third Way and Beyond*. London: Demos.

Harman, H. (1999) 'Keeping mum with New Labour', *The Times*, 13 October.

Harris, M. (1999) New Labour: government and opposition. *Political Quarterly*, 70, 52–61.

Hassan, G. (1995) Blair and the importance of being British. *Renewal* 3(3), 11–20.

Hattersley, R. (1997a) Just one percent on top tax wouldn't hurt. *The Guardian*, 24 June.

Hattersley, R. (1997b) Why I'm no longer loyal to Labour. *The Guardian*, 26 July.

Hay, C. (1994) Labour's Thatcherite revisionism: playing the politics of catch-up. *Political Studies*, 42, 700–7.

Hay, C. (1997) Blaijorism: towards a one-vision polity. *Political Quarterly*, 68, 372–8.

Hay, C. (1999) *The Political Economy of New Labour*. Manchester: Manchester University Press.

Hay, C. (2000) Globalization, social democracy and the persistence of partisan politics: a commentary on Garrett. *Review of International Political Economy*, 7, 138–52.

Hazell, R. (1999) *Constitutional Futures: A History of the Next Ten Years*. Oxford: Oxford University Press.

Hazell, R. (2001) Reforming the constitution. *Political Quarterly*, 72, 39–49.

Hazell, R. and Cornes, R. (1999) Financing devolution: the centre retains control. In R. Hazell, *Constitutional Futures*, Oxford: Oxford University Press.

Heath, A., Jowell, R. and Curtice, J. (eds) (1994) *Labour's Last Chance? The 1992 Election and Beyond*. Aldershot: Dartmouth.

Heffernan, R. (1998) Labour's transformation: a staged process with no single point of origin. *Politics*, 18, 101–6.

Heffernan, R. (2001) *New Labour and Thatcherism: Political Change in Britain*. Basingstoke: Palgrave.

Held, D. (1995) *Democracy and the Global Order*. Cambridge: Polity.

Held, D. (1998) The timid tendency. *Marxism Today*, November/December.

Held, D. (2000) Regulating globalization. *International Sociology*, 15, 394–408.

Held, D., McGrew, A., Goldblatt, D. and Perraton, J. (1999) *Global Transformations: Politics, Economics and Culture*. Cambridge: Polity.

Hemerijck, A. and Visser, J. (2001) Dutch lessons in social pragmatism. In S. White (ed.), *New Labour*, Basingstoke: Palgrave.

Hennessy, P. (1998) The Blair style of government: an historical perspective and an interim audit. *Government and Opposition*, 33(1), 3–20.

Hennessy, P. (2000) *The Prime Minister: The Office and its Holders since 1945*. London: Allen Lane.

Hewitt, P. (1996) Family and work. In G. Radice (ed.), *What Needs to Change: New Visions for Britain*, London: HarperCollins.

Hill, C. (2001) Foreign policy. In A. Seldon (ed.), *The Blair Effect*, London: Little, Brown.

Hirschman, A. (1996) Politics. In D. Marquand and A. Seldon, *The Ideas that Shaped Post-War Britain*, London: Fontana.

Hirst, P. (1999) Has globalisation killed social democracy? In A. Gamble and T. Wright (eds), *The New Social Democracy*, Oxford: Political Quarterly/Blackwell.

Hirst, P. and Thompson, G. (1996) *Globalization in Question: The International Economy and the Possibilities of Governance.* Cambridge: Polity.

HM Treasury (1998) *Persistent Poverty and Lifetime Inequality: The Evidence*, London: HM Treasury/Centre for Analysis of Social Exclusion.

HM Treasury (1999) *The Modernisation of Britain's Tax and Benefits System, 4: Tackling Poverty and Extending Opportunity.* London: HM Treasury.

HM Treasury (2000a) *Spending Review 2000: New Public Spending Plans, 2001–2004. Prudent for a Purpose: Building Opportunity and Security for All.* London: HM Treasury.

HM Treasury (2000b) *Investing in the Future: Departmental Investment Strategies.* London: HM Treasury.

Hobsbawm, E. and Jacques, M. (eds) (1981) *The Forward March of Labour Halted?* London: Verso.

Home Office (1999) *Supporting Families: Summary of Responses to the Consultation Document.* London: HMSO.

Hoyle, C. and Rose, D. (2001) Labour, law and order. *Political Quarterly*, 72, 76–85.

Hughes, G. and Little, A. (1999) The contradictions of New Labour's communitarianisms. *Imprints*, 4(1), 37–62.

Hutton, W. (1995) *The State We're In*. London: Jonathan Cape.

Institute for Fiscal Studies (2000) *Green Budget.* London: IFS.

Jaenicke, D. (2000) New Labour and the Clinton presidency. In D. Coates and P. Lawler (eds), *New Labour in Power*, Manchester: Manchester University Press.

Jencks, C. (1997) The hidden paradox of welfare reform. *American Prospect*, May–June.

Jenkins, S. (1995) *Accountable to None: The Tory Nationalisation of Britain.* Harmondsworth: Penguin.

Jenkins, S. (1997) Blair's major-generals. *The Times*, 7 May.

Johnson, N. (2001) The personal social services. In S. Savage and R. Atkinson (eds), *Public Policy Under Blair*, Basingstoke: Palgrave.

Jones, N. (1995) *Soundbites and Spindoctors.* London: Cassell.

Jones, N. (1997) *Campaign 1997: How the General Election was Won and Lost.* London: Indigo.

Jones, T. (1996) *Remaking the Labour Party: From Gaitskell to Blair.* London: Routledge.

Jordan, B. (1998) *The New Politics of Welfare: Social Justice in a Global Context.* London: Sage.

Jospin, L. (1999) *Modern Socialism.* London: Fabian Society.

Kaldor, M. (1999) *New and Old Wars*. Cambridge: Polity.

Kavanagh, D. and Seldon, A. (1999) *The Powers Behind the Prime Minister*. London: HarperCollins.

Kelly, G. (ed.) (1999) *The New European Left*. London: Fabian Society.

Kelly, G. and Gamble, A. (2000) Stakeholding and individual ownership accounts. Paper to Political Studies Association Conference, London, 10–12 April.

Kelly, J. (1997) The single currency of the imagination. In M. Jacobs, *Creative Futures: Culture, Identity and National Renewal*, London: Fabian Society.

Kenny, M. and Smith, M. (2001) Interpreting New Labour: constraints, dilemmas and political agency. In S. Ludlam and M. Smith (eds), *New Labour in Government*, Basingstoke: Macmillan.

King, D. (1995) *Actively Seeking Work: The Politics of Unemployment and Welfare Policy in the United States and Great Britain*. Chicago: University of Chicago Press.

King, D. and Wickham-Jones, M. (1998) Training without the state: New Labour and labour markets. *Policy & Politics*, 26, 439–55.

King, D. and Wickham-Jones, M. (1999) From Clinton to Blair: the democratic (party) origins of welfare to work. *Political Quarterly*, 70, 62–74.

Labour Party (undated) *Getting Welfare to Work*. London: Labour Party.

Labour Party (1997a) *New Labour: Because Britain Deserves Better*. London: Labour Party [manifesto].

Labour Party (1997b) *Create the Future*. London: Labour Party.

Labour Party (2001) *Ambitions for Britain: Labour's General Election Manifesto*. London: Labour Party.

Ladrech, R. (2000) *Social Democracy and the Challenge of European Union*. London: Lynne Rienner.

Land, H. (1999) New Labour, new families. In H. Dean and R. Woods, *Social Policy Review 11*, Luton: Social Policy Association.

Larkin, P. (2001) New Labour in perspective: a comment on Rubinstein. *Politics*, 21(1), 51–5.

Latham, M. (2001) The third way: an outline. In A. Giddens (ed.), *The Global Third Way Debate*, Cambridge: Polity.

Lawler, P. (2000) New Labour's foreign policy. In D. Coates and P. Lawler (eds), *New Labour in Power*, Manchester: Manchester University Press.

Leadbeater, C. (1998) Welcome to the knowledge economy. In I. Hargreaves and I. Christie (eds), *Tomorrow's Politics*, London: Demos.

Leadbeater, C. (1999) *Living on Thin Air*. London: Viking.

Lees, C. (2001) Social democracy and the structures of governance in Britain and Germany: how institutions and norms shape political innovation. In L. Martell et al. *Social Democracy*, Basingstoke: Palgrave.

Leggett, W. (2000) New Labour's third way: from 'new times' to 'no choice'. *Studies in Social and Political Thought*, 3, September, 19–31.

Le Grand, J. (1998) The third way begins with cora. *New Statesman*, 6 March.

Lent, A. (1997) Labour's transformations: searching for the point of origin. *Politics*, 17(1).

Leonard, D. (ed.) (1998) *Crosland and New Labour*. Basingstoke: Palgrave.

Leonard, M. (1997) *BritainTM: Renewing our Identity*. London: Demos.

Levitas, R. (1998) *The Inclusive Society? Social Exclusion and New Labour*. Basingstoke: Macmillan.

Lewis, J. (1998) Work, welfare and lone mothers. *Political Quarterly*, 69, 4–13.

Lindgren, A.-M. (1999) Swedish social democracy in transition. In G. Kelly (ed.), *The New European Left*, London: Fabian Society.

Lister, R. (1999) Reforming welfare around the work ethic: new gendered and ethical perspectives on work and care. *Policy & Politics*, 27, 233–46.

Lister, R. (2000a) To Rio via the third way: New Labour's welfare reform agenda. *Renewal*, 8(4), 9–20.

Lister, R. (2000b) Towards a citizens' welfare state: the 3+2 Rs of welfare reform. Paper to the Social Policy Association Annual Conference.

Little, R. and Wickham-Jones, M. (2000) *New Labour's Foreign Policy*. Manchester: Manchester University Press.

Lloyd, J. (1998) How the left hijacked the family. *New Statesman*, 27 November.

Lo, C. Y. H. and Schwartz, C. (1998) *Social Policy and the Conservative Agenda*. Oxford: Blackwell.

Lovecy, J. (2000) New Labour and the 'Left that is left' in Western Europe. In D. Coates and P. Lawler (eds), *New Labour in Power*, Manchester: Manchester University Press.

Ludlam, S. (2001a) The making of New Labour. In S. Ludlam and M. Smith (eds), *New Labour in Government*, Basingstoke: Macmillan.

Ludlam, S. (2001b) New Labour and the unions: the end of the contentious Alliance? In S. Ludlam and M. Smith (eds), *New Labour in Government*, Basingstoke: Macmillan.

Ludlam, S. and Smith, M. (eds) (2001) *New Labour in Government*. Basingstoke: Macmillan.

McGowan, F. (2001) Social democracy and the European Union: who's changing whom? In L. Martell et al., *Social Democracy*, Basingstoke: Palgrave.

McGrew, A. (ed.) (1997) *The Transformation of Democracy: Globalization and Territorial Democracy*. Cambridge: Polity.

McLaughlin, E., Trewsdale, J. and McCay, N. (2001) The rise and fall of the UK's first tax credit: the working families' tax credit, 1998–2000. *Social Policy & Administration*, 35, 163–80.

Mandelson, P. (1997) *Labour's Next Steps: Tackling Social Exclusion*. London: Fabian Society.

Marquand, D. (1996) Moralists and hedonists. In D. Marquand and A. Seldon, *The Ideas that Shaped Post-War Britain*, London: Fontana.

Marquand, D. (1997) Reaching for the levers. *Times Literary Supplement*, 11 April, 3–4.

Marquand, D. (1998) In D. Halpern and D. Mikosz, *The Third Way*, London: Nexus.

Marquand, D. (1999) Premature obsequies: social democracy comes in from the cold. In A. Gamble and T. Wright, *The New Social Democracy*. Oxford: Political Quarterly/Blackwell, 17.

Marr, A. (2000) *The Day Britain Died*. London: Profile.

Marsh, D., Buller, J., Hay, C., Johnston, J., Kerr, P., McAnulla, S. and Watson, M. (1999) *Postwar British Politics in Perspective*. Cambridge: Polity.

Martell, L. (1993) Rescuing the middle ground: neo-liberalism and associational socialism. *Economy and Society*, 22, 100–13.

Martell, L. van der Anker, C., Browne, M., Hooper, S., Larkin, P., Lees, C., McCowan, F. and Stammers, N. (2001) *Social Democracy: Global and National Perspectives*. Basingstoke: Palgrave.

Marxism Today (1998) Wrong. November/December.

Massey, A. (2001) Policy, management and implementation. In S. Savage and R. Atkinson (eds), *Public Policy Under Blair*, Basingstoke: Palgrave.

Mead, L. (1986) *Beyond Entitlement: The Social Obligation of Citizenship*. New York: Free Press.

Mead, L. (1992) *The New Politics of Poverty: The Nonworking Poor in America*. New York: Basic Books.

Mead, L. (1997) From welfare to work: lessons from America. In A. Deacon, *From Welfare to Work: Lessons from America*, London: Institute of Economic Affairs.

Merkel, W. (2001) The third ways of social democracy. In A. Giddens (ed.), *The Global Third Way Debate*, Cambridge: Polity.

Meyer, T. (1999) From Gödesborg to the Neue Mitte: the new social democracy in Germany. In G. Kelly (ed.), *The New European Left*, London: Fabian Society.

Millar, J. (1998) Social policy and the family. In P. Alcock, A. Erskine and M. May, *The Student's Companion to Social Policy*, Oxford: Blackwell.

Miller, D. (1989) *Market, State and Community*. Oxford: Oxford University Press.

Miller, D. (1995) *On Nationality*. Oxford: Oxford University Press.

Miller, D. (1997) What kind of equality should the Left pursue? In J. Franklin, *Equality*, London: Institute for Public Policy Research.

Ministerial Group on the Family (1998) *Supporting Families*. London: HM Stationery Office.

Mitchell, J. and Seyd, B. (1999) Fragmentation in the party and political systems. In R. Hazell, *Constitutional Futures*, Oxford: Oxford University Press.

Morgan, P. (1999) *More Damage to the Family*. London: Centre for Policy Studies.

Murray, C. (1984) *Losing Ground: American Social Policy, 1950–1980*. New York: Basic Books.

Murray, C. (1994) What to do about welfare. *Commentary*, 98(6), 26–34.

Nairn, T. (1977) *The Break-Up of Britain: Crisis and Neo-Nationalism.* London: New Left Books.

Nairn, T. (1998) Breaking up is hard to do. *Marxism Today*, November/December, 40–3.

Nissan, D. and Le Grand, J. (2000) *A Capital Idea: Start-Up Grants for Young People.* London: Fabian Society.

Norris, P. (1997) Political communications. In P. Dunleavy, A. Gamble, I. Holliday and G. Peele, *Developments in British Politics 5.* Basingstoke: Macmillan.

O'Connor, J. (1998) US social welfare policy: the Reagan record and legacy. *Journal of Social Policy*, 27(1), 37–61.

Office for National Statistics (2001) *Social Trends.* London: HM Stationery Office.

Oppenheim, C. (1999) Welfare reform and the labour market: a third way? *Benefits*, April/May, 1–5.

Oppenheim, C. (2001) Enabling participation? New Labour's welfare-to-work policies. In S. White (ed.), *New Labour*, Basingstoke: Palgrave.

Parekh, B. (1998) Home at last? *Marxism Today*, November/December, 54.

Pattie, C. (2001) New Labour and the electorate. In S. Ludlam and M. Smith (eds), *New Labour in Government*, Basingstoke: Macmillan.

Peck, J. (1998) Workfare in the sun: politics, representation and method in US welfare-to-work strategies. *Political Geography*, 17, 535–66.

Peck, J. (1999) New labourers? Making a New Deal for the 'workless class'. *Environment and Planning C: Government and Policy*, 17, 345–72.

Peck, J. and Theodore, N. (2000) 'Work first': workfare and the regulation of contingent labour markets. *Cambridge Journal of Economics*, 24, 119–38.

Performance and Innovation Unit (2001) *Social Mobility: A Discussion Paper.* London: Cabinet Office.

Perri 6 (1997) *Holistic Government.* London: Demos.

Phillips, A. (2000) Equality, pluralism, universality: current concerns in normative theory. *British Journal of Politics & International Relations*, 2, 237–55.

Phillips, M. (1999) *The Sex Change Society.* London: Social Market Foundation.

Plant, R. (2001) Blair and ideology. In A. Seldon (ed.), *The Blair Effect*, London: Little, Brown.

Powell, M. (ed.) (1999) *New Labour, New Welfare State? The 'Third Way' in British Social Policy.* Bristol: Policy Press.

Powell, M. (2000) Something old, something new, something borrowed, something blue. *Renewal*, 8(4), 21–31.

Radice, G. and Pollard, S. (1994) *Any Southern Comfort?* London: Fabian Society.

Rake, K. (2001) Gender and New Labour's social policies. *Journal of Social Policy*, 30, 209–31.

Rawnsley, A. (2001) *Servants of the People: The Inside Story of New Labour*. Harmondsworth: Penguin.

Redwood, J. (1999) *The Death of Britain*. Basingstoke: Macmillan.

Rees-Mogg, W. (1997) Ring out the old, ring in the new. *The Times*, 2 May.

Rees-Mogg, W. (2001) Hurrah for the new Tory government. *The Times*, 25 June.

Reich, R. (1997) *Locked in the Cabinet*. New York: Knopf.

Reich, R. (1999), We are all third wayers now. *American Prospect*, 43, 46–51.

Rentoul, J. (1995) *Tony Blair*. London: Little, Brown.

Rhodes, M. (2000) Desperately seeking a solution: social democracy, Thatcherism and the 'third way' in British welfare. In M. Ferrera and M. Rhodes, *Recasting European Welfare States*, London: Frank Cass.

Rhodes, R. (1996) The new governance: governing without government. *Political Studies*, 44, 652–67.

Richards, D. and Smith, M. (2001) New Labour, the constitution and reforming the state. In S. Ludlam and M. Smith (eds), *New Labour in Government*, Basingstoke: Macmillan.

Riddell, P. (1997) Cracks in cabinet cement. *The Times*, 10 November.

Riddell, P. (1998) RIP, Cabinet government. *The Times*, 5 January.

Rosenbaum, M. (1996) *From Soapbox to Soundbite: Party Political Campaigning in Britain since 1945*. Basingstoke: Macmillan.

Rowthorn, B. and Ormerod, P. (2001) Happy ever after. *The Guardian*, 25 March.

Rubinstein, D. (2000) A new look at New Labour. *Politics*, 20, 161–7.

Salvati, M. (2001) Prolegomena to the third way debate. In S. White (ed.), *New Labour*, Basingstoke: Palgrave.

Sassoon, D. (1996) *A Hundred Years of Socialism: The Western European Left in the Twentieth Century*. London: I. B. Tauris.

Sassoon, D. (1999) Introduction: convergence, continuity and change on the European Left. In G. Kelly (ed.), *The New European Left*, London: Fabian Society.

Savage, S. and Atkinson, R. (eds) (2001) *Public Policy Under Blair*. Basingstoke: Palgrave.

Savage, S. and Nash, M. (2001) Law and order under Blair: New Labour or Old Conservatism? In S. Savage and R. Atkinson (eds), *Public Policy Under Blair*, Basingstoke: Palgrave.

Scruton, R. (1996) *The Conservative Idea of Community*. London: Conservative 2000 Foundation.

Seldon, A. (ed.) (2001) *The Blair Effect: The Blair Government, 1997–2001*. London: Little, Brown.

Select Committee on Education and Employment (2000) *New Deal for Young People: Two Years On*. London: House of Commons.

Sen, A. (1992) *Inequality Reexamined*. Oxford: Clarendon Press.

Seyd, P. and Whiteley, P. (2001) New Labour and the party: members and organization. In S. Ludlam and M. Smith (eds), *New Labour in Government*, Basingstoke: Macmillan.

Shaw, E. (1996) *The Labour Party Since 1945*. Oxford: Blackwell.
Shaw, E. (2000) What matters is what works: the 3rd way and the case of the PFI initiative. Paper to conference on 'The Third Way and Beyond', Sussex University, 2 November.
Shaw, M. (2001) Social democracy in the global revolution: an historical perspective. In L. Martell et al., *Social Democracy*, Basingstoke: Palgrave.
Smart, C. and Neale, B. (1999) *Family Fragments*. Cambridge: Polity.
Smith, C. (1998) *Creative Britain*. London: Faber & Faber.
Smith, M. J. (1994) Understanding the 'politics of catch-up': the modernization of the Labour Party. *Political Studies*, 42, 708–15.
Smith, M. J. (1999) *The Core Executive in Britain*. Basingstoke: Macmillan.
Smith, M. J. (2001) Conclusion: the complexity of New Labour. In S. Ludlam and M. Smith (eds), *New Labour in Government*, Basingstoke: Macmillan.
Smith, S. (1999) Arguing against cuts in lone parent benefits. *Critical Social Policy*, 19, 313–33.
Social Exclusion Unit (1999) *Teenage Pregnancy*. London: Cabinet Office.
Teles, S. (1996) *Whose Welfare? AFDC and Elite Politics*. Lawrence: University of Kansas Press.
Thompson, P. (1995) Nations, states and identities. *Renewal*, 3(3).
Tomaney, J. and Hetherington, P. (2000) *Monitoring the English Regions: Report No. 1*. Centre for Urban and Regional Development Studies, University of Newcastle upon Tyne.
Torfing, J. (1999) Workfare with welfare: recent reforms of the Danish welfare state. *Journal of European Social Policy*, 9(1), 5–28.
Toynbee, P. and Walker, D. (2001) *Did Things Get Better? An Audit of Labour's Successes and Failures*. Harmondsworth: Penguin.
US General Accounting Office (1999) *Welfare Reform: Information on Former Recipients' Status*. Washington, DC: USGAO.
Vandenbroucke, F. (1998), *Globalisation, Inequality and Social Democracy*. London: Institute for Public Policy Research.
Vandenbroucke, F. (2001) European social democracy and the third way: convergence, divisions and shared questions. In S. White (ed.), *New Labour*, Basingstoke: Palgrave.
Vincent, A. (1998) New ideologies for old. *Political Quarterly*, 69, 48–58.
Walker, R. (1998) Does work work? *Journal of Social Policy*, 27, 533–42.
Watson, M. (1999) Globalization and the development of the British political economy. In D. Marsh et al. (eds), *Postwar British Politics in Perspective*, Cambridge: Polity.
Weaver, R. K. (1998) Ending welfare as we know it. In M. Weir (ed.), *The Social Divide*, Washington, DC: Brookings Institution/Russell Sage Foundation.
Weaver, R. K. (2000) *Ending Welfare as We Know It*. Washington, DC: Brookings Institution.
Webster, P. (2001) Tory tax cuts for married parents. *The Times*, 21 February.

Weir, M. (2001) The collapse of Bill Clinton's third way. In S. White (ed.), *New Labour*, Basingstoke: Palgrave.

White, S. (1997) What do egalitarians want? In J. Franklin, *Equality*, London: Institute for Public Policy Research.

White, S. (1998) Interpreting the third way: not one road, but many. *Renewal*, 6(2), 17–30.

White, S. (ed.) (2001) *New Labour: The Progressive Future?* Basingstoke: Palgrave.

White, S. and Giaimo, S. (2001) Conclusion: New Labour and the uncertain future of progressive politics. In S. White (ed.), *New Labour*, Basingstoke: Palgrave.

Wickham-Jones, M. (1995) Recasting social democracy: a comment on Hay and Smith. *Political Studies*, 43, 698–702.

Wickham-Jones, M. (2000) New Labour in the global economy: partisan politics and the social democratic model. *British Journal of Politics and International Relations*, 2(1), 1–25.

Wilkinson, H. (1996) The making of a young country. In M. Perryman (ed.), *The Blair Agenda*, London: Lawrence & Wishart.

Wilkinson, H. (1998a) Still the second sex. *Marxism Today*, November/December, 58–9.

Wilkinson, H. (1998b) The family way: navigating a third way in family policy. In I. Hargreaves and I. Christie, *Tomorrow's Politics*, London: Demos.

Wilkinson, H. (1999) Celebrate the new family. *New Statesman*, 9 August.

Wilkinson, H. (ed.) (2000) *The Family Business*. London: Demos.

Willetts, D. (1998a) *Welfare to Work*. London: Social Market Foundation.

Willetts, D. (1998b) *Who Do We Think We Are?* London: Centre for Policy Studies.

Williams, M. (2000) *Crisis and Consensus in British Politics: From Bagehot to Blair*. Basingstoke: Palgrave.

Wilson, W. J., Mulgan, G., Hills, J. and Piachand, D. (1998) *Welfare Reform: Learning from American Mistakes*. London: London School of Economics [CASE report 3].

Wiseman, M. (1996) Welfare reform in the United States: a background paper. *Housing Policy Debate*, 7, 595–648.

Worcester, R. and Mortimore, R. (1999) *Explaining Labour's Landslide*. London: Politico's.

Wright, T. (1997) *Why Vote Labour?* Harmondsworth: Penguin.

Young, R. A. (2000) New Labour and international development. In D. Coates and P. Lawler (eds), *New Labour in Power*, Manchester: Manchester University Press.

Index